CW00742511

CAVALRY TRAINING.

40 / W.O. / 2290

1912.

(Reprinted, with Amendments, 1915.)

The Naval & Military Press Ltd

Published by

The Naval & Military Press Ltd

Unit 5 Riverside, Brambleside
Bellbrook Industrial Estate
Uckfield, East Sussex
TN22 1QQ England

Tel: +44 (0)1825 749494

www.naval-military-press.com
www.nmarchive.com

This Manual is issued by command of the Army Council. It deals with the elementary training of Cavalry and with the general principles which are to govern the further training in peace and the employment in war of that arm.

The attention of commanders is drawn to "Training and Manœuvre Regulations," Section 3. Any enunciation by officers responsible for training of principles or practice of methods differing in principle from those laid down in this Manual is forbidden, as tending to cause confusion of thought and to prejudice successful co-operation in war.

R. H. Brade

WAR OFFICE, S.W.,
    11th MARCH, 1915.

Subsequent amendments are indicated by black lines in the margins of the pages.

$$\frac{P\ 14}{431}$$

CONTENTS.

PART I.—TRAINING.

CHAPTER I.

GENERAL PRINCIPLES OF TRAINING.

x   (33)25119   Wt 31357—251   20,000   3/15   (S)   A 2

CHAPTER II.

DRILL ON FOOT AND PRELIMINARY INSTRUCTION IN HANDLING THE ARMS.

DRILL WITHOUT ARMS.

THE SWORD ON FOOT.

THE LANCE ON FOOT.

THE RIFLE.

DRILL OF THE MACHINE GUN SECTION.

CHAPTER III.

EQUITATION AND THE HANDLING OF THE WEAPONS MOUNTED.

Saddlery.

Riding.

The Use of the Weapons Mounted.

TRAINING THE YOUNG HORSE.

RETRAINING AWKWARD AND BADLY TRAINED HORSES.

NOTES ON DRIVING.

CHAPTER IV.

MOUNTED DRILL.

GENERAL INSTRUCTIONS FOR DRILL.

DRILL OF THE TROOP.

DRILL OF THE DIVISION.

CHAPTER V.

FURTHER PRELIMINARY INSTRUCTION.

CHAPTER VI.

TRAINING IN FIELD OPERATIONS.

PART II.—WAR.

CHAPTER VII.

GENERAL PRINCIPLES OF THE EMPLOYMENT OF CAVALRY IN WAR.

CHAPTER VIII.

MOVEMENTS.

CHAPTER IX.
INFORMATION AND INTER-COMMUNICATION.

CHAPTER X.
GENERAL PRINCIPLES OF CAVALRY TACTICS.

CHAPTER XI.
MOUNTED ACTION.

CHAPTER XII.
DISMOUNTED ACTION.

CHAPTER XIII.
HORSE ARTILLERY, MACHINE GUNS, AND ENGINEERS.
HORSE ARTILLERY.

CAVALRY TRAINING.
1912.
(*Reprinted* 1915.)

INTRODUCTION AND DEFINITIONS.

I.—ORGANIZATION.

1. The higher formations of cavalry are the brigade and division. The division is a grouping of two or more brigades, in which the horse artillery, engineers, and administrative troops are grouped as divisional troops. For details *see* "War Establishments."

2. A cavalry brigade forming part of a cavalry division consists of brigade headquarters and three regiments. When not forming part of a division horse artillery, engineers and the necessary administrative units are attached to it.

3. A *Regiment* consists of:
    Regimental headquarters.
    3 squadrons.†
    Machine gun section.

4. A *Squadron* consists of:
    Squadron headquarters.
    4 troops.

5. A *Troop* consists of 3 or 4 sections.

6. A *Section* consists of from 4 to 8 men under the immediate control of a non-commissioned officer or selected soldier called the section leader.

---

† Regiments in India are organized in 4 squadrons.

The men and horses of a section should. as far as possible, be kept together in barracks as well as in the field. The section leader should know his men and horses thoroughly. He will be responsible generally for the discipline and efficiency of his section.

It is preferable that sections should be designated by the names of their commanders rather than by numbers.

II.—DEFINITIONS.

Alignment.—Any straight line on which a body of troops is formed or is to form.

Covering.—The act of a body placing itself correctly in rear of another.

Deployment.—The formation of line from column.

Depth.—The space occupied by a body of troops from front to rear.

Directing Body.—The body on which the direction, pace, and alignment, or relative positions of, the several parts of a formation depend.

Distance.—The space between men or bodies of troops from front to rear.

Divisional Cavalry.—Squadrons which form an integral portion of a division of all arms.

Dressing.—The act of taking up an alignment correctly.

Files.—The term used to denote the strength of the front rank of a body of troops in line.

  A **File.**—A front rank man with his coverer.

  A **Single File.**—One man.

Firing Battery.—Consists of 6 guns and the 6 ammunition wagons which accompany the guns into action.

Flank—

  Inner Flank.—The flank which serves as a pivot when a body is changing direction.

  Outer Flank.—The flank opposite the inner flank.

Frontage.—The extent of ground covered laterally by troops.

Horse-Length.—A term of measurement (8 feet).

Incline.—The movement by which ground is gained to the front and flank simultaneously.

Interval.—The lateral space between men or units, measured from flank to flank.

> **Deploying Interval.**—The interval between columns necessary to enable them to form line to the front.

> **Close Interval.**—A reduction of interval to suit requirements.

Markers.—Men employed in certain cases to mark points on which to march or form.

Order.—The increased distance taken by the rear rank on some occasions on parade, *i.e.*, three horse-lengths.

> **Extended Order.**—A line of men extended at intervals of 4 yards from each other, or at such other intervals as may be directed.

> **Close Order.**—The ordinary distance between front and rear rank when formed in line, also the ordinary interval between files in line or column.

Pace.—A measurement of distance on foot (30 inches).

Parade Line.—The line on which troops form for review.

Passing Line.—The line on which troops march past at a review.

Patrol.—A few men under a leader detached to reconnoitre. Speaking generally, the term patrol implies a force less than a troop.

Pivot.—The flank on which a body wheels. The man on that flank is termed the " pivot man," or simply the " pivot."

> **Fixed Pivot.**—The term applied to the pivot, when during the wheel the *pivot man* is halted and turns upon his own ground.

> **Moving Pivot.**—The term applied to the pivot, when during the wheel the pivot man moves on the arc of a circle.

Point.—The man or men riding immediately in advance of a patrol, advanced party, or similar detachment.

Rank.—A line of men side by side.

Scouts.—Men detached singly to reconnoitre, or individual members of a patrol.

> **Ground Scouts.**—Men employed to ascertain whether the ground in the immediate vicinity is passable.

Section.—One of the divisions of a troop. It consists of four front rank men with their coverers, if any. , *See* also under "ORGANIZATION," p. 1.

> **Half-section.**—Two front rank men with their coverers.
>
> **A section of artillery** consists of two guns with their detachments and ammunition wagons.

Serrefiles.—Such officers, N.C. officers, and men as may be detailed to ride in rear of the squadron, their duty being to keep the ranks closed and to prevent straggling.

Shouldering.—Wheeling on a moving pivot with an indefinite radius.

Squad.—A small number of men formed for drill or for work.

Troop Guides.—N.C. officers or men placed in the centre and on the flanks of the front rank of each troop.

Wheel.—A movement by which a body changes direction on a fixed or moving pivot.

Wing.—The half of a regiment or larger body. Wings are termed "Right" and "Left" when in line, and "Leading" and "Rear" when in column or échelon. When a regiment is formed in wings, the first and second squadrons form the right or leading wing, and the third (and fourth) squadron the left or rear wing.

III.—TERMS OF FORMATIONS.

1.—*Column.*

Column.—Bodies of troops formed one in rear of the other.

Close Column.—A column with distances reduced to suit requirements.

Open Column.—Bodies of troops at a distance from one another equal to their own frontage plus the interval required in line if any.

Half Column.—*See* under *Echelon*, p. 6.

Quarter Column.—A close column of squadrons at such distances that a wheel of troops to either hand will bring them into mass.

Column of Half Squadrons.—Half squadrons in column at troop distance.

Column of Masses.—A column of two or more regiments each formed in mass one behind the other at 30 yards distance.

Column of Sections.—Sections in column at half a horse-length distance between the front rank of one section and the rear rank of the preceding section.

Column of Squadrons.—Squadrons in open column.

Column of Troops.—Troops in open column.

Squadron Column.—A squadron with its troops in open column.

Troop Column.—A troop in column of sections.

2.—*Line.*

Line.—Men or bodies of troops formed on the same alignment.

Line of Squadron Columns.—A line of squadrons at deploying interval each with its troops in open column.

Line of Troop Columns.—A line of troops, normally at deploying interval, each in column of sections.

Line of Brigade or Divisional Masses.—*See* under *Mass.*

3.—*Mass.*

Mass.—A line of squadron columns, closed to five yards interval.

Line of Regimental Masses.—A line of two or more regiments each in *mass* with deploying interval plus 16 yards between them.

B 2

Brigade Mass or Divisional Mass.—A *Brigade or Divisional Line of Regimental Masses* at close interval, normally 16 yards.

Column of Masses.—*See* under *Column.*

4.—*Echelon.*

Echelon.—A formation of successive and parallel units facing in the same direction, each ou a flank and to the rear of the unit in front of it.

Double Echelon.—A form of *Echelon* in which the centre body is in advance with the others on its left and right rear.

Half Column.—A form of *Echelon* in which the several bodies composing it are so placed that a half wheel to one flank brings them into line with the proper intervals (if any), whilst a half wheel to the other flank brings them into open column.

5.—*Formations of artillery.*

Column of Route.—A column of single carriages in which each gun is followed by its ammunition wagons.

Battery Column.—A battery with the sections following one behind the other in open column.

Line of Battery Columns.—*Battery columns* in line at deploying interval.

Mass.—A line of *battery columns* at 25 yards interval.

IV.—DISTANCES AND INTERVALS.

1. *Distances.*

Distances between mounted troops are measured from the tail of a horse to the head of the one behind it. Between dismounted troops they are measured from heel to heel.

Line - • - -	Troop leaders to front rank, front to rear rank, rear rank to serrefile rank.	1 horse-length (on foot 3 paces).
Column or half-column	Front to rear rank.	½ horse-length (on foot 3 paces).
Open column - -	Between units -	Wheeling distance plus interval in line.
Echelon - • -	Between units in échelon.	As in *open column.*
Column of sections or half-sections.	Between squadrons.	10 yards.
	Between regiments.	20 yards.

2. *Intervals.*

Intervals between mounted troops are measured from knee to knee. For intervals for men on foot, *see* Sec. **27.**

Line - - -	Between files	-	6 inches.†
„ (*Extended order*)	„ „	-	4 yards, unless a different interval is ordered.
„ - - -	„	squadrons	8 yards.
„ - - -	„	regiments	16 yards, exclusive of band and staff.
„ - - -	„	brigades -	16 yards.
Line of squadron columns.	„	squadrons	Frontage of all the rear troops of one squadron, plus 8 yards.
Mass - - -	„	„	5 yards.
Any *line of columns*	„	regiments	Deploying interval, plus 16 yards.
„ „ -	„	„	Deploying interval, plus 16 yards.
„ „ (at close interval)	„	{ regiments { brigades -	16 yards.* 16 yards.*

† Including intervals between files each horse in the ranks occupies approximately a frontage of 1 yard.
* May be reduced in rendezvous formation.

V. SIGNALS.

1. The following signals will be used; it is important that they should be made distinctly. *See* also Sec. 118.

SIGNAL.	TO INDICATE.
i. Arm swung from rear to front below the shoulder, finishing with the hand pointing to the front.	"*Advance*" or "*Forward.*"
ii. Arm circled at its full extent above the head, finishing up by pointing in the direction in which the retirement is to be made.	"*Retire.*"
iii. Open hand raised in line with the shoulder, elbow bent and close to the side.	"*Walk*" or "*Quick time.*"
iv. Clenched hand moved up and down between thigh and shoulder, forearm pointing in such a direction that the movement can be seen by those for whom the signal is intended.	"*Trot*" or "*Double.*"
v. Circular movement of hand below the shoulder, as in turning the handle of a small grinding machine.	"*Gallop.*"
vi. Arm raised at full extent above the head.	"*Halt.*"
vii. Body or horse turned in the required direction and arm extended in a line with the shoulder.	"*Incline.*"
viii. Slow circular movement of the extended arm in line with the shoulder in the required direction.	"*Shoulders.*"
ix. Arm waved from above the head to a position in line with the shoulder pointing in the required direction.	*Troops right* (or *left*) *wheel*. *Troops half right* (or *left*).
x. Arm waved horizontally from right to left and back again as though	1. *Form squadron column* (from line).

SIGNAL.	TO INDICATE.

cutting with a sword, finishing with the delivery of a point to the front.

2. *Form line of squadron columns* (from line, mass, column, or échelon of squadron columns).

3. *Form line—*
    i. From *line of squadron columns.*
    ii. From *line of troop columns.*

xi. Arm held extended above the head as for halt and hand at once moved rapidly right and left.

" *Rally* " or " *Mass* " if in closed order, or " *Close* " if in extended order, or dispersed.

NOTE.—This signal denotes " *Close on the centre.*" If it is desired to close on a flank, finish the signal by pointing towards that flank.

xii. Two or three slight movements of the open hand towards the ground (palm downwards).

" *Dismount* " or " *Lie down.*"

xiii. Two or three slight movements of the open hand upwards (palm uppermost).

" *Mount.*"

\ Arm raised as for "Halt," and then pointed to the ground.

" *For action, dismount.*"

xv. Arm at full extent over head and waved a few times slowly from side to side, bringing the arm down at each wave on a level with the shoulder.

" *Extend.*"

NOTE.—This signal denotes extensions to both flanks. If the extension is to be made to the right, finish the signal by pointing to the right. If the extension is to be made to the left, finish the signal by pointing to the left. If an extension greater or less than 4 yards is required the distance will be given by word of mouth.

xvi. Arm swung from rear to front above the shoulder.

" *Reinforce.*"

xvii. Weapon held up above, and as if guarding the head.

" *Enemy in sight in small numbers.*"

xviii. As in xvii, but weapon raised and lowered frequently.

" *Enemy in sight in large numbers.*"

xix. Weapon held up at full extent of arm, point or muzzle uppermost.

" *No enemy in sight.*"

Signals such as "*Halt*" or "*Incline*" should be maintained. Signals of movements, such as "*Advance*" or "*Shoulder*," should be repeated until it is clear that they are understood.

2. The following signals are used by ground scouts :—

Impassable ground.—Halt and raise the right arm perpendicularly ; then ride towards whatever point appears practicable, pointing towards it with the hand. If the ground within view in front and on either side is quite impracticable, a scout will raise his right arm, and ride into the squadron to report.

3. The whistle will be used—

    i. To draw attention to a signal about to be made—" a short blast." On a " short blast " being blown on the whistle when the troops are in action dismounted, men will cease fire momentarily, if necessary, and will look towards their commander and remain looking at him until he has completed the signal and dropped his hand or until the order is understood. If men are on the move they will continue the movement, while looking towards the commander.

    ii. To denote "Bring up the led horses"—"two long blasts."
    iii. To denote " Rally "—" a succession of short blasts."

4. **Machine gun signals.**—The following signals will be used for machine guns :—

    i. Semaphore code to be used by observers in reporting on the fire of the guns.

P = Plus : meaning fire observed at least 50 yards beyond target.
M = Minus :   „   „   „   „ „ „ „ short of „
T = Right :   „   „   „   to right of target.
L̄ = Left :   „   „   „   to left of target.
C = Centre :   „   direction of fire correct.
U = Unobserved : meaning no observation obtained.
Q = Query : meaning fire observed but its position uncertain.
R = Range :   „   range correct.

The signaller at the observation post should give the "call-up" to show that the observers are ready. "P" and "M" may be repeated for multiples of 50 yards, thus, "PP" would mean fire observed at least 100 yards beyond the target. Signals should be repeated from the gun position if this can be done without disclosing the position to the enemy.

    ii. On all occasions when guns are firing, the following signals should be used in controlling fire :—

By No. 2.—Hand up	- - - -	"*Gun ready to open fire.*"
By controlling officer.	Hand up - -	"*Preparatory to opening fire.*"
	Hand dropped -	"*Open fire.*"
	Elbow close to the side, forearm waved horizontally.	"*Cease fire.*"

VI. Field Calls.

1. The following field calls may be used if required (*see* "Trumpet and Bugle Sounds") :—

"Forward" or "Advance."	"Squadron columns."
"Walk."	"Change direction, right."
"Trot."	"Change direction, left."
"Gallop."	"Pursue."
"Charge."	"Rally."
"March."	"Mass."
"Halt."	"Attention."
"Annul" or "As you were."	"March " or "Sit at ease."
"Troops, half right."	"Stand to your horses."
"Troops, right wheel."	"Mount."
"Troops, half left."	"Dismount."
"Troops, left wheel."	"1st Brigade."
"Form line."	"2nd Brigade."
"Retire" or "Troops, right or left about wheel."	"3rd Brigade."
	"4th Brigade."

2. With the exception of the regimental call no special call devised to supplement or improve on the above are to be used.

CAVALRY TRAINING.

PART I.—TRAINING.

CHAPTER I.
GENERAL PRINCIPLES OF TRAINING.

1. *General instructions for training.*

1. The object of the training is to prepare leaders, men, and horses for war.

All training must therefore be based on the principles of the employment of cavalry which are described in "Field Service Regulations, Part I.," and in Part II. of this manual.

2. General instructions for training, designed to ensure the above object, are given in the "Training and Manœuvre Regulations," on which the instructions in this manual are based.

3. The thorough instruction of the individual horse and man is the foundation of success.

2. *Responsibility for training.*

1. All commanders, from troop leaders to general officers, are responsible for the training of their commands.

In order to develop a proper sense of responsibility and initiative in their subordinates, and to stimulate their interest, the training of units will be entrusted to their respective commanders, the superior in each grade exercising such supervision as he may find advisible to ensure that the desired result is attained. Considerable freedom should be allowed to subordinates as to the methods they adopt, so long as these appear to be suitable and in accordance with the principles laid down.

2. In addition to his responsibility for the instruction of his officers in their duties in war and peace the regimental commander, assisted by the senior major, the adjutant, and at home stations by the assistant adjutant, must ensure that the numbers and efficiency of the officers, non-commissioned officers, and men required for special duties are maintained in accordance with the regulations. He will also arrange and supervise such training of the recruit as cannot be carried out in the squadron.

3. It is of particular importance that the squadron should be treated as a self-contained unit, and that the regimental commander, having indicated the standard of efficiency required, should then allow the squadron leader as much freedom as possible.

3. *Training periods.*

1. The varying conditions under which troops are trained in the different parts of the Empire make strict adherence to any one method of training undesirable. The system described in the following sections is to be taken as a general guide however, so far as the circumstances of each case permit.

2. Training is divided into :—
> i. Individual training.
> ii. Collective training.

3. At home stations the period November, December, January and February should be devoted to individual and the first stage of collective training (Sec. 9). The second period, 1st March to the 31st of October, is to be devoted to collective training, commencing with squadron training.

4. The time which should be apportioned to each item of collective training must vary with circumstances, but ample time should be devoted to squadron training.

5. During the training of larger formations, commanders of the smaller must take advantage of all opportunities to continue the instruction of their commands.

6. Whenever possible, musketry training will be spread over the whole year.

4. Standard required of leaders.

1. Leaders must be capable of imparting efficient instruction in every item of military duty required in war, of fighting with the weapons of their men, and of leading their men efficiently under all circumstances. They must also be physically fit to take part in an arduous campaign.

2. The troop leader should be the best all-round man in his troop.

Every non-commissioned officer of, and above, the rank of sergeant should be qualified to replace the troop leader, and should be capable of writing a concise report accompanied by an explanatory sketch.

Every section leader should be able to give practical instruction to the men of his section in horse management, interior economy, and elementary field duties.

5. Duties of instructors.

1. Great care should be taken to arouse and maintain the interest of the soldier in his work. To this end practical instruction should be accompanied by short lectures and explanations, and the soldier should be made to understand at all periods of his training how the various parts of his course are arranged so as to fit him for his duties in war.

2. For purposes of instruction it is necessary to divide the preparation of the soldier for war into various branches. The instructor should make the soldier understand that the knowledge of each item is by itself of minor use, and that it is a combination of the knowledge so acquired which produces general efficiency.

3. Instructors must be proficient in their subjects, and understand the general principles of the employment of cavalry in war and its training in peace.

6. *The development of the soldierly spirit.*

1. Soldierly spirit is the product of a high sense of personal honour and of duty; of self-reliance and of mutual confidence between all ranks.

A sound soldierly spirit cannot be developed by rules, but much can be accomplished by force of example in teaching high ideals of personal conduct. Officers and N.C.O.'s must be careful, therefore, on all occasions to set a high moral, intellectual, and physical standard to their men.

Men should be taught by example to meet privations cheerfully and never to grumble at hard work or hardship.

2. Efficient instruction and good example will instil into individuals absolute confidence in their superiors and comrades. Instructors must endeavour to increase the soldier's initiative, self-confidence, and self-restraint; to train him to obey orders, or to act in the absence of orders for the advantage of his unit under all conditions; and finally to produce such a high degree of courage and disregard of self, that in the stress of battle he will be able to use his weapons and his brains coolly and to the best advantage.

3. In order to impress him with the necessity of upholding the reputation of the army, of our cavalry, and of his own regiment, the soldier should be instructed in the deeds which have made each famous.

Manly games have a great effect on the military spirit, especially if they are arranged so that all ranks generally, and not only selected teams, take part.

Drill is also an important factor, producing that habit of instant obedience which is so essential in war.

7. *The individual training of recruits.*

1. The training of recruits will begin under carefully chosen officers and non-commissioned officers as soon as they join at the depôts and be continued when men are drafted to their units.

2. The daily programme of work will be arranged with as great variety as possible, and must be suited to the aptitude of the individual recruit; monotony, with its consequent loss of interest, must be avoided.

Clearness and simplicity in the instruction are of great importance.

3. The time for the conclusion of the course is not to be gauged by the number of drills performed, but by the proficiency of the individual recruit.

4. The course* will include :—

    i. The development of the soldierly spirit.

    ii. Instruction in barrack and camp duties.

    iii. Physical training under qualified instructors as laid down in the " Manual of Physical Training."

    iv. Chapters II. and III. of this Manual.

    v. Instruction in horsemastership (" Animal Management ").

    vi. Instruction in the use of ground for cover and observation.

    vii. Elementary instruction in night operations.

    viii. Map reading.

    ix. Musketry instruction and firing of the recruit's course (" Musketry Regulations, Part I.").

    x. Visual training and judging distance (" Musketry Regulations, Part I.").

    xi. Instruction in semaphore signalling (" Training Manual—Signalling.").

    xii. Instruction in the use of the sword and lance.

5. Recruits will be exempted from stable and other duties and will not be allowed to commence riding until they have undergone an uninterrupted course of twelve weeks physical training.

---

* A specimen syllabus for a course of 12 weeks' training is given in the Appendix to assist officers charged with the training of recruits in framing their programme of training.

8. *The individual training of officers, non-commissioned officers, and trained soldiers.*

This will consist of :—

   i. Such training of every officer, non-commissioned officer, and man in the handling of his weapons as will ensure that each is efficient and fully capable of fighting with them.

   ii. The training of officers in professional duties as laid down in "King's Regulations" and in "Training and Manœuvre Regulations."

   iii. The training of non-commissioned officers and privates likely to become non-commissioned officers in the solution of small tactical problems with and without troops ("Training and Manœuvre Regulations.")

   iv. Equitation—Indifferent riders and awkward horses will receive further instruction. At the end of the training each man shall have full control of the horse he is riding (Chapter III.).

   v. Horsemastership ("Animal Management").

   vi. Musketry training: officers and other leaders in giving fire orders; practice in judging distance and in aiming under varied conditions; the improvement of indifferent shots; when possible, range practice and the practice of rapid fire on moving and vanishing targets once a month ("Musketry Regulations, Part I.").

   vii. Physical training. Soldiers must at all times be kept physically fit for their work. When necessary, they should carry out the physical exercises for trained soldiers as laid down in the "Manual of Physical Training," supplemented by running and obstacle training. Officers will also encourage and arrange active games amongst their men.

   viii. Map reading. Every cavalry soldier will be practised in map reading ("Manual of Map Reading and Field Sketching"), and a few men in each squadron should be taught rapid sketching

ix. Field engineering (Sec. **156** and "Manual of Field Engineering").

x. Signalling. One man in each section should be practised in semaphore signalling; the Morse signallers will be brought up to strength and trained ("Training Manual—Signalling").

xi. Scouting and patrol duties. Estimating distances, observing and reporting. Selected men will receive a special training as scouts (Sec. **157**).

xii. Machine gun training. The detachments will be kept up to strength, and the preliminary training will be carried out (Sec. **11**).

xiii. Training in packing and loading all available descriptions of transport, and, where facilities exist or can be improvised, the entrainment and embarkation of animals and vehicles ("Field Service Manual—Cavalry Regiment," "Animal Management," and Chapter VIII. of this Manual).

xiv. Training of transport drivers ("King's Regulations," and Secs. **105** and **106** of this Manual).

The training of the non-commissioned officers and men in the above subjects will be carried out under the direction of the troop leaders.

xv. Training in sanitation ("Manual of Elementary Military Hygiene").

9. *The training of the section and the troop.*

Squadron leaders will allot such time as they think desirable for the collective training of sections under the section leaders, and of troops under the troop leaders. This training will usually be carried out concurrently with individual training. At the conclusion of section and troop training, sections and troops should be fit in all respects to take their places in the squadron.

10. *The training of the squadron.*

1. The object of squadron training is to produce a squadron fit to take its place in the regiment, and prepared for any situation it may be called upon to face in war.

The squadron, from its size and organization, is the best school of instruction in all field duties.

2. The training of the squadron will consist of :—

     i. The development of the military spirit of all ranks.

     ii. The continuance of the instruction carried out during the period of individual training (Sec. 8).

     iii. Drill.

     iv. Tactical training.

     v. Musketry training (as laid down in "Musketry Regulations, Part I.").

3. Each squadron will be struck off all duties on the days which have been allotted to it for squadron training. Every officer, non-commissioned officer and man will be trained, with the exception of the machine gun section and of those exempted from the annual course of musketry ("Musketry Regulations, Part I."). Those unavoidably prevented from being trained with the squadrons to which they belong will be trained with other squadrons of the regiment.

4. The course should begin with elementary work and drill and then proceed to simple tactical exercises and manœuvres ; later, one squadron should operate against another, and occasionally a squadron may be made up to war strength by men and horses attached temporarily from another squadron.

5. Squadron leaders will prepare a general programme for the whole training, so arranged as to utilize the ground at their disposal to the best advantage. This programme will be liable to alteration, should the squadron leader think a change desirable. Each day's work should be carefully considered, and prepared with the object of teaching certain lessons.

11. *The training of machine gun sections.*

(*See* "Handbook for Maxim Machine Gun" and Secs. **46** to **49** and **166** of this Manual.)

1. An officer will be selected in each regiment to command and train the machine gun section, under the orders of the regimental commander.

2. The non-commissioned officers and privates shown in the war establishment of a machine gun section will be trained as the regimental machine gun section. A reserve section will be trained as opportunities occur.

3. Soldiers selected for duty with a machine gun section should possess, as far as possible, the following qualifications :—good physique, calm temperament, fair education, and mechanical aptitude ; their eyesight should be tested by a medical officer. The standard of eyesight required is the possession of full distant vision ($V = \frac{6}{6}$), without glasses, with either eye, as tested with the Army Test Types at 20 feet. The refraction of the eyes must be such that with a + 1.D. spherical glass the distant vision of either eye is rendered inferior to that with the naked eye.

4. Officers, non-commissioned officers, and men selected for the machine gun should remain with it as long as possible in order that they may acquire a high standard of skill.

The men of the regimental machine gun section will fire the practices prescribed in "Musketry Regulations, Part I.," with one of the squadrons of the regiment, but at all other times until regimental training commences they will be at the disposal of the machine gun officer for instruction. The classification of detachments will be determined by regimental commanders after the annual machine gun course.

5. The elementary training, which may be carried out in the neighbourhood of barracks, will consist of instruction in the mechanism of the gun (*see* handbook of the gun) ; in mounting and dismounting the gun, and in loading ; in the drill

C 2

and methods of laying, ranging, and firing; in packing and unpacking with limbered wagons, and with pack transport; and in a theoretical knowledge of the general characteristics of the gun.

6. As soon as the men of a section are thoroughly conversant with the mechanism of the gun they will be exercised in firing it ("Musketry Regs., Part I.") and will carry out further training in open country away from barracks. During this training the sections should be practised in bringing the gun into action, both from the limbered wagons and from the pack transport; in fire discipline; in fire control; in laying and ranging in every variety of country; in utilizing natural cover when advancing into action; and in constructing cover from both view and fire. The men should also be trained in range taking, judging distance, and in the use of field glasses.

7. When the section is proficient in the above the commanding officer will arrange for its tactical training with one or more squadrons which have reached the more advanced stages of squadron training. It may thus obtain practice in co-operating with other troops, and in dealing with such situations as would confront it in war.

8. It is important that the machine guns of a brigade should be capable of acting together when required. Machine gun sections therefore should undergo a further course of tactical training grouped as a unit under a selected officer who is not the machine gun officer of one of the regiments.

12. *The training of the regiment.*

1. Regimental training will begin on the conclusion of squadron training.

2. The object of regimental training is to fit the regiment to take part in any operation it may be required to carry out when acting alone, when brigaded with other regiments, or when operating with other arms.

13. *The training of the brigade and division.*

1. The training of cavalry regiments in brigade, and that of brigades in division with the proper complement of horse artillery and field troops is important both to ensure co-operation and to give practice to the higher leaders and their staffs.

2. A short period of the time available for such training should be devoted to drill to render the force supple and handy.

14. *Inspections.*

(*See* " King's Regulations.")

1. Formal inspections on fixed dates should be avoided.

2 Squadron leaders should usually attend the inspection by the regimental commander of other squadrons of their regiment, in order that they may study combination between squadrons and gather information which may be of use when training their own commands. Similarly troop leaders should attend the inspection by the squadron commander of the other troops in their squadron.

CHAPTER II.

DRILL ON FOOT AND PRELIMINARY INSTRUCTION IN HANDLING THE ARMS.

NOTE.—Throughout the details of drill given in this book the description or name of the formation or movement is printed in italics, and the actual word of command to be used is printed in small capital letters.

DRILL WITHOUT ARMS.

15. *General instructions.*

1. Recruits as soon as they join will be formed for instructional purposes in squads of a few men each; the maximum number of men in a squad should not exceed ten.

Drills will be short and frequent. Long drills cause the instructors and recruits to lose interest in their work.

2. The instructor must be clear, firm, concise, and patient, and should make allowance for the different capacities of the men and avoid discouraging nervous recruits.

He will teach as much as possible by illustration, performing the movements himself, or making a smart recruit perform them.

Recruits should be allowed to stand at ease frequently. During these pauses opportunity should be taken to talk to them, to encourage them to ask questions, and so to develop their confidence and common sense.

Recruits will be advanced progressively from one exercise to another, men of inferior capacity being put back to a less advanced squad.

At first the recruit will be placed in position by the instructor, afterwards he should not be touched, but made to correct himself when faults are pointed out.

When the various motions have been learnt, instruction by numbers will cease.

3. Commands must be pronounced distinctly, and sufficiently loud to be heard by all concerned.

The way in which a word of command is given has a great influence on the manner in which the movement ordered is executed.

Commands which consist of one word will be preceded by a caution. The caution, or cautionary part of a command will be given deliberately and distinctly; the last or executive part which usually consists of only one word or syllable, will be given sharply: as TROOP—HALT. A pause will be made between the caution and the executive word. Men will be taught to act upon the last sound of the executive word of command. Care should be taken that they do not move before it is given.

When the formation is moving, executive words will be completed as the men begin the pace which will bring them to the spot on which the command is to be executed. The caution must be commenced accordingly.

Young officers and non-commissioned officers will be practised frequently in giving words of command. They should stand well away from the squads they are commanding, and speak with the head well raised so that the voice may travel.

4. The squads should be formed up for instruction in single rank at an arm's length interval between recruits.

If want of space renders it necessary the squads may be formed in two ranks, in which case the men of the rear rank will cover the intervals between the men in the front rank, so that in marching they may take their own points, as directed in Sec. 22.

16. *The position of attention.*

" ATTEN--TION."   Spring up to the following position :—

Heels together and in line. Feet turned out at an angle of about 45 degrees. **Knees** straight. Body erect and carried evenly over the thighs, with the shoulders (which should be level, and square to the front) down and moderately back—this should bring the chest into its natural forward position, without any straining or stiffening. Arms hanging easily from the shoulders as straight as the natural bend of the arm, when the muscles are relaxed, will allow; the hands level with the centre of the thighs. Wrists straight. Palms of the hands turned towards the thighs, and the heel of the hand and the inside of the finger tips lightly touching them, fingers hanging naturally together and slightly bent. Neck erect. Head balanced evenly on the neck and not poked forward, eyes looking their own height and straight to the front.

The weight of the body should be balanced on both feet, and evenly distributed between the fore part of the feet and the heels.

The breathing must not be restricted in any way, and no part of the body should be either drawn in or pushed out.

The position is one of readiness, but there should be no stiffness or forced unnatural straining to maintain it.

17. *Standing at ease and standing easy.*

1. " STAND AT—   Keeping the legs straight, carry the left foot
    EASE."   about one foot-length to the left so that the
                 weight of the body rests equally on both feet, at

the same time carry the hands behind the back
and place the back of one hand in the
palm of the other, grasping it lightly with
the fingers and thumb, and allowing the arms
to hang easily at their full extent. (It is
immaterial which hand grasps the other.)

Note.—When a recruit falls in for instruction
he will *stand at ease* after he has got his
dressing.

2. " STAND—   The limbs, head, and body may be moved,
EASY." but the man will not move from the ground on
which he is standing.

Note.—Troops " *standing easy* " who receive
a caution such as " *squad*," "*squadron*," etc.,
will assume the position of " *stand at ease.*"

18. *Dressing.*
(*See* Sec. **114**.)

1. *Dressing when on the move.*—It must be impressed on
the recruit that (except at the *incline, see* Sec. 27, 6) he
maintains his dressing by looking to his front, by uniformity of
pace, and by keeping the correct distance either from his leader
or from his front rank man. For this reason no squad should
be drilled without a leader, who may either be an assistant
instructor or a more advanced recruit.

2. *Dressing a squad at the halt.*—(Not at ceremonial.)

No word of   When soldiers are on the alignment they
command. have to occupy, they will, except at ceremonial
drill, take up their own dressing without orders.
When a squad halts each man will look
towards the centre with a smart turn of the
head and commencing with the man nearest
the centre guide will move up or back to his
place successively. Each man will look to his
front as soon as he has got his dressing.

3. *Dressing by the flank.* (N.B.—Only for ceremonial purposes when halted.)

"EYES—RIGHT." The head will be turned, and the eyes directed to the right.

"DRESS." Each recruit, except the right-hand man, will take up his dressing in line by moving with short quick steps, until he is able to see the lower part of the face of the second man from him, taking care to keep his body in the position of attention.

If the squad is at arm's length interval, all but the right-hand man will extend the right arm, back of the hand up, finger tips just touching the shoulder of the man on the right.

"EYES—FRONT." Head and eyes will be turned smartly to the front, and the arm, if raised, dropped, and the position of attention resumed.

19. *Turnings.*

1. "RIGHT TURN" —"ONE." Keeping both knees straight and the body erect, turn to the right on the right heel and left toe, raising the left heel and right toe in doing so.

On the completion of this preliminary movement, the right foot must be flat on the ground and the left heel raised, both knees straight, and the weight of the body, which must be erect, on the right foot.

"TWO." Bring the left heel smartly up to the right without stamping the foot on the ground.

2. "LEFT TURN" —"ONE." Turn to the left, as described above, on the left heel and right toe, the weight of the body being on the left foot on the completion of the movement.

" Two."	Bring the right heel smartly up to the left without stamping the foot on the ground.

3.　"About Turn "—" One."
　　　" Two."
　" About—Turn." } Turn fully about to the right as described, for the " *Right turn* " by numbers or judging the time.

4. *Inclining to the right or left.*

" Right (Left) —Incline " or " Half Right (Left)—Turn." } As described above, but turning half right or left.

5. In turning " judging the time," the commands are Right (or Left) Turn, Right (or Left) Incline ; the movements described above will be carried out on the word Turn or Incline, observing the two distinct motions.

20. *Saluting.*

1. *To the front by numbers.*

"Salute by Numbers—One."	Bring the right hand smartly, with a circular motion, to the head, palm to the front, fingers extended and close together, point of the forefinger one inch above the right eye, thumb close to the forefinger ; elbow in line, and nearly square with the shoulder.
" Two."	Cut away the arm smartly to the side.

2. *To the front judging the time.*

"Salute."	Go through the motions as in para. 1, and, after a pause equal to two paces in quick time, cut away the arm.

Saluting to the side is carried out as in para. 2, except that, as the hand is brought to the salute, the head will be turned towards the person saluted. The salute will be made with the hand further from the person saluted.

When several men are together, the man nearest to the point will give the time.

When a soldier passes an officer he will salute on the third pace before reaching him, and will lower the hand on the third pace after passing him; if carrying a cane, he will place it smartly under the disengaged arm, cutting away the hand before saluting.

A soldier, if sitting when an officer approaches, will stand at attention, facing the officer, and salute with the right hand; if two or more men are sitting or standing about, the senior non-commissioned officer or oldest soldier will face the officer, call the whole to *Attention*, and salute (as above).

When a soldier addresses an officer he will halt two paces from him, and salute with the right hand. He will also salute before withdrawing.

When appearing before an officer in a room, he will salute without removing his cap.

A soldier, without his cap, or when carrying anything other than his arms, will, if standing still, come to attention as an officer passes; if walking, he will turn his head smartly towards the officer in passing him.

When riding a bicycle he will turn his head smartly towards an officer in passing him, and will not move his hands from the handle bar.

A soldier driving a vehicle will bring his whip to a perpendicular position, with the right hand resting on the thigh, and turn his head smartly towards an officer when passing him.

A soldier riding on a vehicle will turn his head smartly towards an officer when passing him.

When wearing a sword he will salute with the right hand.

The term "officer" includes naval officers, certain naval warrant officers,* and military and naval officers of foreign powers. (*See* King's Regulations.)

---

* Chief gunners, chief boatswains, chief carpenters, chief artificer engineers, and chief schoolmasters in the Royal Navy rank as 2nd Lieutenants in the Army and will be saluted by warrant officers, N.C.O.s, and men.

Officers or soldiers passing troops with uncased colours will salute the colours and the C.O. (if senior), and when passing a military funeral will salute the body.

Officers and soldiers in command of unarmed parties, when paying or returning a compliment will give the command " EYES —RIGHT (or LEFT)" and at the same time salute with the right hand.

21. *Length of pace and cadence.*

1. *Length of pace.*—In *slow* and *quick time* the length of pace is 30 inches. In *stepping out* it is 33 inches, in *double time* 40, in *stepping short* 21, and in the *side pace* 15 inches.

2. *Time.*—In *slow time* 75 paces are taken in a minute. In *quick time* and in the *side pace* 120 paces, and in *double time* 180 paces are taken in a minute.

22. *Instruction in marching.*

1. The legs should be swung forward freely and naturally from the hip joints, each leg as it swings forward being bent sufficiently at the knee to enable the foot to clear the ground. The foot should be carried straight to the front, and, without being drawn back, placed firmly upon the ground with the knee straight, but so as not to jerk the body.

The body should be maintained as erect as possible, its relative position being as described for the position of " *Attention*," well balanced over the legs and carried evenly forward without swaying from side to side, and with head erect.

The arms must not be stiffened, but should swing freely and naturally from the shoulders, the right arm swinging forward with the left leg and *vice versâ*. If the arms are swung in this way they will bend naturally at the elbow as they swing forward and will straighten as they swing back, the movement being free without being forced.

2. Before the squad is put in motion, the instructor will take care that each man is square to the front and in correct line with

the remainder. Each soldier must be taught to take up a straight line to his front by fixing the eye upon some distant object straight to his front; he will then observe some nearer point in the same straight line, such as a stone, tuft of grass, or other object, about 50 yards distant, and in marching will keep these two objects in line.

23. *Marching in quick time.*

1. " QUICK— MARCH." The squad will step off together with the left foot, in quick time, observing the rules in Sec. **22**.

2. " SQUAD— HALT." The moving-foot will complete its pace, and the other will be brought smartly up in line with it without stamping.

3. *Stepping out when marching in quick time.*

" STEP—OUT." The moving foot will complete its pace, and the soldier will lengthen the pace by 3 inches, leaning forward a little, but without altering the time.

Note.—This step is used when a slight increase of speed, without an alteration of time, is required; on the command *Quick— March*, the usual pace will be resumed.

4. *Stopping short when marching in quick time.*

" STEP—SHORT." The foot advancing will complete its pace, after which the pace will be shortened by 9 inches until the command " *Quick—March* " is given, when the quick step will be resumed.

5. *Marking Time.*

i. *From quick march.*

"MARK—TIME." The foot then advancing will complete its pace, after which the time will be continued, without advancing, by raising each foot alternately about six inches, keeping the feet almost parallel with the ground, the knees raised to the front, the arms steady at the sides, and the body steady. On the command "*Forward,*" the pace at which the men were moving will be resumed.

ii. *When at the halt,* the word of command is "QUICK—MARK—TIME."

6. *Stepping back from the halt.*

"——PACES STEP Step back the named number of paces of 30
BACK— inches straight to the rear, commencing with
MARCH." the left foot.

Note.—Stepping back should not exceed four paces.

24. *The double march.*

1. "DOUBLE— Step off with the left foot and double on the
MARCH." toes with easy swinging strides, inclining the body slightly forward but maintaining its correct carriage. The feet must be picked up cleanly from the ground at each pace, and the thigh, knee, and ankle joints must all work freely and without stiffness. The whole body should be carried forward by a thrust from the rear foot without unnecessary effort, and the heels must not be raised towards the seat but the foot carried straight to the front and the toes placed lightly on the ground. The arms

should swing easily from the shoulders and should be bent at the elbow, the forearm forming an angle of about 135 degrees with the upper arm (*i.e.* midway between a straight arm and a right angle at the elbow), fists clenched, backs of the hands outward, and the arm swung sufficiently clear of the body to allow of full freedom for the chest. The shoulders should be kept steady and square to the front and the head erect.

2. " SQUAD—   As in Sec. **23**, at the same time dropping
    HALT."   the hands to the position of *Attention*.

3. *Marking time in double time, from double march.*

" MARK—TIME."   Act as in Sec. **23**, the arms and hands being carried as when marching in double time, but with the swing of the arms reduced.

25. *The side step.*

1. " RIGHT (or   Each soldier will carry his right foot 15
    LEFT)   inches direct to the right, and instantly close
CLOSE—MARCH." his left foot to it, thus completing the pace ; he
    or   will proceed to take the next pace in the same
"—PACES RIGHT manner. Shoulders to be kept square, knees
    (or LEFT)   straight, unless on rough or broken ground.
CLOSE—MARCH." The direction must be kept in a straight line to the flank.

2. " SQUAD—   The command " *Halt* " will be given only
    HALT."   when the number of paces has not been specified. Then men will complete the pace they are taking, and remain steady.

Note.—Soldiers should not usually be moved to a flank by the side step more than twelve paces.

26. *Turning when on the march.*

1. "RIGHT (or LEFT)—TURN."	Each soldier will turn in the named direction, and move on at once, without checking his pace.

Note.—A soldier will always turn to the right on the left foot; and to the left on the right foot. The word "*Turn*" will be given as the foot on which the turn is to be made is coming to the ground; if it is not so given the soldier will move on one pace and then turn.

2. "ABOUT—TURN."	The soldier will turn right-about on his own ground in three beats of the time in which he is marching. Having completed the turn about the soldier will at once move forward, the fourth pace being a full pace.
3. "RIGHT (or LEFT)—INCLINE."	Make a half-turn in the required direction.

27. *Squad drill in single rank.*

1. Recruits will at this stage be formed in single rank without intervals, each man occupying a lateral space of 30 inches. An assistant instructor or more advanced recruit will be placed as leader. The man immediately in rear of the leader is called the centre guide.

2. *Numbering a squad.*

"SQUAD—NUMBER."	The squad will number off from the right-hand man, the right-hand man calling out "one," the next on his left "two," and so on. As each man calls out his number he will turn his head smartly towards his left and then at once turn it to the front again.

x 25119   D

3. *Proving.*

"Even (or Odd) Numbers— Prove."	Those ordered to prove stretch out their right hands to the full extent of the arm, palm of the hand to the left, fingers extended and close together, thumb close to the forefinger and in line with the top of the shoulder.
"As You Were."	Those proving bring their right hands smartly to the side, bending the elbow in so doing.

4. *Marching in squad.*—The caution will be given "The Squad will Advance." The leader will take up a point to march on.

"Quick March."	As in Sec. 23. Each man will preserve his position in the general line by an occasional glance towards the leader.

The recruit will be practised in changing the pace, without halting, from quick to double, by the command, "Double March." On the command "Quick March," the arms will be dropped to the usual position.

The instructor will ensure that the leader selects two distant points to march on, and that, before approaching the first, he takes another in advance on the same line, and so on.

5. *Opening and closing a squad.*

"Open Ranks —March."	The odd number* will take two paces forward; when the paces are completed the whole squad will look to the centre and correct the dressing quickly, looking to the front as soon as the dressing is correct.
"Reform— Ranks— March."	The odd numbers will step back two paces; when the paces are completed the squad will dress.

---

* If the centre-guide happens to be an even number he will move forward with the odd numbers.

6. *The incline or diagonal march.*

"RIGHT—   The men will all turn half right together,
INCLINE."   and march in that direction, each regulating
             his pace so that his own shoulders are parallel
             with the shoulders of the man on his right.
             The dressing will be by the right, consequently
             the right hand man must see that he inclines
             the same degree as the leader.

"FORWARD."   Every man will move forward together in
             the original direction.

             Note.—If the incline is properly performed
             the squad, after the word " *Forward,*" will be
             parallel to its original position.

7. *Dismissing.*

"DIS—MISS." The squad will turn to the right, and, after
             a pause, break off quickly and leave the parade
             ground.   If an officer is on parade the men
             will salute together as they break off.

8. *Wheeling.*

The method of wheeling will be the same as laid down in
the mounted drill.   (Sec. 116.)

Recruits will first be taught to wheel from the halt, after
which they will be instructed to wheel while on the march.   It
will be explained to the squad that, in wheeling, the flank which
is brought forward is termed the outer flank; the other, the
inner or pivot flank.

9. *Movements by sections, half-sections, and single files.*

These will be performed in accordance with directions for
mounted formations.

28. *Preparatory instruction for mounted drill.*

1. The recruits, when thoroughly grounded in the foregoing,
will be practised on foot in two ranks, as a troop, the rear rank
at three paces distance from the front rank.

D 2

The troop will be told off as laid down for mounted drill, two of the most intelligent recruits being posted as leader and centre guide. The troop leader will be posted three paces in front of the centre of the troop.

2. Dressing, inclining, wheeling, movements by sections, increasing and diminishing the front are executed in the same manner as laid down in mounted drill.

3. When the troop is standing easy, the instructor should ask questions on what the men have been learning. Occasionally the more advanced recruits should be called out to drill the troop.

4. During extended order drill the words of command will at first be preceded by the whistle sound, and accompanied by the corresponding signal. As the training progresses the men will be taught to work by whistle and signal only. For signals, *see* pages 8–11.

5. When extending or closing from the halt the men who have to change their position move at a walk, halting and standing at ease on arrival at their new position. The man who does not have to change his position stands at ease as soon as the order to extend or close is given.

6. When extending or closing on the march, the man from whom the extension is made or on whom the squad is closing will continue at the same pace; the remainder will double to their places, resuming the original pace on arrival.

THE SWORD ON FOOT.

29. *General principles.*

1. Instructors will base their instruction on the general principles for fighting mounted, as laid down in Sec. 82. They should impress upon the recruit from the first that he is provided with a sword for one purpose only, namely, to enable him to kill with it in war, when he will almost invariably use it mounted, and that instruction on foot is little more than a

necessary preliminary to the training which he will receive later on in mounted fighting.

2. Instruction in the use of the sword as a weapon should be taught in three stages.

1st Stage.—The various positions and movements used in fighting on foot, eliminating as much as possible the intricacies of the art and anything that is not applicable to mounted work.

Attention should be paid to strengthening the right wrist and muscles of the right arm.

2nd Stage.—The application of these movements, commencement of *assaulting lessons* and *loose play.*

3rd Stage.—Constant instruction in *assaulting lessons* and *loose play*; also instruction in the various points and parries in any direction, from the mounted position on foot, or preferably on low dummy horses.

3. Swordsmanship can only be taught by individual instruction. The best way to give this is by the method of "instructor and pupil," followed by two pupils opposing one another under the instructor's supervision.

Not more than three or four pupils should be allotted to one instructor at a time, and these should remain under his instruction throughout the complete course.

4. Assaulting lessons and loose play enable the men to see, step by step, the application to fighting of each detail which they have been taught. They also relieve the dullness of routine work, encourage the spirit of emulation, and give, from quite an early stage of instruction, some idea of actual fighting.

5. Work with single stick and any form of practice which might lead the men to cut instead of to point is prohibited.

6. Exact adherence to the details of the various positions and movements is not required, and much time should not be spent on them; the men should be taken on quickly to the practical lessons of "Instructor and Pupil." In teaching these lessons care must be taken to observe the order laid down and to improve gradually the pupil's execution of the movements.

30. *Parts of the sword.*

The sword consists of two parts, viz.: hilt and blade.

The *hilt*, which serves to protect the hand, and also to assist in turning an attack, is made up of the *guard* (or *shell*), the *resistance piece*, the *handle* (or *grip*), and the *pommel*.

The *blade* is straight and has a sharpened *point*.

The blade, from hilt to point, is divided into *forte*, *feeble*, and *middle*. The *forte* is that part of the blade nearest the hilt; the *feeble* the part nearest the point; and the *middle* is the part between the forte and feeble.

31. *Sword drill.*

1. *Position at attention.*—The sword will be held upright by the side, the shoe of the scabbard resting on the ground close to the left foot and just in front of the heel. The left arm will be extended, the hand round the scabbard, thumb in front, fingers in rear, back of the hand outwards.

2. *To stand at ease with the sword in the scabbard.*

"STAND AT—   Both legs to be kept straight. The left foot
EASE."   to be carried about one foot length to the left, the scabbard being carried off with the left leg. The shoe of the scabbard will rest on the ground close to the left foot, and just in front of the heel. The palm of the left hand, fingers in front, will rest on the top of the hilt, which will be pushed to the front, the right arm hanging by the side.

3. *To stand at ease with the sword drawn.*

"STAND AT—   Both legs to be kept straight. The left foot
EASE."   to be carried about one foot length to the left, the scabbard being carried off with the left leg and allowed to fall to the front, palm of the left hand resting on the bell of the scabbard. Sword to be sloped.

4. *Drawing swords by numbers.*

"DRAW SWORDS —ONE." Raise the scabbard until the little finger of the left hand is in line with the elbow, grasping the back (for officers' swords, upper) ring with the thumb and forefinger, the remaining fingers closed in the hand, the thick part of the forearm against the side; at the same time pass the right hand smartly across the body to the sword knot, place it on the wrist, give it two turns inwards to secure it, and as the handle is grasped draw out the blade slowly until the hand is in line with the elbow, turning the edge to the rear and straightening the left arm in rear of the thigh. the right arm close to the body, shoulders square to the front.

"TWO." Draw the sword from the scabbard, edge to the rear, in rear of the left shoulder, and lower the hand until the upper part of the hilt is opposite the mouth, the blade perpendicular, edge to the left, thumb in the thumb seat, elbow close to the body. This forms the position of *recover swords.*

"THREE." Bring the sword smartly down until the hand is in front of the elbow, and little finger in line with it, the elbow close to the body, blade perpendicular, edge to the front, forefinger and thumb round the resistance piece, hilt resting on the upper part of the hand. This forms the position of *carry swords.*

5. *Sloping swords.*

"SLOPE— SWORDS." Release the grasp of the last three fingers, and, without disturbing the position of the hand, allow the back of the sword to fall lightly on the shoulder midway between the neck and the point of the shoulder.

6. *Returning swords by numbers.*

"RETURN
SWORDS—
ONE."
Carry the hilt smartly to the hollow of the left shoulder, blade perpendicular, edge to the left, elbow level with the shoulder, at the same time bringing forward the mouth of the scabbard about three inches, grasping the back (for officers' swords, upper) ring with the thumb and forefinger; then, by a quick turn of the wrist, drop the point in rear of the left shoulder into the scabbard and resume the position at the end of the first motion of *draw swords*, shoulders being kept square to the front throughout this motion.

"TWO."
Let the sword fall smoothly into the scabbard, release the sword knot by giving it two turns outwards, the right hand remaining across the body in line with the elbow, fingers extended and close together, back of the hand up, and bring the sword to the position of *attention*.

"THREE."
Drop the right hand smartly to the side, as in the position of *attention*.

7. *To carry the sword in order to march.*

"QUICK—MARCH."
Raise the sword smartly with the left hand at the first pace, without stooping or disturbing the position of the body, and grasp the scabbard at the point where the sword balances when held at an angle of 45°, the fingers round the scabbard, the thumb along the edge, the arm fully extended, the hilt touching the back part of the arm.

8. *Halting.*

"SQUAD—HALT."
Lower the sword to the ground and assume the position of "*Attention.*"

9. *Paying compliments with the sword.* — When saluting an officer a soldier with sword drawn will come to the *carry*; when wearing a sword he will always salute with the right hand.

An officer when marching will salute a senior by coming to the *carry*.

10. *Officer's salute at the halt.**

First motion.	Bring the sword to the *recover*.
Second motion.	Lower the sword until the point is twelve inches from the ground and directed to the front, edge to the left, right arm straight, hand just behind the thigh, thumb flat on the handle of the sword.
Third motion.	Bring the sword to the *recover*.
Fourth motion.	Bring the sword to the *carry*.

32. *The first stage in teaching the recruit how to fight with the sword.*

1. *Method of grasping the sword (see Figs.* 1 *and* 2).—Grasp the handle of the sword with the right hand, first joint of the forefinger touching the base of the resistance piece, thumb in the groove on the back of the handle, central line of the thumb directly over the central line of the back of the handle, fingers pressing the back of the handle against the heel of the hand. In using the sword the wrist is not to be bent.

2. *The "first position."*—Heels together, feet at right angles to one another, right foot pointing straight to the front, with the left heel immediately behind the right. Body erect; with the right side, head and eyes turned in the direction of the adversary. Sword and arm in one straight line, edge of the sword to the right front, and the point about 8 inches from the ground.

---

* For the officer's salute when marching past, *see* "Ceremonial."

Fig. 1.   Fig. 2.

 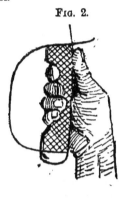

3. *The position of "sword in line."*—From the "First Position," keeping the sword and arm in one straight line, raise the sword with the arm fully extended to the level of the shoulder, the edge to the right and inclined slightly upwards.

4. *The position of the "engage."*—From the position of "Sword in Line" advance the right foot in the direction of the adversary about 2½ feet, bending the knees well in doing so.

In this position both legs below the knee should be perpendicular; body erect, its weight evenly balanced between each leg, head and eyes looking towards the adversary; forearm and blade in one line, pointing in the direction of the adversary, edge of the blade to the right, and inclined upwards; elbow bent near the right side and free from the body; left shoulder well back and left hand on the hip, wrist bent downwards.

· The body and limbs should not be rigid and the direction of the weapon should vary according to the position of the adversary.

5. *To lunge or point.*—From the position of "**Engage**," and keeping the left foot flat on the ground, straighten the right arm and force the body forward to the fullest extent, at the same time straightening the left leg with the utmost rapidity; the right foot raised not more than an inch, must be advanced at least a foot's length in the direction of the adversary, and placed sharply and firmly on the ground. The weight of the body, thus inclined forward, must rest principally on the right leg, the left hip being neither raised nor depressed. The point should be delivered with the back of the hand to the left, little finger uppermost.

6. *The position of "rest."*—Straighten the legs, drop the left hand to the side, and bring the sword to the position of the "Slope."

The pupil should come to rest from any position the easiest way.

7. *The parries.*—These are described as if made from the "*engage*"; they should, however, be executed from any position, *e.g.*, a parry should be made from the final position of any other parry, or from the lunge, &c.

A parry is a movement of defence and not a fixed position; it is made with the object of taking off the adversary's attacking blade with the edge of the sword. The edge of the sword is used on account of the extra strength obtained. In making a parry the adversary's blade should be met with the forte, and not with the feeble.

When a parry is made correctly the adversary's blade should not only be met by the edge and forte of the blade, but should finally be brought to rest by the hilt.

The height at which a parry is made should vary according to the height of the adversary's attack; it will be seen that most of the parries practically merge into one another, and that as long as the body is protected, it is not important which is used, or whether it is made higher or lower than as described.

It is always advisable to parry an attacking blade as far in front of the body as possible; and this is best effected by giving a slight forward movement to the parry.

All parries are effective against either a point or cut.

    i. *Right parry.*—Straighten the right arm so as to meet the attack, directing the point towards the adversary, and high or low as required, edge of the blade to the right, and turned slightly upwards.

    ii. *Left parry.*—Carry the sword across the body to the left to meet the adversary's attack, arm slightly bent, the blade high or low as required, edge to the left, without allowing the point to move too far from the central line.

    iii. *Head parry.*—Carry the sword upwards, straightening the arm, hand in line with the head, the point about 6 inches higher than the hand and directed over the head of the adversary, the edge turned upwards, eyes looking under the forte of the blade.

8. *The disengage.*—When two adversaries are engaged with their blades in contact in one line, and one of them carries his blade into another line, the movement is termed the " disengage." The blades cannot, however, be in contact in one line and the line closed (*i.e.,* the body protected on that side) without an opening being left for attack in another line. An attack can therefore be made at such opening by a *point with disengage* delivered as follows :—

By a quick and close movement of the whole arm detach the blade from the adversary's blade, carry it with a spiral motion (over or under that of the adversary) passing close to his hilt and arm and deliver the point at the opening aimed at. The whole movement to be executed with great rapidity combined with steadiness.

9. *The deviation.*—When an opponent keeps the point of his sword persistently directed towards the body, it is impossible to attack him without running on his point, until the blade is removed from its threatening position. His blade may be removed by a *deviation* executed as follows :—

Make any one of the parries described above, then with a slight forward movement press smoothly but quickly with the forte of the blade against the feeble of the adversary's until the direction of his blade has been changed sufficiently to give an opening for a point—then immediately deliver a direct point or a point with disengage, as required.

10. *Feints.*—A " feint " is a false or pretended attack made by a movement of the sword and body with the intention of causing the adversary to believe that a determined attack is about to be delivered. The object of making a feint is to induce the adversary to form a parry to protect the line threatened, and so uncover some other part of his body, thereby making an opening for the real attack. The feint should be made by inclining the body slightly but energetically forward and straightening the arm (if it be not already straight) so as to simulate an attack with a direct point. If the feint is made well, the adversary will at once form a parry, and it is while he is forming this parry that a disengage and point should be made at the part of his body he has uncovered. In attacking with a feint it is very important not to dwell on the feint, but (anticipating the parry that the adversary will form) to disengage immediately, so that you may hit him while he is making the parry. A feint, to be of any use, must be made with such decision that it conveys to the adversary's mind a firm conviction that it is a real attack, and so compels him to form the necessary parry to meet it. A feint can be made with a cut in a similar manner, but the subsequent attack should always be with the point.

33. *The second stage in teaching the recruit how to fight with the sword.*

1. The following lessons are progressive, and will be taught in the order in which they are given below. A reasonable degree of proficiency is required in each lesson before proceeding with the next, repetition being made as found necessary.

Their object is to teach the recruit how to apply the various movements and positions described above in Sec. 32.

2. Lesson i: *Lunging with the point.*

> "First position."
> "Sword in line."
> "Engage."
> "Lunge" (*i.e.*, with direct point).
> "Rest."

The above will at first be taught without a sword, and afterwards with sword in hand, the men being taught how to hold the sword while resting between the various movements.

3. Lesson ii. *The parries.*

> "Right parry."
> "Left parry."
> "Head parry."

The instructor will at first illustrate the parries with the aid of an assistant who knows them. He will then take each pupil separately and, holding his own sword in the required position, will show him a threatening attack and make him parry it, indicating the part to be defended rather than the name of the parry. By this means the pupil will be made to realise from the beginning exactly what he has to parry, and the necessity for it.

4. Lesson iii. *Lunging with point at "wall pad."*

This lesson is indispensable for teaching men to aim at and hit something with the point, to judge their distance properly, and to increase their reach, speed, and energy.

5. Lesson iv. *The direct attack.*

> Instructor shows opening.
> Pupil lunges with point and hits instructor.
> Repeat this from different openings till pupil attacks well with the point.

6. Lesson v. *Parry and return.*

Instructor threatens pupil with point or cut.
Pupil parries instructor's attack and " returns " with
the point, hitting instructor.
Repeat in different lines.

7. Lesson iv. *Combination of lessons iv and v.*

Instructor shows opening.
Pupil attacks with point.
Instructor parries and returns at pupil.
Pupil parries and returns with the point, hitting the
instructor.
Repeat in different lines.

8. Lesson vii. *Direct assault.*

Two pupils, on guard, facing each other at lunging
distance.
The one attacks direct with point and tries to hit his
opponent.
The other endeavours to parry the attack and, if he
succeeds, to return with the point immediately.

In this assaulting lesson the attacker chooses his own
time to make the attack, and must make it with great speed
and determination. No words of command will be given.
All subsequent instruction will finish with a few minutes
of this assaulting lesson, until Lesson xi is reached, when
either may be used to conclude the day's instruction.

9. Lesson viii. *The disengage.*

Teach iv, v, vi, and vii, commencing with a " Disengage."

10. Lesson ix. *The deviation.*

Teach iv, v, vi, and vii, commencing with a " Deviation."

11. Lesson x. *The feints.*

Teach iv, v, vi, and vii, commencing with one feint.

Instructor shows opening.

Pupil feints with the point at the opening, and (as instructor parries) disengages and hits with the point.

12. Lesson xi. *The assault either direct or with feint.*

Two pupils, on guard, as in Lesson vii.

The instructor will order which of the two is to attack.

The one attacks either direct or with feint trying to hit with the point.

The other parries and returns with the point (*i.e.*, acts according to which of the two ways he is attacked) trying to hit with the point in his return if he is able to parry successfully.

This lesson gives scope for developing the true fighting instinct by teaching the men to make either a good direct attack, or a good feint, which will really deceive the adversary (*see* also remarks on Lesson vii).

13. Lesson xii. *The assault or loose play.*

This will be practised first of all with the instructor and afterwards with other pupils under the supervision of the instructor. In this lesson either man attacks when he thinks fit. The men must be taught to acknowledge points by " recovering " the sword.

14. Men will now be passed on to the third stage even though not thoroughly proficient in what has already been taught. Backward pupils will be given additional lessons in the assault as required, either at once or later on.

34. *The third stage in teaching the recruit how to fight with the sword.*

1. The great object of all these lessons, mounted and dismounted, is to give the man such control of his sword, as

will enable him to adopt methods suitable to the occasion in an actual fight. The pupil will be placed in the mounted position on foot, or seated astride on a barrack room form, or preferably on the low dummy horse.

There are some differences in the positions and movements used in mounted fighting to those used when dismounted. These differences, though very slight, are to a certain extent inevitable. The principles are the same.

2. *The position of the engage.*—Forearm and blade in one line, pointing in the direction of the adversary, edge of the blade to the right and arm slightly bent at the elbow, which should be free from the body. There should be nothing stiff about this position, and the direction of the weapon should vary according to the position of the adversary.

When charging, the arm should be straight, back of the hand to the left, little finger uppermost, body bent well forward, the direction of the point being controlled from the shoulder without bending the elbow or wrist.

The instructor will place himself in the position of the opponent, and then move round the pupil, making him follow him with his sword, as though he were engaged with an enemy.

3. *The point.*—The point will be delivered with the utmost promptitude, horizontal at cavalry and low at infantry, in any required direction, as follows :—

> Keeping the sword and forearm in line with one another, direct the point of the sword at the object, and straighten the arm vigorously, at the same time bending the body forward to gain extra reach.

Without in any way checking the speed with which the point is delivered, the instructor must be careful to ensure that it is made with steadiness and accuracy, so as to prevent any vibration of the sword. To this end lungeing at a wall pad from a seated position must be practised constantly.

4. *The "parries."*—As described in Sec. **32**, **7**. :

When mounted, the best way to deal with an adversary on the left rear is to manœuvre by means of good horsemanship for some better position.

5. In all the instruction in this stage the instructor will move round the pupil as required, the pupil following him round with his sword at the *engage*, as described above. The instructor will then (from any direction) show an opening for the pupil to attack, or will attack the pupil to make him form the correct parry as the case may be. All the hits and parries will thus be made with reference to the instructor's movements. To quicken the movements of an advanced pupil two, three, or even four men may be placed round him to attack or to be attacked by him in turn.

6. Stuffed heads or dummies will be placed in various positions, and the pupil made to run his point through them quickly.

THE LANCE ON FOOT.

35. *General instructions.*

1. The instructions will be based on the principles of mounted fighting described in Sec. **82** and will be divided into three portions :—

   i. *Lance drill*—

     Necessary for ceremonial purposes.

   ii. *Lance practice*—

     The object of lance practice is to teach the points, parries, butts and waves, and to strengthen the grip and give freedom in handling the weapon.

   iii. *Preliminary instruction in fighting with the lance.*

36. *Parts of the lance.*

The lance consists of the following parts : the point, the butt, the pole, the point of balance, the sling. The sling should be fitted as for mounted work, so that the bottom of it comes two inches nearer the butt than the point of balance.

37. *Lance drill.*

1. *Position at attention.*—The man stands as in Sec. **16.** The lance is held between the thumb and fingers of the right hand at the full extent of the arm, thumb inside the pole, fingers outside, back of the hand to the right, butt close to the ball of the right foot.

This is the position of the *order.*

2. *The stand at ease from the order.*
" STAND AT EASE." Carry the left foot to the left.

3. *The carry from the order.*
" CARRY—LANCE." Raise the hand with the back to the front and grasp the pole, thumb level with top of the shoulder, back of the hand to the front, elbow down. Lance to be kept perpendicular.

4. *The shoulder from the order.*
" SHOULDER—LANCE." Bring the lance to the shoulder by raising the arm from the elbow, still holding the lance as at the " *Order,*" right elbow close to the hip, hand in front and in line with the elbow, lance sloping backwards and resting on the right shoulder. (This is the position in which the lance is carried when marching on foot.)

5. *The support from the order.*
" SUPPORT LANCE —ONE." Raise the hand to the balance, placing the thumb in front, and the fingers in rear of the pole.

" TWO." Raise the arm from the elbow, back of the hand down, so that the butt is brought across the body to the left front, the lance resting on the right forearm, the butt about six inches lower than the point.

E 2

6. *The order from the support.*

"ORDER LANCE—"   Lower the butt and resume the first posi-
   "ONE."   tion of the support.
   "TWO."   Move the hand to the position of the
                 order.

7. *The dismiss.*

"DIS—MISS."   As when dismissing without arms. Men
                 will leave the parade ground with lances at
                 the shoulder.

8. *Paying compliments with the lance.*—When a soldier carry‧
ing a lance passes an officer he will do so at the *shoulder* and
will turn his head towards the person saluted. A soldier with a
lance, if halted when an officer passes, will turn towards him
and *carry lance*. A sentry on the approach of an officer will
halt, turn towards him and *carry lance*.

9. *Guards, sentries.*—Guards including reliefs will march
with lances at the *shoulder*.

Sentries are to walk with their lances at the *support*.

38. *Lance practice.*

1. The recruits may be taught lance practice individually, or
they may be formed for instruction in small squads of about ten
men each.

2. Each series of points, parries, etc., should be carried out
by word of command, either by numbers or in drill time; the
practice should not be carried out continuously from beginning
to end on one word of command.

3. The order in which the words of command are given should
be varied, so that the men may be accustomed to deliver a rapid
attack in any direction. The direction of the attack should also

be changed frequently; for instance, instead of "FRONT FIRST POINT," the command may be given "HALF RIGHT LOW FIRST POINT."

4. The men should be formed for lance practice so that each man has a clear space round him of at least four yards, and before the practice begins the instructor must make certain that this space has been taken.

5. *From the carry.*

"ENGAGE."   Let the hand slide smartly down the pole to full extent of the sling, thumb inside it, lance upright; raise the butt six inches from the ground and lower the point direct to the front till the lance is horizontal, catching the pole under the closed arm; as the lance is being lowered carry the right foot 20 inches to the right, feet pointing straight to the front, bridle hand in the mounted position.

6. "ROUND WAVE   Carry the point smartly to the right. Hold
   —ONE."   the pole firmly under the arm and bend both knees, keeping the weight of the body on the left leg.

"TWO."   Carry the point round in the same horizontal line to the left, changing the weight of the body on to the right leg.

"THREE."   Carry the point to the front.

7. "FRONT FIRST   Deliver the point to the full extent of the
   POINT—ONE."   arm; back of the hand to the left, body inclined in the direction of the point to add force to the blow.

"TWO."   Withdraw the lance to the engage.

8. "RIGHT FRONT   Lower the lance horizontally : point to the
   FEINT AND   right front, hand in rear of and as low as the
   SECOND POINT   hip; both knees bent and the weight of the
   —ONE."   body on the left leg.

"Two."   Feint by bringing the hand about 18 inches
                to the front and quickly withdrawing it; then
                without a pause deliver the point to the full
                extent of the arm, back of the hand to the left.

"Three."   Withdraw the lance to the first position.

9. "Right Front Make a strong parry by carrying the lance
Glance Parry,   forwards and outwards, point of the lance
Feint, and   slightly raised and to the right front, hand in
Butt—One."   line with the shoulder.

"Two."   Raise the point and circle it upwards by the
                left to the rear, using the heel of the hand in
                doing so; butt to be directed to the right
                front as high as the breast, arm bent, hand
                over the elbow, elbow a little higher than the
                shoulder.

"Three."   Move the butt to the front about 18 inches,
                withdraw it quickly, and without a pause
                deliver the butt in a downward direction to
                the full extent of the arm, relaxing the grasp
                with the last two fingers.

"Four."   Return to the second position.

10. "Right Rear, Lower the butt and parry strongly out-
Stop Parry   wards to the right rear, lance perpendicular, arm
and Third   slightly bent, hand in line with the shoulder.
Point—One."

"Two."   Raise the butt with the heel of the hand so
                as to clear the horse's head; bring the right
                hand smartly towards the left, back of the
                hand down, and let the pole rest on the bridle
                arm, point to the right rear.

"Three."   Deliver the point to the full extent of the
                arm to the right rear, back of the hand down,
                arm in line with the shoulder, leaning the
                body well over and throwing back the right
                shoulder.

"Four."   Withdraw the lance to the second position.

11. "LEFT REAR, FOURTH POINT —ONE." Raise the lance horizontally over the head by straightening the arm; circle the point smartly to the left rear and lower the lance until it rests horizontally on the bridle arm, the right hand drawn back about 18 inches from the left, elbow well raised; at the same time turn the body well to the left on the hips and change the weight from the left to the right leg.

"Two." Deliver the point catching the pole firmly under the arm.

"Three." Withdraw the lance to the first position.

12. "LEFT, STOP PARRY—ONE." Raise the hand straight above the head, lance horizontal; circle the butt to the left and lower it on the near side of the horse, lance perpendicular, arm bent, hand and elbow in line with the shoulder.

"Two." Parry with force to the left front, extending the arm to its full extent.

13. "LEFT FRONT, FEINT AND BUTT—ONE." Raise the hand upwards to the right rear with the butt direct to the left front and as high as the breast, arm bent, hand over the elbow, elbow a little higher than the shoulder.

"Two." Feint by moving the butt to the left front about 18 inches and quickly withdrawing it; without a pause deliver the butt in a downward direction to the full extent of the arm, relaxing the grasp of the last two fingers.

"Three." Withdraw the lance to the first position, but with the arm straightened and hand more to the rear.

14. "LEFT FRONT, FIFTH POINT— ONE." Circle the point round by the rear to the left front; lower the lance horizontally on to the bridle arm, right hand drawn back about 18 inches from the left elbow, well raised.

"Two."	Deliver the point to the full extent of the arm, pole outside the arm, back of the hand to the left.
"THREE."	Withdraw the lance to the first position.
15. "LEFT FRONT, FEINT, AND FOURTH POINT —ONE."	Feint low at the body by bringing the hand forward 12 inches and quickly withdrawing it, sliding the lance on the bridle arm; then without a pause deliver the point to the left front, catching the pole firmly under the arm.
"Two."	Withdraw the lance to the first position.

39. *Preliminary instruction in fighting with the lance.*

The principles of instruction in fighting with the sword are equally applicable in the case of instruction in fighting with the lance. When once the recruits know the various points, parries, butts and thrusts described in the lance practice they should be given individual instruction by the instructor in the way these movements may be turned to account. Later two recruits may oppose one another under the instructor's supervision. One should be mounted on a dummy horse and armed with a dummy lance or sword; the other armed with a dummy lance should attack at the double from the front from a distance of about ten yards.

THE RIFLE.

40. *General rules.*

1. The recruit should first be taught the different parts of the rifle, and the care of arms, as laid down in "Musketry Regulations, Part I."

2. He should then be instructed in drill with the rifle, with the object of teaching him how to handle it in various circumstances and at the same time to strengthen his muscles.

These exercises will not be performed at inspections, and will only be practised by units larger than a squad as may be necessary for purposes of ceremonial.

The movements described in Sec. 41 should be thoroughly taught and be carried out with smartness and precision; but the same precision is not required of those included in Sec. 42, and but little time should be spent in learning them.

3. Squads with arms will be practised in the different marches and variations of step. During these practices, the closest attention must be paid to the position of each individual recruit.

The disengaged arm will be allowed to swing naturally as described for marching in quick or double time without arms.

41. *Rifle exercises, Part I.*

1. *Falling in with the rifle.—The order.*—The recruit will fall in as directed in Sec. 16 with the rifle held perpendicularly at his right side, the butt on the ground, its toe in line with the toe of the right foot. The right arm to be slightly bent, the hand to hold the rifle at or near the band (with the L.E. or L.M. rifle near the lower band), back of the hand to the right thumb against the thigh, fingers together and slanting towards the ground.

When each man has got his dressing he will *stand at ease*.

2. *To stand at ease from the order.*

"STAND AT—   Keeping the legs straight, carry the left foot
EASE."'   about one foot-length to the left so that the
                 weight of the body rests equally on both feet,
                 at the same time incline the muzzle of the
                 rifle slightly to the front with the right hand,
                 arm close to the side, the left arm to be kept in
                 the position of *attention.*

3. *The attention from stand at ease.*

"SQUAD—   The left foot will be brought up to the right
ATTENTION."   and the rifle returned to the order.

4. *The slope from the order.*

"SLOPE ARMS"— Give the rifle a cant upwards with the right
" ONE."   hand, catching it with the left hand behind the
                backsight and the right hand at the small of
                the butt, thumb to the left, elbow to the rear.
"TWO."   Carry the rifle across the body and place it
                flat on the left shoulder, magazine outwards
                from the body. Seize the butt with the left
                hand, the first two joints of the fingers grasp-
                ing the outside of the butt, the thumb about
                one inch above the toe, the upper part of the
                left arm close to the side, the lower part
                horizontal, and the heel of the butt in line with
                the centre of the left thigh.

"THREE."   Cut away the right hand to the side.

5. *The order from the slope.*

"ORDER ARMS"—   Bring the rifle down to the full extent of the
" ONE."   left arm, at the same time meeting it with the
                right hand just above the back sight, arm close
                to the body.
"TWO."   Bring the rifle to the right side, seizing it
                at the same time with the left hand just below
                the foresight, butt just clear of the ground.
" THREE."   Place the butt quietly on the ground, cutting
                the left hand away to the side.

6. *The present from the slope.*

"PRESENT ARMS" Seize the rifle with the right hand at the
—" ONE."   small, both arms close to the body.

"TWO."   Raise the rifle with the right hand perpen-
                dicularly in front of the centre of the body,
                sling to the left; at the same time place the

left hand smartly on the stock, wrist on the magazine, fingers pointing upwards, thumb close to the forefinger, point of the thumb in line with the mouth; the left elbow to be close to the butt, the right elbow and butt close to the body.

"THREE." Bring the rifle down perpendicularly close in front of the centre of the body, guard to the front, holding it lightly to the full extent of the right arm, fingers slanting downwards, and meet it smartly with the left hand immediately behind the back sight, thumb pointing towards the muzzle; at the same time place the hollow of the right foot against the left heel, both knees straight. The weight of the rifle to be supported by the left hand.

7. *The slope from the present.*

"SLOPE ARMS"— Bring the right foot in line with the left and
   "ONE." place the rifle on the left shoulder as described in the second motion of *Slope* from the *Order.*

   "TWO." Cut away the right hand to the side.

8. The recruit having been thoroughly instructed in the foregoing motions of the rifle by numbers, will be taught to perform them in quick time, the words of command being given without the numbers, and executed as above detailed, with a pause of one beat of quick time between each motion. Arms will be sloped from the *stand easy,* on the command "SQUAD—SLOPE—ARMS"; and when at the *slope* the squad will be taught to go through the motions of the *order, stand at ease* and *stand easy* on the command "STAND—EASY."

9. *Dismissing.*

   "DIS—MISS." As in Sec. 42, 6.

42. *Rifle exercises, Part II.*

1. *To trail arms from the order.*

   "TRAIL ARMS."   By a slight bend of the right arm give the
   rifle a cant forward and seize it at the point of
   balance, bringing it at once to a horizontal
   position at the right side at the full extent of
   the arm, fingers and thumb round the rifle and
   behind the seam of the trousers.

2. *To order arms from the trail.*

   "ORDER ARMS."   Raising the muzzle, catch the rifle at the
   band, and come to the order.

3. *The short trail.*

   (*No word of*   Raise the rifle about three inches from the
   command.) ground, keeping it otherwise in the position
   of the *order.*

   If standing with ordered arms, and directed
   to close to the right or left, to step back, or
   to take any named number of paces forward,
   men will come to the *short trail.*

4. *To ground arms from the order.*

   "GROUND ARMS."   Place the rifle gently on the ground at the
   right side, magazine to the right.   The right
   hand will be in line with the toe as it places
   the rifle on the ground.   Then return smartly
   to the position of *attention.*

5. *To take up arms and return to the order.*

   "TAKE UP ARMS."   Bend down, pick up the rifle and return
   to the order.

6. *Dismissing.*

"DIS—MISS." The squad will turn to the right, and after a pause break off quickly and leave the parade ground with sloped arms.

Note.—Arms will be sloped before the squad is dismissed.

43. *Inspection of arms.*

1. *To port arms for inspection on parade from the order.*

"FOR INSPECTION PORT—ARMS." Cant the rifle, muzzle leading, with the right hand smartly across the body, guard to the left and downwards, the barrel crossing opposite the point of the left shoulder, and meet it at the same time with the left hand close behind the backsight, thumb and fingers round the rifle, the left wrist to be opposite the left breast, both elbows close to the body.

Turn the safety catch completely over to the front with the thumb or forefinger of the right hand. (Charger loading L.E. rifle, lower the safety catch with the thumb of the right hand.) Pull out the cut-off if closed, first pressing it downwards with the thumb, then seize the knob with the forefinger and thumb of the right hand, turn it sharply upwards, and draw back the bolt to its full extent, then grasp the butt with the right hand immediately behind the bolt, thumb pointing to the muzzle.

2. *To ease springs and come to the order.*

   i. *If the magazine is to be emptied.*

"EASE-SPRINGS." From the position described above, work the bolt rapidly backwards and forwards until all cartridges are removed from the magazine and chamber,* allowing them to fall to the ground, then close the breech (with L.E. or L.M. rifle, the cut-off should first be closed), press the trigger, close the cut-off by placing the right hand over the bolt and pressing the cut-off inwards, turn the safety catch over to the rear, and return the hand to the small.

ii. *If the magazine is to be kept charged.*

"Lock Bolt." Close the breech (with L.E. or L.M. rifle, the cut-off should first be closed), then turn the safety catch over to the rear and return the hand to the small.

"Order—Arms" Holding the rifle firmly in the left hand,
—"One." seize it with the right hand at the band (with L.E. or L.M. rifle, at the lower band).

"Two." As in the second motion of the order from the slope.

"Three." As in the third motion of the order from the slope.

3. When arms are inspected at the *port* only, as when inspecting a squadron on parade, the officer will see that the wind-gauge is properly centred, the fine adjustment at its lowest point, the keeper screw and the screw on the right charger guide in proper position, and that the magazine platform works freely.

Each soldier, when the officer has passed the file next to him, will, without further word of command, *Ease springs, Order arms* and *Stand at ease.*

4. If it is necessary to *Examine arms*, the men, when in the position of *For inspection, Port—arms*, will be cautioned to remain at the *Port.*

---

* This precaution will be also adopted when rifles are not loaded.

5. *To examine arms from the position, for inspection,*
port arms.

"EXAMINE ARMS." Both ranks will come to the position for loading (*see* "Musketry Regulations, Part I"), with the muzzle so inclined as to enable the officer to look through the barrel, the thumb nail of the right hand being placed in front of the bolt to reflect light into the barrel.

The soldier, when the officer has passed the next file to him, will unload, order arms, and stand at ease.

44. *Paying compliments with the rifle.*

1. When a soldier carrying a rifle passes or addresses an officer he will do so at the *slope* and will salute by carrying the right hand smartly to the small of the butt, forearm horizontal, back of the hand to the front fingers extended. He will salute at the same number of paces before reaching the officer, and cut the hand away, as directed when saluting without arms.

2. In passing an officer the soldier will always turn his head towards him in the same manner as when unarmed.

3. A soldier if halted when an officer passes will turn towards him and stand at the *order*.

45. *Guards, sentries.*

1. Guards, including reliefs, rounds, and patrols, will march with sloped arms.

2. Sentries are to walk with their arms at the *slope*, and when saluting otherwise than by presenting arms, will carry the right hand to the small of the butt as directed above.

3. Further instructions concerning guards and sentries are given in "Ceremonial."

DRILL OF THE MACHINE GUN SECTION.

46. *Elementary training.*

1. The elementary training of the machine gunner will be carried out as directed in Sec. **11,** 5. During this training, untrained numbers should attend on any occasion when firing is being carried out. They should also be present when the gun is stripped by the armourer.

2. The machine gunner must be taught at an early stage to hold the gun so that sufficient pressure is applied to the handles to check its vibration without transferring the vibration to the mounting.

Machine guns vary considerably, and such variations can be counteracted only by a thorough knowledge of the particular gun and by skilful holding. Whenever the gun is laid, the holding should be such as would be employed in actually firing service ammunition.

An early opportunity should be taken to demonstrate with a few rounds of ball ammunition at 30 yards range the necessity for correct holding. This may be done by a trained number firing a series of 2 or 3 rounds when pressing the handles down, when pressing the handles up, and then when holding correctly.

47. *Allocation of duties.*

1. The duties of the *section officer* are to command his section in accordance with his orders and the tactical situation; to observe and to control fire generally; to regulate the ammunition supply; and to give instructions regarding the movement of limbered wagons. If guns are brigaded, he should repeat and pass orders of the brigade machine gun officer, watch for signals, and act as the brigade machine gun officer may direct.

2. The duties of the *serjeant* are to act as leader when the section commander moves on ahead of the guns to choose a position, and to supervise guns coming into action as the section officer may direct. He must be prepared to take command of the section in the event of the officer becoming a casualty.

3. The *corporal* will supervise the ammunition supply and filling of belts, direct the limbered wagons as required, and watch for signals from the section officer. When the guns are in action he will remain with the ammunition wagons. He will be prepared to take the place of the serjeant should the latter become a casualty.

4. The following are the duties of the various numbers :—

No. 1, is the firer. He will clean and look after his gun ; ensure that the mechanism is working smoothly. On going into action he will carry the tripod and place it in a suitable position and assist No. 2 in mounting the gun. He repeats all orders received.

No. 2, assists No. 1 at the gun, carries the gun into action, and mounts it with the assistance of No. 1. In action he will watch for signals from the section or brigade machine gun officer, attend to the feeding of the gun, and generally assist No. 1.

Fig. 3.

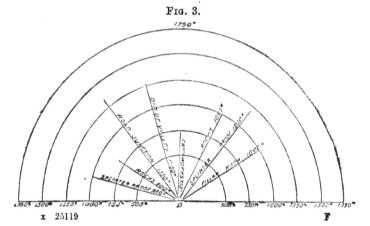

Nos. 3 and 4, are ammunition carriers. No. 3 takes the first supply of ammunition to the gun, assisted by No. 4, who also carries the spare parts box. No. 4 takes ammunition from the limber to No. 3 as a further supply is required.

No. 5, acts as scout, as ordered by the section officer.

No. 6, is the rangetaker. He will take ranges and prepare range cards. (*See* Fig. 3.)

No. 7, is horse holder.

5. In allotting the various duties, section officers should select the men who show a particular aptitude for each particular duty, and for this purpose they will keep careful record of the characteristics and particular aptitude of each number. The results obtained in table " C," (*see* " Musketry Regulations ") in rangetakers' tests, and tests in belt filling, will assist section officers in detailing the numbers. Nos. 1, 2, and 3 should be the best in that order of merit at laying and holding, Nos. 5 and 6 at range taking, and No. 4 at belt filling. During training, the numbers should frequently change round, so that each may be trained in the duties of all numbers under various conditions.

The serjeant should similarly be practised in the duties of section officer and the corporal in the duties of serjeant and of section officer.

48. *Section drill, without transport.*

1. The guns, with tripod and ammunition boxes, will be placed on the ground, muzzles to the front and in line, legs to the rear, straps buckled and clamps sufficiently tight to prevent the legs hanging loose when the tripod is lifted off the ground; the traversing clamp should be sufficiently loose to enable the gun to be deflected by a sharp tap with the hand on the rear cross piece, guns on the right, ammunition boxes three paces in rear of the guns. The guns to be a convenient distance apart, but not closer than eight paces.

2. On the command " FALL IN " the detachments for the two guns will fall in in two ranks, 5 paces in front of the interval between the guns; the serjeant on the left of the front rank, covered by the corporal in the rear rank. The front rank will

provide the right gun detachment, the rear rank the left gun detachment.

On the command "NUMBER" the men will number off from the right as in squad drill (Sec. 27, 2).

On the command "TAKE POST," detachments turn outwards and double to their respective guns (the serjeant and corporal on the outer flank, where they can superintend). Nos. 1 and 2 fall in on the left of the tripod and right of the gun respectively, No. 3 on the left of the ammunition box. If the ground is suitable, these Nos. should lie down.

Nos. 4, 5, 6, and 7 fall in, in single rank, in rear of No. 3.

3. A landscape target should be placed about 25 yards from the guns, and a point of aim indicated. The instructor having pointed out a spot, not more than 5 yards away, where each gun will come into action, will give the command "MOUNT GUN." No. 1 picks up the tripod, having previously seen that both elevating screws are exposed the same distance, carries it to the spot ordered, and places it in position. In adjusting the tripod he must make certain that the crosshead and sights are upright and that the legs are clamped tight. He must learn by experience the adjustment that suits him best for the position ordered and for the nature of the ground, so that he will not be cramped when firing and will not have to alter the tripod after the gun has been mounted.

As soon as the tripod is nearly in position, No. 2 picks up the gun and carries it to the right side of the tripod, holding the rear cross piece with the left hand, with the gun, muzzle to the rear, under the right arm. He then kneels on the left knee, facing the tripod, and supporting the weight of the gun on the right knee, places it on the tripod, drives in and turns down the crosshead joint pin, and removes the cork plug from the steam escape hole. No. 1 fixes the elevating joint pin, and directs the gun towards the mark. Meanwhile, No. 2 sits down, places the ammunition box in position, opens the lid and holds the tag of the belt ready to load.

No. 2 should time his advance so as to reach the tripod at the moment its adjustment is completed.

F 2

When No. 3 sees the gun is nearly mounted, he carries the ammunition box forward and places it within reach of No. 2. The ammunition must be at hand directly No. 2 is ready for it. No. 3 then retires to his original place.

4. On the command "LOAD" No. 2 passes the tag of the belt through the feed block. No. 1 turns the crank handle on to the buffer spring, and with his left hand pulls the belt straight through as far as it will go, and then lets go the crank handle; he releases the strain on the belt, turns the crank handle on to the buffer spring; he pulls the belt to the left front and lets go the belt and crank handle. The gun is loaded and ready to fire. Each motion should be distinct.

"AT —" (name the aiming mark). No. 2 releases the traversing clamp, and No. 1 lays the gun approximately. No. 2 alters the position of the ammunition box if necessary.

"——" (Elevation required in yards). No. 1 repeats the order for his own gun, raises the tangent sight, adjusts the slide to the distance given and aims, maintaining the same pressure on the handles while laying as when firing.

5. When the gun is laid, No. 1 says "CLAMP," and No. 2 acts accordingly. No. 1 then raises the automatic safety catch with the forefinger, and prepares the fire. When No. 1 is ready, No. 2 holds up his left hand. As proficiency increases the pause between naming the object and the range should be slight.

On the command "FIRE," No. 1 presses the double button.

On the command "CEASE FIRE," No. 1 releases the automatic safety catch, and remains steady.

6. Frequent instruction will be given in traversing fire. The firer must first ensure that the traversing clamp is just sufficiently loose to enable the gun to be deflected by means of a sharp tap with the hand on the rear cross-piece. Each man must learn by experience the exact degree of clamping he requires and before firing he should ensure that the clamp is correctly adjusted to suit himself.

The target will be the instructional machine gun target described in "Musketry Regulations, Part II."

Traversing fire is applied by means of a series of groups fired at regular intervals within certain limits indicated by such figures on the target as may be ordered by the instructor.

In horizontal traversing the instructor having described the figures between which fire is to be directed, will order "TRAVERSING FIRE." The firer will lay the gun on the flank figure named and press the button, then tap the gun to approximately the centre of the interval to the next figure, again press the button, then tap and so on until the limit ordered has been reached. The firer should be taught to fire groups of about 8 rounds by maintaining pressure on the button for about 1 second at each group. By this method he learns to tap the gun with the necessary force in order to avoid firing more than one group at the same place and also to avoid leaving gaps in the line he is traversing.

As proficiency increases instruction should be given in diagonal traversing. The target will be three bands each with three figures as for horizontal traversing. The bands will be joined so that each of the outer bands is in the same vertical plane as the centre band and forms an angle of 120 degrees with it. In this case the firer is taught to combine the use of the elevating wheel with tapping for deflection. The same principles apply for this diagonal as for horizontal traversing.

Instruction should be afforded in traversing from right to left as well as from left to right.

* During the instruction fire should be stopped at least twice in order to check the aim and also to measure the distance traversed. By comparing the distance traversed with the number of groups fired, an estimate can be made as to the value of the traversing fire. For example:—Traversing fire is ordered from the 1st to the 6th figure; fire is stopped after the 4th group. If the traverse has been correctly carried out the gun should be laid on the interval between the 2nd and 3rd figures.

7. On the command "UNLOAD," No. 1 lowers the tangent sight, turns the crank handle twice in succession on to the buffer

spring, letting it fly back each time on the check lever; then presses up the finger pieces on the lower pawls, while No. 2 withdraws and repacks the belt in the box; this must be done correctly and the lid closed and fastened; No. 1 clears the ejector tube and lock, and releases the lock spring by pressing the double button.

8. On the command "DISMOUNT GUN," No. 1 removes the elevating joint pin, No. 2 passes the ammunition box to No. 3, removes the gun as in mounting, and replaces it in its original position in rear. No. 1 follows with the tripod. On reaching the original position, he folds and clamps the legs and sees that the joint pins are home and turned down.

9. Instruction should be afforded in bringing the gun into action in the several positions of the tripod, and in various natures of ground. Firing up, down and along the side of steep hills should be practised. Practice should also be afforded in mounting the gun from the prone position, in firing from the lying position, and when kneeling on both knees, as well as when sitting.

49. *Belt filling.*

1. The corporal, all the numbers, and also the drivers of the limbered wagon and S.A.A. cart when available should be instructed and frequently practised in belt filling, both by hand and with the belt filling machine.*

---

* For description and method of using the belt filling machine, *see* the handbook of the gun.

CHAPTER III.

EQUITATION AND THE HANDLING OF THE WEAPONS MOUNTED.

50. *The standard required of men and horses.*

1. Every cavalryman should be a good military horseman that is to say he should :—

    i. Have a strong seat.

    ii. Be able to apply correctly the aids by which the horse is controlled.

    iii. Be capable of riding across country.

    iv. Be capable of covering long distances on horseback with the least possible fatigue to his horse.

    v. Be able to use his horse to the utmost advantage in a mounted fight.

    vi. Under proper directions be able to train an unbroken horse, and improve a badly-trained one.

    vii. Have a practical knowledge of the care of horses both in barracks and in the field, understand how to detect and treat the minor ailments to which they are liable, and be a good groom.

All officers, in addition to being good military horsemen and instructors in riding, must be able to train, and direct the training of, remounts.

2. A trained charger or troop horse must be :—

    i. Well balanced and capable of carrying a heavy weight over long distances, without loss of condition.

    ii. Handy and quick in obeying the correct aids.

    iii. Steady both in and out of the ranks.

    iv. Capable of being ridden with one hand at any pace either in the company of other horses or alone.

v. Active on his legs and a good jumper over all kinds of
obstacles.

vi. Unafraid of entering deep water or of swimming.

51. *Horsemastership.*

(*See* also " Animal Management.")

1. The importance of being a good horsemaster should be
impressed upon every cavalry soldier. He should be taught to
look upon his horse as his best friend, to study it, and to take a
pride in its appearance. He should receive instruction in the
prevention and cure of the minor ailments of a horse, in
feeding and watering, and in the treatment of a horse on the
march, in the field, in bivouac and in billets.

2. Men should be taught to water their horses whenever an
opportunity occurs, particularly on hot days. Many a horse
has died on service through his rider neglecting what proved
to be the only chance of watering his horse during a long day.
Horses accustomed to be watered from buckets drink slowly at
a shallow stream, and consequently should be given plenty of
time. They never suffer from being watered when heated,
unless they are put to fast work immediately or are left to stand
and get chilled.

If they are required for fast work very soon after being
watered, they should not be allowed to drink more than six to
ten swallows.

Opportunities for giving the horses a small feed at frequent
intervals and for giving them grazing, even a few mouthfuls,
should never be neglected.

3. Even the lightest cavalryman is a heavy burden* and every
minute that weight is removed from the horse's back is a
refreshing period of relief. When the men are working independently during long days, they should be taught to dismount
whenever possible. Instructors should impress on recruits the

---

* On service the total weight on a horse's back is more than 17 stone.

necessity for making them dismount frequently for a few minutes at a time.

Horses can be taught to lead well at a walk, and can be trained to move at the rate of 4 miles an hour, though this is too fast a pace for the men to maintain for long. It should seldom be necessary for a man to sit on his horse at the halt. He should be accustomed to dismount at every opportunity, and if his horse is at all blown to turn its head towards the wind excepting in very wet or cold weather.

4. The two most frequent causes of sore backs are :—i. Continued friction at one place ; ii. the stoppage of the circulation at one place by continued pressure.

Either of these is liable to occur if the saddle is left on for hours without being moved or if the girths are not slackened.

Even when there is not time to off saddle, the action of loosening the girths and shifting the saddle eases the horse greatly. The off saddle can be effected rapidly if it is regularly practised. It is advisable in warm weather to off saddle once a day on the drill ground, or in the open country, whenever the horses are absent from their stables for any length of time. When the saddles are removed, the backs should be immediately hand-rubbed or slapped with the flat of the hand for a few minutes, with steady pressure against the direction of the hair in order to restore circulation. In cold weather the girths should only be slackened, and the saddle moved, as taking the saddle off may cause a chill.

5. Men should be taught to pay special attention both at stables and in the field to their horses' shoes. The least sign of a shoe loose, or clinches broken or knocked up, should be reported without delay.

6. A roll in sand will often refresh horses considerably, but care should be taken that any sand or dirt remaining on their backs after a roll is removed before they are saddled up again.

A sand bath is useful in barracks to teach the horses to roll. It should be not less than 20 feet square with sand 1 foot deep.

52. *The paces of the horse.*

1. The following are the regulation paces for drill and manœuvre :—

. Walk 4 miles an hour, at which rate 117 yards are passed
over in one minute, or ¼ mile in 3 minutes 45 seconds.

Trot 8 miles an hour, at which rate 235 yards are passed over
in 1 minute, or ¼ mile in 1 minute 52 seconds.

Gallop 15 miles an hour, at which rate 440 yards (¼ mile)
are passed over in 1 minute.

2. The canter, about nine miles an hour, and the jog or slow
trot, six miles an hour. should be employed constantly, both in
teaching recruits to ride and in training young horses. At the
walk, however, horses should always be made to maintain the
regulation pace of 4 miles per hour.

3. In marching, especially along a road, and when men are
riding singly or in small groups not at drill, a slower trot should
be used than the regulation drill or manœuvre trot of 8 miles an
hour. Trotting at a greater rate than 8 miles an hour should
seldom be permitted.

53. *Terms used in equitation.*

1. " *Right rein* " and " *Left rein*."—A horse is said to be on
the " right rein " when he is going round turning to the right,
or on a circle to the right. The term " left rein " is used when
be is proceeding to the left in a similar manner.

To avoid confusion the instructor as far as possible should
use the terms " Right " or " Left " instead of " Outward " or
" Inward " when giving explanations.

2. " *The true canter* " is a pace of three time. The legs of a
horse should move in such a manner that whichever foreleg
leads, the hind leg on the same side must also lead.

3. " *The true gallop* " is a pace of four time, in which the feet
follow one another in succession, with an interval of suspension
between the coming down of the leading fore foot and that of

the opposite hind foot. As when cantering, whichever fore leg leads, the hind leg on the same side must also lead.

4. " *Cantering disunited* " or " *galloping disunited.*"—When a horse is cantering or is galloping in such a way that the leading hind leg is on the opposite side to the leading fore leg, *e.g.*, when he leads with the off fore and near hind legs, he is said to be "disunited." It is a common fault with bad riders in changing the bend of their horses to allow them to change their fore legs but not their hind legs. This results in the horse going " disunited," a faulty action which should not be allowed.

5. " *Cantering false* " or " *galloping false.*"—A horse is said to be cantering false or galloping false, when at either of these paces, he goes on a circle to the left with the off fore and off hind leading, or to the right with the near fore and near hind leading.

6. *Balance.*—A horse on the move is said to be balanced when he carries his head and neck in the right position for balancing his weight and that of his rider.

7. *Collected.*—A horse is said to be collected when he is made to bring his limbs properly under him so that he has the maximum control over them. The collected paces are the school or regulation walk or trot and the canter. The extended paces are the walk out, the trot out, and the gallop.

SADDLERY.

54. *How to fit a saddle.*

1. The following are the chief points of importance in fitting a saddle :—

    i. The withers must not be pinched nor pressed upon.

    ii. There must be no pressure upon the horse's spine.

    iii. The shoulder-blade bones must have free and uncon-
        trolled movement.

    iv. The weight must not be put on the loins but upon the
        ribs through the medium of the muscles covering them.

2. In fitting a saddle there are several sizes to choose from, and in making the choice the bare tree should be first tried on the back.

The saddle should be placed on the horse's back so that the front arch is above the hollow behind the shoulder.

The arch and seat should then be clear of the spine. This is not always possible with horses possessing high withers, but it is desirable in order to ascertain the fit of the side bars. The front arch must be wide enough to admit the hand on either side of the wither. The side bars, which must not be too long, must bear evenly on the back, or as nearly so as possible. The points of the tree must be wide enough apart to clear the ribs, and the edges of the side bars must not press into the withers or ribs.

The saddle is then taken off, fitted with numnah pannels and replaced. The saddletree will now be considerably raised and the proper thickness of the blanket can be estimated.

It must be remembered that the addition of a numnah or a blanket reduces the width of the front arch, and narrows the saddle across the top of the side bars.

The blanket is then folded and placed on the horse's back with the tree on it. The blanket must be well pressed up into the front arch, and before the girths are tightened it should be noticed whether the burrs are off the shoulders and the fans off the loins; if they are not, the thickness of the blanket beneath the side bars must be increased by turning it up on either side. The girths are now pulled up and a man placed in the saddle.

3. The fit of a saddle cannot be determined until the saddle is inspected with a man sitting in it, for parts which appear well clear when no weight is in the saddle, may be brought dangerously close by the pressure of a man's weight.

First ascertain that the withers are free from pressure. Make the rider carry his weight forward; then pass the whole hand beneath the blanket and over the top, and along both sides, of the withers. If there is any difficulty in inserting the hand, the saddle does not fit.

Next see that the shoulder-blade bones are free from pressure. This is done by passing the hand beneath the blanket to the play of the shoulder; if there is pressure, the hand can only be introduced with difficulty. Assuming that the hand can find its way in, the horse's fore leg should be advanced to its full extent by an assistant. This should be possible without the examiner's fingers being pinched between the shoulder-blade and side bar, even if the man is leaning forward in the saddle. If the fingers are pinched the shoulder-blade will also be pinched, and the saddle must be raised by fitting thicker numnah pannels on the side bar or by making an extra fold in the blanket. Both sides must be tested.

The fans should then be tested for loin pressure; with the man leaning back in the saddle, the flat of the hand should find ready admission under the fans.

4. Then ascertain whether the pressure of the side bars is evenly distributed; this can be done in the following way.

The saddle having been ridden in for about half an hour is carefully ungirthed, and the tree lifted from the blanket without disturbing it. The blanket will be found to bear the imprint of the side bars, and an examination will show at a glance whether they are pressing evenly from top to bottom and from front to rear.

The examination must be made without delay, as the elasticity of the blanket soon causes it to lose the impression of the side bars.

The commonest places to find excessive pressure are the top edge of the side bar behind the front arch, and the bottom edge in front of the rear arch. If there is a deeper impression on the blanket in these places than elsewhere, we may say with certainty that the pressure is not evenly distributed, and that the corresponding part of the horse's back is receiving an undue amount of the weight. With a horse in condition, or with a good blanket and numnah, this may not necessarily cause a sore back; but it will certainly do so should the animal lose condition or the blanket or pannel be thin, for this will bring the tree nearer to the bony framework of the horse.

The irregularity in the fit of the side bars may be remedied by the introduction of pieces of numnah to fill up the space between the side bars and blanket.

Once the pieces of felt have been cut to the required shape they must be fixed in position. In peace this can be done with glue, but in the field they may have to be tied on, or secured with tacks, or bound in position by means of a piece of leather (basil) which can be tacked to the edge of the side bar or laced with string across the top.

By means of these strips of felt the most radical alterations in the fit of a side bar can be effected in a few minutes by a man who has but little technical skill.

55. *Saddling.*

1. The front of the *saddle* should not be so far forward that it interferes with the play of the shoulder. The pannels of the saddle should lie flat on the top of the horse's ribs, the weight of the rider being borne by the part between the front and back arches. The burrs and fans should bear no weight. The front arch, when numnah or stuffed pannels are attached, should clear the withers to the breadth of not less than 2 fingers when the rider is in the saddle. The saddle, to afford a suitable seat for the rider, should be level, neither dipped in front nor in rear.

2. The *blanket* should be raised well off the withers by putting the hand under it.

It can be folded in several ways. With a horse of normal shape and condition the following method is recommended:—
The blanket is folded lengthways in three equal folds, one end is then turned over 24 inches, and the other turned into the pocket formed by the folds; the blanket thus folded is placed on the horse's back with the thick part near the withers. Size when folded 2' 0" × 1'. The folding of the blanket may be modified to suit special horses and to meet alteration in shape consequent upon falling away in condition, or from other causes. In the

case of a horse which has fallen away in condition, and for certain shapes of back, a useful method is the 'channel fold.' The blanket is folded lengthways in three equal parts, each end is then turned over and folded towards the centre (two or three folds may be taken as required to suit the horse's back), leaving a channel in the centre.

3. The *girth* should be sufficiently tight to keep the saddle in its place and no tighter. It should be tightened gradually, and not with violence, care being taken that the skin is not wrinkled. It is recommended that the girths of all except young and growing horses should be fitted with the buckle in the second or third hole from the free end of the tab.

4. The *surcingle* should lie flat over the girth, and be no tighter than it.

5. *Adjustment of the " V " attachment.*—The V attachment fitted to the saddle as issued, admits of limited adjustment to suit the conformation of the horse.

The front strap of the V attachment, Mark II or III, should not be buckled and unbuckled daily when girthing, nor utilized for shortening or lengthening the girth.

The normal position of the attachment is with the buckle in the centre hole of the three—6½ inches from the rivet—this position will suit a very large number of horses ; the upper and lower holes are provided for the adjustment; additional holes are not to be punched. If the saddle has a tendency to work forward, this strap should be shortened by buckling it in the lower hole.

The front strap holds the saddle in place and should be nearly in a straight line with the girth. The rear strap is intended to balance and steady the hinder part of the saddle, it should never be tighter than the front strap. In no case is the attachment to be worn as a true V, *i.e.*, the front and rear straps of equal length, for this would depress the hinder part of the saddle, and cause other difficulties.

Care should be taken in all cases to buckle the near and off straps in corresponding holes.

56. *Bridling.*

1. The *bridoon* should touch the corners of the mouth, but should hang low enough not to wrinkle the lips.

2. The *bit* should be adjusted in the horse's mouth in such a manner that the mouth-piece is above the tush or corner tooth and that, when the reins are pulled, the curb chain (*see* para. 4) lies in the chin groove and not above it. The smooth side of the mouth-piece should be next the horse's tongue.

These instructions can only be laid down as a general guide, as so much depends on the shape and sensitiveness of the horse's mouth and on his temper.

3. Figs. 4 and 5 represent bits with and without a port with a section of the horse's tongue and lower jaw.

The tongue is less sensitive than the bars of the mouth. A straight mouth-piece rests on the tongue and bars of the mouth. When the reins are pulled the tongue is able to take the greater part of the pressure. A mouth-piece with a port rests chiefly on the bars. When the reins are pulled the tongue slips into the port and is unable to relieve the bars of the greater part of the pressure. A bit with a straight mouth-piece is therefore less severe than one with a port.

Care should be taken to fit each horse with a bit of the correct size. A narrow bit pinches the horse's lips, and a wide bit moves from side to side and bruises them.

Fig. 4.   Fig. 5.

4. The *curb chain* should be laid in the chin-groove, and be so adjusted that when the bit is pulled back to its greatest extent the angle which the bit forms with the mouth should never exceed 45° even with the lightest mouthed horse, and should vary between that and 30° according to the degree of hardness of the mouth. The curb chain should be fixed permanently on to the off curb-hook. The adjustment to the near hook should be made by twisting the chain to the right until it is quite flat, putting the last link on to the hook, and then taking up as many more links as may be necessary.

5. The *headstall* should be parallel to and behind the cheek-bone.

6. The *noseband* should be two finger-breadths below the cheek-bone and should admit two fingers between it and the nose.

7. The *throat lash* should fit loosely, being only sufficiently tight to prevent the headstall slipping over the horse's ears.

8. The *bridoon rein* should be of such a length that, when held by the middle, in the full of the left hand, with a light feeling of the horse's mouth, it will touch the rider's waist.

57. *The breastplate and martingale.*

1. The *breastplate* is not, as a rule, required. When used it should be so fitted that the upper edge of the rosette or leather is three finger-breadths above the sharp breast bone.   It should admit the breadth of the hand between it and the flat of the shoulder.

2. The *martingale* should only be used for exceptional horses. It may be either running or standing, according to whichever is found to suit the horse best. It should be fitted at such a length that it will not interfere with the horse until he gets his head above the proper position. If shorter than this it will tend to make him set his head and neck, and lean against it.

If a running martingale is used on reins other than those sewn to the bit or bridoon, they should be fitted with "stops" to prevent the rings of the martingale being caught by the buckles or studs which fasten the reins to the bit or bridoon. Running martingales should, as a rule, be put on the bit reins and sufficiently loose to have no bearing on the reins till the horse attempts to raise his head.

The standing martingale should, as a rule, be fastened to the noseband, but under exceptional circumstances it may be fastened to the bridoon or cheek of the portmouth bit.

58. Care of saddlery.

1. The leather work of all saddlery should be kept soft. The seats and flaps of the saddles and handled parts of the reins should not be polished and leather girths, girth attachments, and sweat flaps should be kept supple with grease.

2. Minor defects in saddlery should be remedied at once. Stirrup leathers should occasionally be shortened one inch at the buckle ends, to bring the wear on fresh holes. The girth tabs require special attention and must be renewed from time to time as the holes wear.

3. All leather work, whether new or old, should be greased before being put away in store, and, especially in hot or damp climates, should be overhauled from time to time.

4. All saddlery and harness should be taken to pieces from time to time and carefully inspected. Once a year all leather work should be dubbed, the leather having first been moistened with a sponge and in cold weather the dubbing warmed; after a few days the dubbing should be rubbed off with a dry brush or rubber.

Soft soap should not be used as it contains an excess of alkali which tends to damage the leather.

Leather must not be washed with soda or soaked in water; very hot water destroys its vitality at once. Washing in lukewarm water with soap, quickly and without soaking, will do the least harm if oil, dubbing, or good saddle soap is applied whilst the leather is still slightly damp.

, The dirt should always be removed from leather before fresh dressing is applied.

5. Stitching should be tested periodically, for the life of thread is shorter than that of leather.

RIDING.

59. General instructions.

1. The instruction should be divided into three stages, and the pupil should be gradually brought on from one to the other, as the proper sequence of instruction is a matter of importance.

2. The *first stage* should be devoted to the attainment of a firm seat independent of the reins.

It is important to maintain the recruit's confidence from the start, so he should be given a quiet, well trained horse. He should be allowed a saddle and stirrups for the first few days, after which some of his work each day should be without stirrups. He should only be allowed a snaffle at this early stage, or if this is not possible the portmouth bit with a single rein attached to the cheek and without a curb chain.

The greater part of the instruction at this stage should be without reins. To save the horse's mouth the pupil should only be allowed to hold the reins when he is allowed the use of his stirrups.

As soon as the recruit begins to be at home in the saddle and can rise in his stirrups, cantering and jumping should commence.

Before he enters the second stage the recruit should be able to control his horse in straightforward movements and simple turns in the school or manège, and be able to ride over low jumps at all paces without reins. From now onwards a considerable portion of the work should be outside the riding school.

3. The *second stage* should be devoted to teaching what are called the aids, that is to say the indication of the rider's will by means of the use of the hand and lower part of the leg, and of the distribution of the rider's weight. (*See* Sec. **70**.)

G 2

The instructor should see that the recruits are free and elastic in the shoulders, arms, and wrists. Stiff shoulder action cramps the play of the elbow-joints and wrists, and makes good hands impossible.

Instruction in riding with arms should commence during this stage.

4. In the *third stage* more advanced instruction in horsemanship is given.

The recruit should learn to combine the play of the body and limbs so that he moves in unison with his horse. Exaggerated movement of any sort must be discouraged, and the necessity for sitting still emphasized.

During this stage recruits should be made thoroughly handy with their weapons mounted, and be taught how to fight with them.

5. Towards the end of the second and during the third stages of their training the men should occasionally be taken out for long rides away from barracks, when some practical knowledge of pace may be acquired.

6. The recruit should not be considered as fit for the ranks until the average horse goes pleasantly with him at any pace. He should be able to ride long distances without distressing a fit horse, and should understand thoroughly how to use his weapons. A good recruit should be fit for the ranks in about eight months after his first riding lesson.

60. *Hints to instructors.*

1. All officers must be practical horsemen, capable of teaching their men, and able and ready at any time to get up on a horse which a man has failed to ride in order to give instruction by personal example.

2. After the first few lessons the recruit's horse should be constantly changed throughout the training.

3. Concurrently with his instruction in riding the young soldier should be taught the points of the horse and other elementary knowledge connected with horses and stables.

4. Recruits should be taught carefully from the first how to put on and fit their saddles and bridles. The bad effects resulting from ill-fitting saddlery should be explained to them. The men should be made to point out mistakes and to rectify them. They should also be taught how the bit acts on the bars of the mouth, and how it should be fitted.

5. An instructor should be mounted. When possible practical illustrations should accompany verbal descriptions. A recruit who has difficulty in learning his work by verbal instruction, may learn quickly by copying an expert horseman.

6. All instructional work should be quiet; the instructor should never shout and must always keep his temper. He should endeavour from the first to create a spirit of emulation amongst his pupils, and avoid delaying the more forward amongst them for the sake of the more backward.

7. Instructors should make their lessons progressive and as interesting as possible. In order that recruits may gain confidence, they may be allowed occasionally to amuse themselves in the riding school with their horses, by doing anything they like provided it is sensible and that the horses are not ill-treated.

When men are working in the open they should occasionally be made to ride about independently, and as they improve should be accustomed to riding under as varied conditions as possible.

8. The first portion of the early training can be pushed on more quickly in an enclosed space than in the open. The horses are under better control, the nervousness natural to beginners and usually felt by recruits is greatly lessened, for they know that the horse cannot run away, and there is nothing to distract the attention of the men or horses. The more advanced training must, however, always be carried out in the open, in order that the recruit may learn real control over his horse.

9. The first object of the instructor is to give his pupils confidence, and to teach them the knee and thigh grip, and to sit well down in the saddle. The lungeing whip should be seldom used, for it does harm rather than good, frightens the other horses and upsets the men; if necessary, the recruit should be allowed to carry a stick or whip.

10. Falls should be avoided, as they tend to spoil the beginner's nerve and thus retard his progress. To avoid falls the recruit's stirrups should be connected in the initial stages of the training by a strap passing under the horse's belly, of such a length that the man's knees are not drawn away from the saddle. The strap saves falls because it prevents the rider's leg from flying out far in any direction and the confidence it engenders enables him to acquire balance more quickly. It should not be used when jumping obstacles over two feet high.

11. More horses are spoilt from being jerked in the mouth than from any other cause; this is particularly the case when jumping; hence the importance of teaching the men from the first to leave their horses' heads alone except for the purpose of control and for applying particular aids.

Men may be taught with advantage to ride with their reins long.

12. Instructors should be careful not to make horses rein back, passage, or bend for long distances. Generally speaking, half the length of the school is sufficient at one time for one of these exercises. It should then be changed. The instructor should avoid giving long explanations whilst his men are reining back or passaging.

13. Men should be practised crossing a V-shaped ditch, about 18 feet wide and 10 feet deep, so that they go down one side and up the other. This is a valuable exercise, as no horse will face the opposite bank unless his head is left free.

14. In order to teach a man to have a strong seat, with the knee firmly in the saddle, and at the same time to keep his feet pressed down home in the stirrups with the leathers taut, he

should be practised frequently in the third period of his training at standing up in his stirrups. This should be done at first with the horse standing still; the man to assist his balance may rest his hand on the horse's neck. Afterwards he should stand in his stirrups at the walk, trot, canter, and gallop. When jumping the recruit should be made at times to stand up in his stirrups between the fences, and even during the actual jump, if the horse is a free jumper and does not require the man to sit down and drive him.

61. *Preliminary instruction.*

1. Before a recruit is allowed to mount a horse he should receive instruction on a dummy horse with a view to :—

    i. Strengthening his riding muscles.

    ii. Giving him the correct seat.

    iii. Giving him balance and confidence in his seat.

    iv. Accustoming him to keep the knee constantly pressed against the horse's side.

This instruction should be given under the direction of a riding instructor.

2. The following are good exercises :—

    i. Swinging the lower part of the leg with a circular motion to the rear, and towards the horse's side.

    ii. Rising from the knee with stirrups.

    iii. Rising from the knee without stirrups.

    iv. Holding the side of the foot with the hand on each side, with and without stirrups in each case without moving either leg.

    v. Leaning forwards and backwards in the saddle, with and without stirrups.

    vi. Pointing with outstretched arm in any given direction.

    vii. Turning round in the saddle to either side to look behind without changing the position of the legs, one hand resting on the horse's neck and the other on the back of the saddle.

viii. Without stirrups and with arms folded to make the
horse rock by swinging the body backwards and forwards, maintaining a firm grip with the thigh.

ix. Swinging the body to either side as the horse is rocked.

3. All the above exercises may be continued with advantage
during subsequent training. Preliminary instruction in mounting, holding the reins, &c., may be given with the aid of the
dummy horse.

62. *First lessons to the recruit with a horse.*

1. Squads should not exceed 12 in number, and should parade
in line, leading their horses.

"STAND TO YOUR HORSES." The man stands at *attention* as in Sec. **16**
on the near side of the horse, his toes in line
with the horse's fore feet, the bridoon reins, if
taken over the horse's head, are held with
the right hand near the rings, little finger
between the reins, back of the hand up; the
right arm bent, the hand as high as the
shoulder, the end of the reins in the left hand,
which hangs down by his side without
constraint.

If the bridoon reins are not taken over, his
position will be the same as the above except
that the reins will be held by the right hand
only near the rings.

This is the position of *attention*.

"STAND AT EASE." The right hand slides down the reins to
the full extent of the arm, the end of the
bridoon reins being retained in the left hand.
The position of the man's legs and feet is the
same as at foot drill (Sec. **17**).

If the bridoon reins have not been taken
over the horse's head, they will be held in
the right hand only, the left arm hanging by
the man's side.

" ATTENTION."   As above.

" IN FRONT OF   Each man will take a full pace forward
YOUR HORSES." with the right foot, turn to the right-about,
and take one rein in each hand near the ring,
still holding the end of them in the left hand,
if the reins are over the horse's head; hands
and elbows to be as high as the shoulders.

This is the position in which a man should
stand when showing a horse to an officer.

" OFF SIDE, STAND   Each man will take a full pace forward with
TO YOUR   the left foot to the horse's off side, turning
HORSES."   right-about, the left hand holding the reins
near the rings, the little finger between them,
and the right hand taking hold of the ends of
the reins and hanging down behind the thigh.

" IN FRONT OF   Each man will take a full pace forward with
YOUR HORSES." the left foot, turn left about, and resume the
position before described, the left hand taking
the end of the reins.

" STAND TO YOUR   Each man will take a full step forward with
HORSES."   the right foot to the horse's near side, and
turn left-about.

" QUICK MARCH."   Each man will move off holding the reins
as above.

" SINGLE FILES   Each man will move off in succession, one
RIGHT (or LEFT)" horse-length from the file in front of him.
" QUICK MARCH."

2. When leading through a narrow gate or doorway, the man
should move slowly taking care that the horse's hips clear the
posts of the door. He should walk backwards holding the head
collar with both hands, one on either side of the horse's head.

In passing an officer the soldier when leading a horse will
look towards the officer.

3. *How to pick up a horse's foot.*—The recruit should be
taught that in picking up a horse's foot, he should face the rear

and run the hand lightly down the leg from the shoulder or
quarter along the back of the knee or hock downwards before
attempting to lift the foot from the ground. When picked up
the foot should be held by the hoof and not by the fetlock.

4. *How to run a horse in hand.*—The reins should be held as
described above in *stand to your horses* and the horse led off.
As soon as he breaks into a steady trot the man should release
the reins with the hand nearest the horse, and only hold the end
of the reins in his outer hand. In turning a horse when in
hand, the man should move round the horse and not swing the
horse round himself. In leading a horse past an officer for
inspection, the man should place himself on the side of the
horse nearest the officer.

63. *Mounting and dismounting.*

1. *Without stirrups.*—The reins hanging evenly on the horse's
neck, the command will be given :—

"PREPARE TO MOUNT."   Each man will turn to the right, and step
6 inches to the right.

Taking the reins in the left hand, properly
separated for riding, he will place the left
hand on the front of the saddle, grasping a lock
of the mane if the horse has one. Though the
reins should be short enough to check any
forward movement of the horse if necessary,
they should be of such a length that the horse's
mouth is not interfered with by the man when
mounting. The right hand will grip the back
of the saddle.

"MOUNT."   When mounting without a saddle the left
hand will be placed in front of the horse's
withers, and the right arm on the horse's loins,
forearm well to the offside, fingers closed.
The man will spring up, assisting himself by
straightening his arms, pass his right leg over
the horse, and lower himself into his seat

"PREPARE TO   The man will place both his hands with a
DISMOUNT."   rein or reins in each on the front of the saddle,
                 and raise himself from the horse's back by
                 straightening his arms.

"DISMOUNT."   He will vault lightly to the ground and
                 assume the position of *stand to your horses.*

When dismounting without saddles, both hands will first be
placed on the horse's withers.

Mounting and dismounting on the offside, which is carried out
in the same manner as on the near side, should also be practised.

2. *With stirrups.—*

"PREPARE TO   Turn to the right about. Take the reins in
MOUNT."   the left hand properly separated as for riding,
                 and with a light and equal feeling on the
                 horse's mouth. Place the left hand on the
                 horse's withers, grasping his mane if he has
                 one, otherwise seize hold of the front of the
                 saddle. Place the left foot in the stirrup,
                 steadying it with the right hand, then place
                 the right hand on the back of the saddle.

"MOUNT."   Spring quietly into the saddle, place the right
                 foot into the stirrup without looking down and
                 assume the position of *attention.* (*See*
                 Sec. 66.)

Mounting on the offside will be taught in the same manner,
and recruits will practise it equally.

"PREPARE TO   Shorten the reins and grasp the mane with
DISMOUNT."   the left hand, place the right hand on the front
                 part of the saddle and take the right foot out
                 of the stirrup.

"DISMOUNT."   Carry the right leg over and lower the right
                 foot gently to the ground: place the left foot in
                 line with the horse's fore-feet, turn to the left,
                 and come to the position of *stand to your
                 horses.*

Whenever the men are dismounted, with or without arms, and have been allowed to *stand easy* from the position of *stand at ease*, they will ·be recalled to *attention* by the command " STAND TO YOUR HORSES."

3. For instructional and ceremonial purposes the order for mounting and dismounting is given in two words of command :

" PREPARE TO MOUNT."—" MOUNT."

" PREPARE TO DISMOUNT."—" DISMOUNT."

Otherwise there is only one word of command in each case: " MOUNT " or " DISMOUNT."

4. From the first recruits should be taught not to allow their horses to move forward, or to turn round, whilst they are in the act of mounting.

64. *The seat.*

1. The recruit must be made to sit evenly on his seat well down in the saddle, and not on his fork ; the flat of the thigh and the inside of the knee pressed against the horse, but not so tightly that the man rides on his thighs, as the weight of the body should rest principally on the seat; below the knee the leg should hang free. In the early stages much attention need not be paid to the position of the body, though from the first the recruit should be taught to get his seat well under him and to avoid any tendency to stiffness.

2. Care should be taken to fit the stirrups to the length suitable to the build of the rider. A man with a short thick leg requires his stirrups shorter in proportion than does a man of equal height, but with a flat thigh and thin leg. If a man standing in his stirrups can just clear the pommel with his fork the stirrups are about the right length. The man should be made to place himself in the saddle with his knees at the most suitable height. The stirrups should then be adjusted so that the bars are in line with the soles of his boots. The stirrups are intended to be an aid and convenience to the rider; if they are too long he

will lose his seat by leaning forward in his endeavour to retain them; if they are too short, the seat becomes cramped and the rider prevented from using the lower part of the leg correctly.

In ceremonial work the stirrups should be kept on the ball of the foot, but at other times the feet should always be pushed right home in the stirrups.

65. *How to hold the reins.*

1. The reins should normally be held in the left hand only, bit reins inside. In the case of beginners, and when riding young or awkward horses, often both hands should be used. Occasionally the left hand may be required to be free, as when leading another horse, in which case the reins of the ridden horse can be held in the right hand.

The hands should be low and close in front of the body, thumbs uppermost, wrists rounded, and back of the hands to the front. Play should be allowed to movements of the horse from the wrists, elbows, and if necessary from the shoulders. Elbows should be kept close to the body.

2. *Reins in left hand.*

i. *Bridoon or cheek reins only.*—Take the two reins in the left hand, the right rein between the first and second fingers and the left rein outside the fourth finger, slack passed across the palm and secured between the thumb and first finger.

ii. *All four reins.*—Place the right bit rein between the second and third fingers, and the left bit rein between the third and fourth fingers. The right bridoon rein between the first and second fingers, and the left bridoon rein outside the fourth finger, the slack of all four reins thrown back over the first finger and secured by the thumb.

3. *Reins in both hands.*—In the first place, whether using single or double reins, take them in the left hand as described above, then take up the right rein or reins in the right hand by placing it in front of the left, and pull sufficient of the slack

forward through the left hand to obtain an even bearing on the
mouth with both hands when held low, just in front of the body
and close to the horse's withers.

FIG. 6.   VIEWED FROM FRONT.

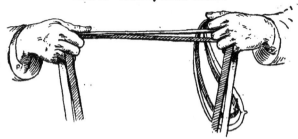

Bit-reins shown shaded.

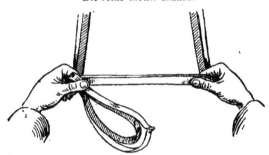

FIG. 7.   VIEWED FROM ABOVE.

In the case of single reins only, the right rein should be held between the third and fourth fingers, and with both bit and bridoon, the two right reins should be separated by the third finger. In each case the right hand should hold only the right rein or reins, the slack of these being secured between the right thumb and forefinger and thence passed back into the left hand, which will hold both the left and right reins, whether the two hands are used or only one. (*See* Figs. 6 and 7.)

4. *To lengthen the reins.*—Allow sufficient rein to slip gently through the fingers.

5. *To shorten the reins.*—Keep the reins in the left hand but drop the slack from between the thumb and forefinger, and take hold of this in the right hand behind the left, slide the left hand forwards until the desired length is obtained. Then as before secure the slack, and if riding with both hands on the reins, take up the right rein or reins again in the right hand.

6. Recruits should be well grounded in the proper method of holding their reins, and of changing them from one hand to both quickly and *vice versâ*, also of shortening and lengthening them at all paces. To make men handier in this respect they should have constant practice, some of which should be given when they have drawn swords or sticks in their hands. The importance of keeping the reins supple and unpolished should be impressed on recruits.

66. *Position in the saddle at attention.*

1. The head and body should be erect and square to the front; upper arm hanging perpendicular; forearm nearly horizontal; thighs flat on the saddle. The legs from the knee down should be almost vertical; the knees turned inwards and the toes pointing towards the front. The heels should be sunk lower than the toes and the feet pressed down into the stirrups. (As in Fig. 8.)

2. On the command " SIT AT EASE " the reins should be relaxed by dropping the left hand on the front of the saddle. The right hand should rest on the left, back up.

Fig. 8.

67. *First movements on horseback.*

1. The recruit should be impressed with the importance of not hanging on by the reins and should be told that if he does so he will injure his horse's mouth and make it difficult to ride.

He should be taught to hold the reins in both hands as described in Sec. **65**, and then be shown how to start his horse at a walk from the halt, that is to say, he should be made to ease the reins slightly, though still keeping a light feel on the horse's mouth, and press him forward with the legs below the knee. He should be prevented from kicking his horse in the ribs with his heels and from pushing his hands forward to slacken the reins. He should be taught next how to halt without jerking his horse s mouth.

These instructions, carefully illustrated by the instructor and fully understood by the recruit, should suffice for the first few days, during which time the recruits may be more or less left to themselves to shake down in their seats; they may then be taught to trot, and afterwards to canter.

2. *How to rise in the stirrups.*—The loins must be perfectly lissom, so that the seat may be easy and comfortable; the back should not be hollowed, but the upper part of the body should be inclined a little forward.

The recruit should not try, by rising, to follow or to anticipate the movements of the horse, but should let himself be raised.

His knees will sustain his movement and will allow him to descend softly into the saddle.

3. At the trot without stirrups the recruit should allow his body to be thrown up at each step, and fall on his seat.

In cantering, the knees, the inside of the thighs, and the seat itself must remain close to the saddle, the small of the back should be drawn in slightly, the whole body pliant and accompanying the movement of the horse, so that with each stride the rider feels a forward thrust through his seat from the animal's back.

4. A few turns and circles may next be introduced, and in executing them the recruit should be told how to use the weight of his body. He should be taught, whilst preserving the grip of his knees and thighs, to incline his weight from the hips the least thing backwards and to the hand to which he is turning.

5. As soon as he has gained confidence and can sit well at a canter, the recruit may be taught to ride without reins; he should then be taught to jump over small obstacles, such as the bar lying on the ground. *See* Sec. **68**.

The recruit should not be allowed to cling with the back of the calf of his leg; it should be explained to him that the use of the lower part of the leg will be taught him later.

6. In about six weeks an average recruit, with careful individual instruction, should have a fair seat and be able to ride at a trot, canter and gallop, and to leap small jumps without reins.

7. Much of the early training should be without reins. The arms if folded should be in front of the body, never behind, as the latter tends to throw the upper part of the body forward.

The exercises mentioned in Sec. **61** for use on the dummy horse should be continued during the later training on the real horse. They should be carried out first when the horse is halted and later when it is moving.

68. *Teaching the recruit how to ride his horse over a fence.*

1. Jumping, when carried out with discretion, both as to the amount of practice given and the state of the ground, is an excellent training for men and horses. Constant practice throughout the recruit's training will enable him to acquire, and afterwards to maintain, a firm seat.

2. The recruit should be taught to jump without reins before being required to do so with them. By this means he learns to rely on balance and grip and become independent of the reins to retain his seat.

3. The men trotting round the school with suitable distances between horses should be made to jump a bar lying on the ground. As the training progresses, the height of the bar should be increased, but so gradually that the men never lose confidence.

The recruit should at first either hold the end of the rein in the flat of one hand, or drop it altogether. The arms should be

folded across the chest; or the men may be made to grasp their
breeches at the thigh. Stirrups should be allowed until the
instructor considers it advisable for the beginner to jump without them. In the first jumping lessons the recruits may be
allowed to hold the mane, head rope, or front of the saddle in
one hand and the reins loosely in the other. With this
assistance they will be found to get confidence, attain their
proper balance in a short time, and be in a position to control
their horses without jerking their mouths.

4. As the horse takes off, the pupil should be instructed to
lean forward and to tighten his leg grip; if he is successful in
this his body will soon swing in harmony with the movement of
the horse. The movements of the body from the hips upwards
when riding over a jump vary so much with different horses
and different fences, that it is impossible to lay down any hard
and fast rule. Balance must be combined with leg grip. The
horse should be eased up gently after a jump, and on no account
should his pace be checked suddenly.

5. When the initial stage is passed frequent change of horses
accelerates progress.

6. The pupil should be gradually trained to handle the reins
when jumping, and care must be exercised to avoid illtreatment
of the horse's mouth during the process. If the shoulder-joints
are given free play when the horse requires more rein all jerky
movements of the arms and wrists will be avoided as the hands
go forward. The reins must be held long, and the man taught
to keep his hands low and allow them to come freely forward as
the horse is descending.

7. Jumping low obstacles is very little exertion to the horse,
and the more the recruit has of it the sooner he will be ready to
enter the third period of instruction. Before he enters this
stage he should sit his horse with ease both with and without
reins, and, when jumping, should be able to keep a light feeling
on the horse's mouth without in any way interfering with it.

During the third period the pupil may be given horses that
require "riding" at their fences, and be taught to handle them

H 2

with resolution. A combination of the qualities of determination and patience is invaluable in a horseman, and should be developed and encouraged at this stage of the training.

The method of dealing with refusers is given in Secs. 77 and 97.

69. *Paying compliments mounted without arms.*

When riding with both hands on the reins a soldier passing an officer turns his head and eyes in the direction of the officer without moving his hands. When holding the reins in one hand only he should drop the right hand to the full extent of the arm behind the right thigh, fingers half closed, back of the hand to the right, and turn his head in the direction of the officer.

70. *The aids.*

1. The aids are the signals used by the rider to assist him in controlling and directing his horse. These signals are made by means of the reins, legs, spurs, shifting the weight of the body, whip, and voice. For instance, the reins can be used to bend, raise, lower, or turn the head to one side, and to make the horse decrease his speed, halt, or rein back.

The pressure of the drawn back leg on one side is employed to make the hind quarters turn towards the opposite side, or to prevent them from turning out towards the side on which the pressure is applied. The pressure on both legs is an indication to the horse to go forward and should normally be applied just behind the girth; the indication is emphasized by increasing the pressure, only in the event of the horse still resisting is it necessary to apply the heels or spurs. When it is necessary to use the spur it should be applied as described in Sec. 72. If, when the horse is on the move, the weight of the body is shifted, say to the right, the horse will be inclined to put out a foot on that side, in order to equalise the distribution of weight on its limbs.

The hind quarters and forehand are respectively lightened by the rider's body being brought forward and back, or by lowering or raising the horse's head. The movement of the body as an aid should be only very slight. It should suffice if the weight is placed a little more on one seat bone than on the other, or the body inclined the least bit forward or backward. Any excessive movement of the rider's body upsets the horse and renders the pressure of the hands on the reins uneven.

The indications of the whip are closely akin to those of the leg and spur.

The instructor should constantly illustrate his explanations by showing how the aids are applied.

2. *To collect the horse.*—In collecting the horse the rider causes the horse to stand, walk, trot or canter, at attention. He makes the horse bring his hindquarters well under him by a pressure of both legs, and causes him to flex his jaw and bring his nose slightly in by a light feeling of the bit rein. The pressure of the legs should precede any feeling of the reins.

3. " *Walk* " or " *Trot.*"—Close both legs to the horse and slightly ease both reins by a slight turn of the wrist. As soon as the horse advances at the desired pace relax the pressure of the legs and feel the reins again as before.

4. " *Halt.*"—Close both legs and feel both reins, at the same time bring the weight of the body slightly back. As soon as the horse halts, relax the pressure of the legs and the feeling on the reins.

5. " *Right Turn.*"—Close both legs to the horse, using more pressure with the left leg to prevent his haunches from flying out to the left, feel the right side of the horse's mouth, press the left rein against his neck, and lean the body slightly back and to the right. Trained horses should never be turned otherwise than on their haunches.

" *Left Turn.*"—Reverse the above.

6. " *Right about Turn.*"—The same as " right turn," except that the rider should lean his body more back and as required apply more continued pressure on the right rein and firmer pressure with the drawn back left leg to compel the horse to turn on his haunches.

7. *To rein back.*—On the command " REIN BACK " the rider will collect his horse, then feels the horse's mouth as an indication to the horse to step backwards; the rider must never have a dead

pull on the horse's mouth, but when the horse has taken a step back, should ease the reins and then feel them again. The horse should be kept up to his bit by a pressure of both legs.

The trained horse should rein back collectedly, with head carried fairly high, and the body balanced on all four legs. He must move in a straight line, and must not be allowed to run back out of hand, but must make each movement in obedience to the properly applied indication of the rider. Nor should he be allowed to halt in an uncollected position.

8.—i. *To canter off fore and off hind leading.*—Collect the horse, feel the left rein gently, and by a strong pressure of the drawn-back left leg make him strike off into a canter. Prevent him from turning his quarters to the right by a supporting pressure of the right leg as required. When cantering the horse's body, head, and neck should be kept in the direction in which he is moving; the horse should be collected and slightly bent in the direction of the leading leg. The horse must always be made to canter true and united.

ii. *To canter near fore and near hind leading.*—Reverse the above aids.

9. *Change from off fore and off hind to near fore and near hind at the canter.*—Close both legs to the horse, turn his head slightly to the right, prevent him from turning his body to the left by the pressure of the left leg, move the weight of the body slightly backwards and cause him to change by a stronger pressure of the drawn-back right leg.

Change from near fore and near hind to off fore and off hind, at the canter.—Reverse the above aids.

10.—i. *Circle right at canter* (from the halt, walk, or trot).— Apply the aids described for the "*canter, off fore and off hind leading*," and guide the horse round to the right.

ii. *Circle left at the canter.*—Apply the aids described for the "*Canter, near fore and near hind leading*," and guide the horse round to the left.

71. *Bending.*

1. Bending affords the advanced recruit a lesson in applying the aids. It is a tiring exercise for the horse and should be practised with discretion.

It is important that the horse when bending should yield his jaw slightly. His neck should be kept straight from the withers onwards to near the poll, the bend being made just behind the latter. His head should be turned in the direction towards which he is moving.

As a rule bending should be done on the move.

2. *To bend a horse :—*

    i. *On the snaffle.*—If to the right, the rider should bend the horse by a gentle pressure on the right rein, at the same time giving to him slightly with the left rein, but still retaining a gentle feeling on the left side of his mouth, and using the pressure of the legs as required ; as soon as the horse bends to the hands, cease bending and make much of him.

    ii. *On the bit.*—The left hand, holding the reins, should have an equal feeling on all four reins. In bending to the right, place the third finger of the right hand between the two right reins and slightly feel the horse's mouth, using the pressure of the legs as required ; when the horse yields to the feeling by relaxing his jaws and bending as required, the hand should immediately yield to him.

Bending to the left is done in the same manner, by placing the forefinger of the right hand between the left reins.

The outer rein in bending should always retain a steady feeling to support the inner and to ensure the bend being made at the poll.

3. *Bending Lesson.*—With beginners bending should be done in the riding school or closed-in manège, but, as the instruction progresses it should be practised outside.

Fig. 9.

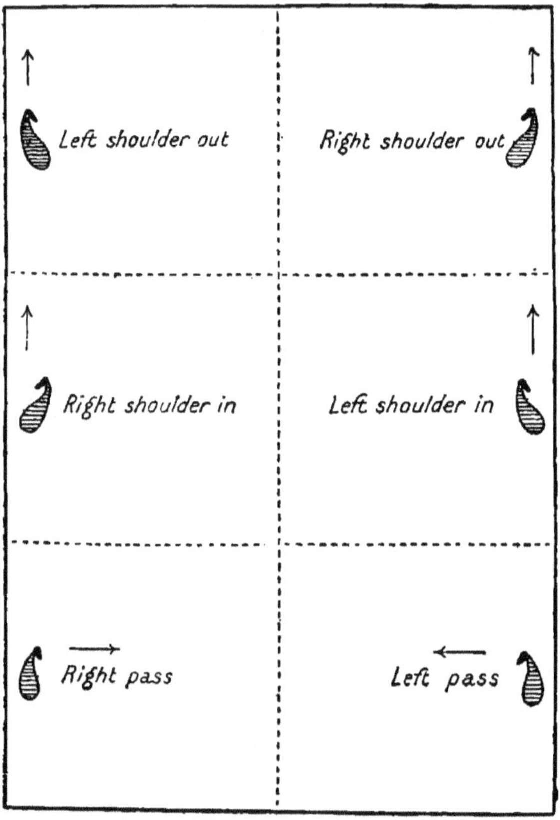

The following movements should be made (*see* Fig. 9) :—

Right shoulder in.

Left shoulder in.

Right shoulder out (moving to the left down the side).

Left shoulder out (moving to the right down the side).

Right pass ⎫
Left pass ⎬ To move across the school or to a flank.

In the *shoulder in* and *shoulder out* the horse's body should be inclined at about a half turn to the direction in which he is to move.

In *right* or *left pass* the horse's body should be kept approximately at right angles to the direction in which he is moving, being inclined only just sufficiently in that direction to enable him to cross his legs.

These movements should all be made in the same way. Thus in *right shoulder in*, the left rein bends and leads the horse assisted by the right rein. The pressure of the rider's right leg makes the horse cross his legs (except in the case of the half passage) whilst the rider's left leg keeps him up to the hand and prevents him from swerving.

Horses should not be turned at the corners when in the position of *shoulder in*. On reaching a corner each horse should be walked forwards and made to *shoulder in* after passing it.

In working the *passage* or *shoulder out* the turn is made on the haunches.

To turn to the right when passaging to the right :—Stay the hind quarters with the right leg, lead the forehand round with the right rein, keep the left leg closed to prevent the quarters from flying out.

In working the shoulder in and passages, fore and hind feet should move on four distinct lines parallel to each other.

4. *Half passage.*—In the *half passage* the horse is placed and bent as above, but instead of crossing his legs, one foot is placed in front of the other, and ground is gained to the front as well as to a flank.

In the *half passage* to the right the horse's forehand is brought in by a feeling of the right rein, at the same moment the left leg should be closed sufficiently to bring his quarters in an oblique direction, shoulders leading.

The right rein bends and leads, and a stronger pressure of the left leg obliges the horse to half cross his legs, placing one foot in front of the other, the right leg being used as required to keep him up to the hand.

72. *Spurs.*

1. When the recruit has learned to preserve his proper seat and balance, and has a knowledge of the aids made with the hands and legs, he may ride with spurs. In making use of spurs he must not open his thighs or move his body forward ; the leg from the knee downwards only should move.

Spurs with sharp rowels should only be allowed in exceptional circumstances.

2. The spurs should be used as little as possible, but when they are necessary the horse must be made to feel them. A continual light touch with the spurs will either make the horse kick or cause him to become insensible to them ; a jerking motion of the leg, with the heel drawn up, should therefore never be allowed.

73. *Various exercises.*

1. *General principles.*—The recruit's course should proceed by degrees according to the progress made, and any or all of the following exercises may be found useful.

Others which suggest themselves to the instructor may be added. Each exercise or game, however, should have some definite object in view, and should be looked on merely as a means to an end.

2. *The circle.*—The ride being told off by sections, " Nos. 1 OF EACH section CIRCLE RIGHT (or LEFT)," each No. 1 will ride his horse in a circle and fall-in in the rear of his section ; Nos. 2, 3, and 4 will do the same when ordered by the instructor.

"ODD (or EVEN) NUMBERS CIRCLE RIGHT (or LEFT)."—Each odd (or even) number will ride in a small circle and fall-in behind the even (or odd) number immediately behind him.

"HEADS OF SECTIONS CIRCLE RIGHT (or LEFT)."—The leading man of each section will ride in a circle followed by 2, 3, 4. They will continue in the circle until they get the command "GO LARGE," when they will cease circling and resume their original formation; or the rein may be changed by the word of command "HEADS OF SECTIONS—CHANGE."

3. *Figure of* 8.—For preliminary training in this movement, which may be carried out either in the riding school or in the open, the horse should be cantered quietly on a large circle or an oblong of about the same length as the school.

FIG. 10.

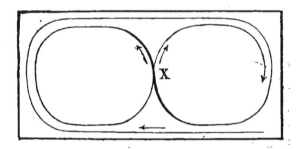

The change of rein and leading legs should be made as soon as the new circle is commenced at X. (*See* Fig. 10.)

In changing the bend, exaggerated movement of the rider's body, or the jerking of the horse's head across from one side to the other, should not be allowed; to compel the horse to change his legs it is necessary to turn his head slightly outwards, the rider at the same time inclining his weight backwards to lighten the forehand and pressing with his outer leg. These movements should be made gently, and as soon as the horse has changed the leading legs, both fore and hind, his neck and head should be turned towards the direction he is going.

4. Striking off at a canter with a named leg leading, when moving at a walk or slow trot either in the open or along one side of the school, is a good exercise for teaching recruits the use of their hands and legs in combination. The horses being at the walk the instructor gives the command " CANTER—OFF (or NEAR) LEGS LEADING," and after proceeding a few yards " TROT," or " WALK." The exercise is continued by alternately cantering and trotting or walking, the leading legs at the canter being constantly varied.

5. *The Serpentine.* ·

FIG. 11.

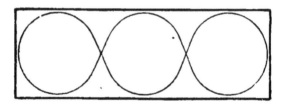

The changes of rein and leading legs to be made as soon as each new circle is commenced in the centre of the school or manège.

6. *Circling at the Corners.*

Fig. 12.

The circles should be made first at a walk, and then at a trot, on both reins before being made at a canter. When cantering it should not be attempted to make the horse do a small circle till he is fairly perfect at a big one. The circle should be gradually reduced in size till the horse makes such a small figure that he almost turns about on his haunches. A horse should be able to do this small circle in every corner at a collected canter on both reins, but it is a difficult figure, and only a well-balanced animal will do it. The horse should be made to go right into the corner, and make almost a square turn, but care must be taken to prevent him making these turns on his forehand.

7. *Ladies Chain.*—The leading file turns about, and rides a slightly zig-zag course through the remainder of the ride, who will be eight or ten yards distant from each other, passing on their right and left hands alternately. When each man in succession has done this, the rear file, at increased pace, will zig-zag through the ride from the rear, and the remainder will follow in succession.

8. *Games on Horseback.*—Progress depends so much on the interest taken by the men that games on horseback should be encouraged. Among the games which can be played are "*follow*

my leader," "throwing and catching balls," "wrestling on horseback," "jumping matches," "bending races," "plucking the handkerchief" from the shoulder of one of their number or from the ground, *"potato races," "figures of 8 round posts or trees," "rounders," "dismounting," "mounting,"* and *"changing horses," "on the move,"* and many others, some of which can be combined with jumping.

9. *Riding in Extended Order.*—A good exercise, for advanced squads of men who can ride fairly well, is for three or four squads of eight men, led by their own instructors, to be grouped under an officer, who should work them together.

The officer can put them over jumps by squads and can work them in close or extended order. Supposing he is working them at 3 yards' interval, in a column of squads at 10 yards' distance with No. 1 squad in front, by the word of command "No. 1 right about turn," he can turn the squad in front about so that the men must ride their horses to meet the squads following, and pass in between the files or by increasing the pace of the rear squad he can make it overtake and ride through those in front. Such exercises can be varied to any extent.

10. *Pursuing Exercise.*—The following exercise will be carried out first at a trot and then at a gallop.

The instructor will prescribe boundaries within which the pursued man may ride; if he crosses beyond them to avoid the pursuer, the pursuit ceases in favour of the latter and both men return to the squad or troop.

The instructor designates two men, one as the pursued, or No. 1, and the other as the pursuer or No. 2; he indicates a point toward which No. 1 will march until the pursuit is ordered. No. 1 leaves the squad and marches at a walk in the direction indicated, followed by No. 2 at a distance of about 15 yards. At any time after they have moved off the instructor commands "PURSUE—TROT OR GALLOP."

No. 2 will try to touch No. 1 on the left shoulder with his right hand. No. 1 will try to prevent this by turning, circling, bending over, dismounting, &c.

The ground for this exercise should be selected with a view to including obstacles, jumps, and broken ground.

74. *Practice of the gallop.*

1. As soon as the recruit has learnt to canter correctly, he must be practised in riding and using his weapons at the gallop, and must be gradually accustomed to the management of his horse when moving at the highest speed over undulating and broken ground.

2. When galloping at speed, the rider should tighten the grip of the knees and thighs, and press the upper part of the inside of his calves to the horse's sides; he should take the weight of his body off the seat bones by inclining the body forward from the hips, supporting his weight on the knees and inside of thighs just above the knees, at the same time putting more weight on the stirrups. Though the horse must be made to gallop freely the reins should not be allowed to flap loosely, and the feeling on the horse's mouth though gentle should be even and continuous, the fingers being closed firmly on the reins.

75. *Leading horses.*

1. When riding one horse and leading another, the led horse should usually be on the near side, so that, when meeting or being overtaken by traffic, the man, by keeping on the left of the road, will have the ridden horse between the led horse and the traffic. The led horse's rein should be held in the left hand lying flat against the reins of the ride horse.

If the led horse is fresh, his rein should be held short in the left hand, about a foot from his head. If the led horse tries to break away, the man should circle the two horses to the left.

2. When leading two horses one should usually be on each side of the rider.

3. When leading three horses one should be on the near side and two on the off side. When leading two horses on the

same side the reins of the outer horse should be passed between
the jaw and the back strap of the head collar of the inner horse
before being gathered up.

76. *Securing horses.*

1. *Tying up a horse.*—In securing a horse by the reins or head
rope to a tree, bush, or fence, he should be tied so that he cannot
injure himself or break his reins by treading on them.

Fig. 13.   Fig. 14.

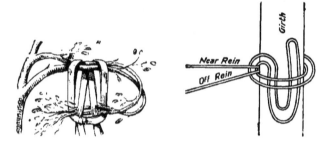

The knot used should be capable of being tied and untied
quickly, and should not become unfastened if the horse becomes
restive.   The following is a useful method for securing a horse
to a bush or small tree.

Take a suitable branch or bunch of branches, place the loop
of the reins under and round it, then double back the end of
the branch, breaking it if necessary, and pass it through the reins
as shown above and tighten up.   A separate piece of stick will
answer the same purpose.   (*See* Fig. 13.)

2. Single horses can also be kept from straying as follows :—

    i. By being trained to stand still whenever the reins are taken over the head and placed on the ground, but at the best this is an uncertain method (*see* Sec. **93**).

    ii. By being hobbled above the knees by a rope or leather thong tied round in such a way as to prevent the horse moving one foot in advance of the other.

    iii. By securing the bit to the stirrup iron by means of the rein or strap.

    iv. By knee-haltering.—One end of a rope is made fast above the knee by a clove hitch, fairly tight, with a keeper knot (half-hitch) round the rope to prevent it becoming loose. The other end is then carried to the head collar and so secured that the horse cannot tread on it. The rope should be from 1 foot to 1 foot 6 inches from the knee to the lower ring of the back strap of the head-collar.

    v. By securing the bridoon rein to the girth on the near side ; this is done by taking the bridoon reins over in the usual way and passing them under the girth from front to rear. They should then be drawn sufficiently tight to bend the horse's head to the left and fastened by a single hitch, but without drawing the slip end through. When mounting in haste the rider can easily loosen the slip knot after mounting, and then pull the reins clear and pass them over the horse's head.

3. *Coupling horses.*—Horses should be turned head to tail and tied each with the bridoon rein to the off back-strap or arch of the saddle of the other, care being taken that the reins, when tied, are not more than 6 to 8 inches long.

With three horses one can be tied to the head collar of either of the two horses so coupled. Four horses are secured by tying a horse to each of the two originally coupled. No horse should have more than one foot length of rein, and the best knot to be used is a slip knot round the rein itself.

   x 25119   **I**

4. *Linking horses.*—The head ropes are taken over the horses' heads clear of the reins, the coil or knot remaining fastened. Each man, facing his horse, hands his rope to the man on his right, who passes it through the upper ring of his own horse's head collar and ties it with two half-hitches.

5. *Ringing horses.*—The reins are taken over the horses' heads, and the flanks of the troop are brought forward until the horses are in a ring. The surcingle or stirrup leather of the right-hand man is then passed through all the reins and fastened.

77. *Riding awkward horses.*

1. The recruit should ride a number of different horses, commencing with easy, quiet animals, and later riding more difficult ones.

Speaking generally, when a horse refuses to do what is required, the rider should sit well down in the saddle, use plenty of firm leg pressure, and keep both hands on the reins with a light feeling on all four of them. The hands should be kept low and close on either side of the horse's withers and should not be held forward or out at right angles.

As a rule the use of stick or whip and spurs are not essential when riding an awkward horse. Speaking to a horse quietly will often have a good effect, but shouting is usually harmful. (*See* also Secs. **94** to **101**.)

2. *Kicking and bucking.*—Sit back and take the reins in both hands; if possible jerk the horse's head up or pull it right round to one side; make him move forward as soon as possible.

3. *Rearing.*—Take the reins in both hands and, as the horse stands up on his hind legs, lean forward leaving his mouth alone. Lean the weight on that part of the reins which passes from one hand to the other over the withers and compel the horse to move forward, if necessary hitting him over the quarters but never on the head, neck, or shoulder.

4. *Refusal to leave the ranks.*—Feel the horse's mouth and do not slacken the reins by pushing the hands forward, press him on

with the legs. Kicking the horse in the ribs with the heels or spurs and slackening the reins will have little effect. If he continues to decline to leave the ranks, rein him back two or three feet, then suddenly press him forward with leg pressure. If he still refuses, he should be reined back and taken out of the ranks backwards; such horses however require retraining (*see* Sec. **99**).

5. *Refusers.*—The best way to prevent a horse refusing is to make him feel that the rider is determined to jump. This is to be communicated to the horse by holding the reins in both hands and feeling his mouth with firmness, but not roughly or with undue pressure, and by pressing him up to the bit with the legs. Care must be taken not to ride the horse at the outside edge of the fence; the rider should be on the look out for the horse swerving round, especially to the near side, to which side horses are more liable to go. The horse should be taken slowly up to within a few lengths of the fence and then put straight at it by the rider increasing his leg pressure and slightly decreasing the feeling on the horse's mouth.

If the horse swerves round, he should be turned back the opposite way to face the fence again, then reined back a short distance and, when quite square, put at it afresh. If necessary this time he should be touched with the spur but the leg pressure should not be relaxed.

6. *Horses that rush at their fences* should be circled round in front of the fence as though they were not going to jump it, until they settle down, when they may be jumped over the obstacle. They should be taught to stand quietly in front of a fence. On no account should they be spurred or have their mouths jerked. After landing over a fence they should be eased up gently to a slow pace and never allowed to get out of hand.

7. *A hard puller or runaway.* — Never let the horse get fully extended. His head should be up if he tries to get it down

I 2

and down if he tries to get it up; do not maintain a dead pull
on the reins, but alternately exert and relax the pull.

8. *Mounting restive horses.*—With the left hand gather up
the reins loosely and seize the cheek piece, hold the stirrup iron
in the right hand, allowing the horse to walk round.   Place the
left foot in the stirrup, and transfer the right hand to the
pommel, off side waist, or other part of the saddle.   The horse,
if he moves, will revolve in a small circle, of which the right toe
of the rider is the centre.   The latter should now be able to
mount without difficulty.

At the first opportunity such horses should be systematically
trained to stand still (*see* Sec. **93**).

THE USE OF THE WEAPONS MOUNTED.

78. *Riding with the sword.* (*Drill.*)

Fig. 15.   Fig. 16

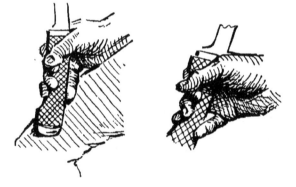

1. *To draw swords.*

"DRAW-SWORDS —ONE." Pass the right hand smartly across the body over the bridle arm, draw out the blade so as to rest the hilt on the bridle arm, place the sword knot on the wrist, give it two turns inward to secure it, and then grasp the handle with the right arm close to the body, shoulders square to the front.

"Two." With an extended arm draw the sword slowly from the scabbard, in the rear of the left shoulder, and bring it smartly to the *Recover*, that is, with the upper part of the hilt in line with the mouth, blade perpendicular, edge to the left, elbow close to the body.

"THREE." Lower the sword smartly to the *Carry*, that is, with the top of the guard resting on the top of the hand, blade perpendicular, edge to the front, the first and second fingers gripping the handle under the resistance piece, the little finger behind the handle to steady it, the wrist resting on the leg and the pommel pressed against the side of it, upper part of the arm close to the body, and the elbow lightly touching the hip. (*See* Fig. 15.)

2. *To slope swords.*

"SLOPE-SWORDS." Bring the lower part of the arm at right angles to the upper, hand in front of the elbow, relax the grasp of the second and third fingers, and allow the sword to fall lightly on the shoulder, midway between the neck and point of the shoulder, the top of the hilt resting on the top of the hand, the little finger still in rear of the hilt. (*See* Fig. 16.)

3. *To sit at ease.*

"SIT AT EASE."   Keeping the sword at the slope, place the
                  hands on the front part of the saddle, with the
                  right hand over the left.

4. "ATTEN-   Come smartly to the position of *Slope*
   TION."   *Swords.*

"CARRY   Resume the grasp of the second and third
SWORDS."   fingers and bring the blade perpendicular, the
                  hilt resting on the thigh, as in the third motion
                  of drawing swords.

5. *To return swords.*

"RETURN   Carry the hilt smartly to the hollow of the
 SWORDS—   left shoulder, blade perpendicular, edge to the
 ONE."   left, elbow level with the shoulder; then by a
                  quick turn of the wrist drop the point in rear of
                  the left shoulder and push it slowly into the
                  scabbard; then resume the position at the end
                  of the first motion in *Draw Swords*, shoulders
                  being kept square to the front throughout this
                  motion.

"TWO."   Push the sword lightly into the scabbard,
                  release the hand from the sword knot by giving
                  it two turns outwards, the right hand remaining
                  across the body in line with the elbow, fingers
                  extended and close together, back of the hand
                  up.

"THREE."   Drop the right hand smartly to the side.

6. When "*Draw Swords*" is ordered at the walk, the men
after drawing will remain at the *carry* until ordered to *slope*; but
if "*Draw Swords*" is ordered at the trot or gallop, the men will
come to the *slope* after drawing.

7. Drawing and returning swords should frequently be practised at the trot and gallop. On such occasions, when returning swords, the scabbard may be steadied by the drawn back heel.

8. *Proving.*—In proving with a drawn sword, the sword is brought to the *carry*, and again sloped on the command " AS YOU WERE."

9. *Paying compliments with the drawn sword.*

i. *Officers' salute in marching past.*

The salute is to commence at ten yards before arrival in front of the reviewing officer, and finish ten yards after passing him, the time being taken from the officer on the right.

> *First motion :* Carry the sword direct to the right to the full extent of the arm, hand as high as the shoulder, back of the hand to the rear, blade perpendicular.
>
> *Second motion :* Bring the sword by a circular motion to the *Recover*, keeping the elbow as high as the shoulder.
>
> *Third motion :* Still keeping the elbow the height of the shoulder, bring the hilt to the right shoulder ; during this motion let the finger nails come in line with the edge of the sword.
>
> *Fourth motion :* Lower the sword to the front to the full extent of the arm, blade 3 inches below the knee, edge to the left, thumb extended in the direction of the point, hand directly under the shoulder. There should be no pause between these motions ; all should be combined in one graceful movement.
>
> The head is slightly turned towards the reviewing officer whilst passing him.
>
> When ten yards past the reviewing officer, the sword is brought to the *Recover* carrying it well to the front, and to the *Carry* in two deliberate movements.

ii. *Officers' salute at the halt.*

The sword being at the *Carry* :—

> *First motion.*—Bring the sword to the *Recover*, but with the thumb pointing upwards.
>
> *Second motion.*—As described in fourth motion of the salute when marching past.
>
> *Third motion.*—Bring the sword to the *recover.*
>
> *Fourth motion.*—Bring the sword to the *carry.*

iii. A soldier, when passing an officer and carrying a drawn sword, should *carry* his sword and turn his head and eyes in the direction of the officer.

79. *Riding with the lance.* (*Drill.*)

1. When standing to his horse at *attention*, the lancer stands square to the front, his toes in line with the horse's fore feet, holding the bridoon rein with the right hand near the bit, and the lance at the *order* in the left hand, which slides down the pole to the full extent of the arm, the thumb next the body, the fingers on the outside of the lance.

2. "**Prepare to Mount.**"*   Grasp the lance just below the sling with the left hand, which at the same time grips the reins and a lock of the mane.

"Mount."   Mount in the usual manner, taking care to keep the point of the lance well up to prevent it from touching the men and horses in the ranks. As soon as seated in the saddle, grasp the lance by the right hand below the balance under the bridle hand; by a second motion bring it smartly up and hold it perpendicularly with the right hand in front of the face, the butt in line with the elbow; after a short pause, lower it carefully into the bucket and come to the position of *carry lance*, which is the position of *attention* when mounted.

---

* This is a word of command for recruits only, except on ceremonial occasions. *See* Sec. **63**, 3.

3. "PREPARE   Let the right hand slide down the pole of
TO DISMOUNT." the lance to the full extent of the arm; bring
the lance smartly up and hold it perpendicularly
with the right hand in front of the face; after
a short pause lower it under the bridle
arm, and grasp it just below the sling by the
left hand, which should already be holding the
reins and mane.

"DISMOUNT."   Dismount as usual, pressing the hand upon
the butt end of the pole, so as to keep the point
well raised, and assume the position of
attention with the lance at the *order* in the
left hand, butt close to the ball of the left foot.

4. "STAND AT   Stand at ease, as after dismounting with
EASE." swords, the lance resting against the left
shoulder.

5. "CARRY   The lance, resting with the butt end in the
LANCE." bucket, is kept upright with the right hand,
which grasps the pole, thumb level with the
top of the shoulder, back of the hand to the
front, elbow down.

6. "ORDER   Let the lance fall against the hollow of
LANCE." the right shoulder, and let the right hand slide
down the pole to the full extent of the arm, as
on foot.

7. If the order " SIT AT EASE " is given when at the *carry*, the
lance is allowed to fall against the hollow of the shoulder as at
the *order*, the left hand is placed on the front of the saddle, the
right hand over the left, with the right arm round the pole.

On the command " ATTENTION " (from *sit at ease*), the position
of " *carry lance* " is at once assumed.

8. "TRAIL LANCE."	Grasping the lance at the balance, raise it out of the bucket, lower the point to the left front, over the horse's near ear, the hand resting on the thigh, little finger in line with the back edge of the stripe of the pantaloons, knuckles down and elbow slightly forward.
9. "SLING LANCE."	(From the *carry*.)—Pass the right hand through the sling, and rest it on the thigh, near the hip, with the knuckles down, elbows bent outwards, without stiffness.
10. "BY NUMBERS.— LEFT ARM SLING LANCE."	Let the right arm slide down the pole of the lance to the full extent of the arm.
"TWO."	Bring the lance smartly up, and hold it perpendicularly with the right hand in front of the face; after a short pause, lower it carefully into the left bucket outside the bridle arm, the right hand resting on the left, the lance sliding through it.
"THREE."	Holding the lance between the thumb and fore-finger, pass the remaining fingers of the right hand over the reins and hold them, with the back of the hand up: pass the left hand thus disengaged through the sling and again take the reins.
"BY NUMBERS.— CARRY LANCE."	Take the reins in the right hand, the back of the hand up, and drop the left hand, taking hold of the lance at the full extent of the arm.
"TWO."	Sweep the lance to the front with the left arm, and, disengaging the arm from the sling, allow the lance to fall against the left shoulder, and immediately take the reins with the left hand.

"THREE." Drop the right hand to the full extent of the arm under the bridle hand, seize the lance and bring it smartly up, holding it perpendicularly with the right hand in front of the face; after a short pause, lower it carefully into the right bucket, and assume the position of *carry lance.*

The recruit will be taught the *left arm sling lance* and *carry lance* by numbers. The trained soldier will go through the motions above described on the word of command "LEFT ARM SLING LANCE."

11. *Dressing.*—On the order "DRESS," when mounted, the lance is brought to the *order.* As soon as the dressing is completed and the command "EYES FRONT" given, the position of *carry lance* is resumed.

12. *Proving.*—In proving the telling off with a lance at the *carry,* the right arm is extended to the front, the hand retaining its grasp. In proving at the *order,* the hand is brought to the position of *carry,* and the arm extended to the front. The original position is assumed on the command "AS YOU WERE."

13. Royal escorts and orderlies attending royal personages or officers on duty will move with their lances at the *trail.* Other orderlies and individual lancers when detached will move with their lances *slung,* except when acting as scouts or when passing guards, armed parties, and officers and others entitled to salutes, when they *carry lance.* Care should be taken to prevent men from getting into the habit of leaning on their lances when at the *carry* or when at the *sling.*

14. When it is desired to ride at ease, the command "SLING LANCE, MARCH (or SIT) AT EASE" will be given, upon which leaders and serrefiles return swords.

When at the halt and it is intended to sit at ease for a short time, afterwards to resume riding at attention, the command will be given "SIT AT EASE," upon which leaders and serrefiles do not return swords but sit at ease as in Sec. **78,** 3.

15. It may sometimes be convenient, *e.g.*, when riding through a wood, to trail lance with the point to the rear : if this is done files should be opened.

80.   *Riding with the rifle.   (Drill.)*

1. Whenever a man dismounts he does so with his rifle.

2. *To mount—by numbers.*

" PREPARE TO MOUNT."
Take hold of the barrel of the rifle with the left hand, about 3 inches below the muzzle, butt downwards, and prepare to mount as in Sec. **63** but with the rifle held in the left hand on the off side of the horse.

" MOUNT."
Mount as usual, raise the rifle with the left hand, seize it with the right hand in front of the magazine, and place it in the bucket.

3. *To dismount—by numbers.*

" PREPARE TO DISMOUNT."
Seize the rifle with the right hand by the small of the butt.

" TWO."
Draw the rifle out of the bucket far enough to allow the hand to re-grasp it just in front of the magazine; raise it so as to clear the front of the saddle.

" THREE."
Lower the butt under the bridle hand, and hold the barrel with the left hand about 3 inches below the muzzle.

" FOUR."
Take a lock of the mane in the right hand and twist it round the thumb of the left, place the right hand in front of the saddle, and quit the right stirrup.

"DISMOUNT." Dismount as usual, bringing the rifle to the position of the *order* in the left hand, and hold the bridle with the right hand.

4. *The Advance.*

" BY NUMBERS, DRAW ARMS." Grasp the rifle at the small of the butt.

" TWO." Draw the rifle out of the bucket far enough to allow the hand to re-grasp it just in front of the magazine.

" THREE." Retaining the same grasp, bring the rifle to the *advance.* In this position the rifle is held with the right hand in front of the magazine, right hand resting on the upper part of the right thigh, thumb and fingers round the rifle, muzzle pointing to the left front, just clear of the horse's near ear, trigger guard to the front.

5. " RETURN ARMS " This is done in one motion as follows :— Raise the butt of the rifle and lower the muzzle into the mouth of the bucket, pressing the rifle well home with the right hand, trigger guard to the rear, taking care that the bolt lever does not catch on the edge of the bucket.

6. " CARRY ARMS." (From the *advance.*)—Without moving the right hand from its grasp of the rifle, place the butt on the upper part of the right thigh, the muzzle leaning to the front and in line with the right eye, trigger guard to the left, back of the hand down, arm slightly bent, elbow close to the side.

81. *Dismounting and mounting when armed with lance and rifle.*

" FOR ACTION FRONT (RIGHT— LEFT)—DIS- MOUNT." Without removing the lance from the bucket, pass it to and hold it with the bridle-hand; then grasp the rifle at the small, withdrawing it (to the rear) from the bucket and

> passing it under the bridle-arm; at the same
> time insert the thumb of the left hand in
> the rifle sling, place the lance in the rifle
> bucket, and dismount as quickly as possible.

"MOUNT."   Grasp the rifle with the left hand in front
of the magazine, muzzle to the rear, trigger-
guard down; withdraw the lance with the
right hand from the rifle bucket, returning
the rifle with the left hand into the bucket,
mount on the offside as quickly as possible.

82. *Use of the weapons in war.*

1. In the charge against both cavalry and infantry each man
should ride at his opponent at full speed with the fixed determination of running him through and killing him. The weapon
should be held firmly (sword at *sword in line* and lance at the
engage) and pointed straight at the chest or stomach of the
opponent.

The hand and arm should be used simply for directing the
point of the weapon; the impetus should be sufficient to drive
the point home. The best method of defence is to put the
opponent out of action before he can strike. It should be
remembered, however, that the sword when in line to a certain
extent guards the body against the enemy's attack.

When delivering the charge, the body should be inclined
forward, the weight being taken off the seat bones; the grip of
the thighs and knees should be as strong as possible, the right
shoulder well forward, the head inclined forward, and the eyes
directed at the target.

2. In the mêlée, if both sides are equally determined, success
depends to a great extent on the handiness of the horse and the
skill of the soldier as a man at arms. Lack of space and speed
may deprive the rider of the impetus which in the charge drives
the point home, and he will be compelled to use a vigorous

thrust to force his weapon through his opponent. In the pursuit, also, owing to the pace of the pursued the thrust will be necessary.

3. The main principles of fighting with the sword are that the swordsman should :—

    i. Keep his point directed on the adversary ;

    ii. Attack rather than await attack ;

    iii. After parrying an attack, immediately return with the point ;

    iv. Make every possible use of the speed and handiness of his horse.

4. The same principles apply to fighting with the lance, but it is perhaps even more important for the lancer to attack at speed and thus obtain full advantage of the terror which the lance inspires. He should, if possible, prevent his adversary gaining his right rear.

5. Firing with the rifle from horseback usually results in waste of ammunition. There are only two occasions when it may be employed :—

    i. When a scout who has fallen into on ambush wishes to inform his comrades of the proximity of the enemy.

    ii. In case of retreat to delay the enemy's advance.

83. *Training in the use of the sword and lance.*

1. Before riding with arms is practised, the men should have acquired good firm seats and light hands, and have been thoroughly trained in handling their weapons on foot.

2. The instruction should be such that every man becomes accustomed to ride with his weapon in his hand and has confidence in his ability to use it with effect. Constant practice should be given in riding with swords drawn and lances at the trail.

3. The soldier should be taught to deliver a vigorous point at dummies on either side of him and at every height. The resistance of the dummies should be such that it is impossible to knock them over with the point of the sword or lance, or to drive the point through them, unless the horse is travelling at speed, and unless the weapon is held firmly with the full weight of the rider and the momentum of the horse behind the point.

To ensure accuracy a target should be marked on the dummies.

The service pattern swords and lances should be used, and the points with the sword should be delivered correctly with the back of the hand to the left, little finger uppermost.

4. Neither at training nor recreation should pointing at balls, rings, or heads which offer no resistance, or which cannot be pierced by the sword or lance, be permitted.

5. Though tent pegging is unnecessary for training it may be permitted for purposes of recreation if the following precautions are taken to avoid making the horses excitable and to prevent damage being done to their legs :—

    i. Only aged horses should be used.

    ii. The exercise should be carried out on soft ground.

    iii. The horses should not be allowed to gallop at full speed until they come within forty yards of the peg, and should be pulled up at eighty yards beyond it.

84. *Instruction in the use of the sword or lance in the mélée.*

1. This instruction will be given in two forms :—

    i. In mounted combats.

    ii. Against single dummies.

2. To attain good results in mounted combats recruits should be mounted on horses trained to the work, for if they ride insufficiently trained horses they will learn little and will probably spoil the horses.

3. *Single combat* if carried out on sound lines (*see* Sec. **86**) under-strict supervision, is a valuable exercise, but unless so carried out it leads to false teaching. It should only be looked on as preliminary instruction for mounted combat by squads.

4. *Mounted combat instruction by squads* should take place in an open space, marked out by boundaries; a manège is too small.

The following rules are given for guidance, others may be arranged as suggest themselves to the instructor :—

i. Opposing sides form up at opposite ends of the ground in extended order. They may consist of any number up to six, not necessarily of equal numbers, nor need they be armed with the same weapons.

ii. The sides may be directed, on receipt of the order to commence, to gallop at each other and fight, or to pass each other, then to wheel about and attack as opportunity offers.

iii. Any man striking his own or his opponent's horse must immediately leave the ring at a gallop.

iv. When a man is hit he must hold up his weapon, and immediately retire out of the ground.

v. Any man going outside the boundary is disqualified.

Unless rule iii and iv are observed as points of honour by the combatants the fight can be neither interesting nor instructive. One director, who should stop the fight if any rule is broken, should be sufficient.

The combat should not last more than two minutes, by the end of which time the whole of one side should have been disposed of. No halting is to be permitted, and, except in the early stages of the training, a gallop should be maintained throughout.

Though in war it will often be to the advantage of a man to wound his opponent's horse, in peace training, rule iii is obviously necessary.

5. In mounted combats, when delivering points or thrusts with dummy lances other than spring dummy lances, the men

should let their hands slide up their lances in order to avoid hurting their opponents, but in the field with service lances when their object is to kill and in practising against dummies they should grip their lances tightly.

6. The other form of training in mêlée fighting is carried out by means of single dummies, placed in a variety of positions on the training ground, in front, behind, and on the wings of the jumps, on undulating as well as on level ground.

Points against these dummies may be delivered either with the arm rigid as in the charge, or with a thrust from the engage according to the pace at which the horse is travelling.

The positions of the dummies should be varied, if possible, from day to day, and no stereotyped form of course should be allowed.

85. *Instruction in the use of the sword or lance in the pursuit.*

1. Men should first be exercised in pursuing one another without arms, a piece of canvas, or handkerchief being placed under the shoulder cord of the pursued, which the pursuer must remove; neither man should be allowed to go outside certain prescribed boundaries.

The practice should be carried out over all descriptions of country.

2. The men being armed with *practice swords*, or *dummy lances* and protected with masks, etc., should be started at some distance apart, one man being told off to attack and the other to parry or avoid the assult; when the combatants have passed one another, the man making the parry should be instructed to turn quickly about and pursue the attacker (whose attack whether successful or not is presumed to have failed), the pursued man being allowed to defend himself as best he can. The pursuer must thrust at the pursued man's back and not at the back of his head.

3. As explained in Sec. **82** it will probably be necessary for the pursuer to deliver his thrust by straightening the arm vigorously from the *engage*. As the thrust is being delivered the man should lunge his body forward end reach well out with his head and shoulder. Practices for instruction should also be carried out with the object of teaching the pursuer to place himself on the most vulnerable side of the pursued.

86. *Rules for single combat mounted, with sword and lance.*

1. With the sword, points only will count as hits; with the lance, points and thrusts with the butt will both count.

2. The combat will continue until a hit is made or until the fight is stopped by the judges. It must cease when a combatant is hit, whether such hit be valid or not.
If no hit is made the judges will stop the bout after it has lasted half a minute.

3. If no hit is scored by either combatant or if a counter is made, *i.e.*, if the attacks of both are simultaneously successful, the bout will be re-fought. If a bout is re-fought for the first of these reasons and for a second time no hit is made, both competitors will be disqualified, except in deciding a final tie, when the prize, if any, will be divided.

4. All parts of the body above the hips are included in the target, with the exception of the hands below the wrists.

5. A competitor will be disqualified for:—

i. Dropping his weapon.
ii. Being unhorsed.
iii. Hitting his own or his opponent's horse.
iv. Dangerous riding.
v. Unfair practices.
vi. Deliberately delaying or avoiding the fight.

K 2

87. *Revolver shooting mounted.*

1. The lessons should begin with blank ammunition; firing at first to the right only, then to the left, and then to the right front and rear, and left front and rear; at first at a walk, and eventually at a gallop.

2. The man should carry the revolver with safety, that is to say, pointed straight down, and with the finger away from the trigger until it is time to fire; he should then throw the arm towards the target and shoot without taking aim along the sights.

3. Ball firing should at first be carried out on foot, the firer walking past the target.

With a little practice, men soon get accustomed to, as it were, "throwing the bullet," much on the principle of throwing a stone. The eyes should be directed on the object and not on the sights.

4. Practice with ball ammunition mounted should not be carried out until a man thoroughly understands the handling of the weapon.

TRAINING THE YOUNG HORSE.

88. *General principles.*

1. The training of the young horse must be gradual, and accompanied by a steady development of his physical powers.

Exactly the same system or length of training is not applicable to every breed and condition of horse and in all climatic conditions. The principles, however, are the same, and must be modified to suit the horse's temperament, age, and condition. Care must be taken to avoid overworking weak horses and rendering others unsound by overtaxing their powers.

2. The training of a horse joining at under five years of age should take at least 18 months divided into three periods.

3. In the first period (5 to 7 months) the object is to develop the horse's physical powers, to make him quiet to ride and to teach him to carry his head at the correct height and move freely forward. (*See* Sec. **89**.)

4. In the second period (4 to 6 months) the object of the trainer is to make the horse balanced and collected, and to teach him to passage, turn on his hocks, rein back, and to obey the aids quickly when ridden with one hand. (*See* Sec. **90**.)

5. The third period (6 to 8 months) will be devoted to training the horse to the sword, lance, and rifle; to go quietly in company, whether in front of, behind, or alongside other horses; to mounted combat, etc., etc.

6. In the case of horses joining in good condition at over five years of age the above stages, especially the first, may be shortened to a total of about 12 months.

Before the third period of training is concluded, a young horse may be taken for light work at squadron and regimental training; he is not, however, to be considered as fit for active service or to be taken to manœuvres until over 6 years of age.

7. Patience, firmness, and courage are necessary to all entrusted with the training of young horses. Some horses are much quicker at learning than others, and no hard and fast rule can be laid down; but only under exceptional circumstances should the training be hurried.

The trainer should communicate to his pupil his appreciation of any progress made by immediately rewarding him with a handful of corn or a carrot.

In no circumstances should the trainer lose his temper with his horse; punishment should only be resorted to when it is certain that the horse understands what he is required to do, but will not do it.

Instructors must not imagine that the animal can learn a lesson only by constant repetition. A horse is quick to receive new impressions, and remembers them after comparatively few lessons, provided they are given properly.

8. It is better to give a young horse two short lessons in a day than one long one, for the tendons and muscles of a young immature animal are easily strained by too much continuous work, and must be gradually strengthened in order to stand the work required.

After the first few lessons the young horse should be taken occasionally for quiet rides well away from his stables, the distance of the ride being gradually increased.

9. Jumping should be constantly practised throughout the training, commencing at an early stage over very low obstacles and always with a due consideration for the horse's legs. When carried out with discretion, it tends to develop and strengthen the muscles of the young horse's back and thighs.

10. The use of long reins in the training of young horses should be confined to those horses which, from weakness or other causes, are not fit for the time being to carry the weight of a man. In giving young horses long rein work care should be taken that the driving is done by experienced men and that the work is not overdone. The horses should be driven equally on both reins ; if driven more on one rein than on another their mouths may become one-sided. Long reins may also be used to re-train a badly broken or awkward horse.

The instructions in the use of long reins for the purpose of re-training given in Sec. **95** apply equally to the first training of a young horse. In the latter case, however, it is advisable to fasten the reins to the head collar and not to the bit for the first few lessons.

11. When the horse is fit for the ranks he should be quiet, handy, and as active as his build will permit him to be. He should also be in good condition and well muscled up.

The squadron commander must himself ride and try each remount before passing him into the ranks.

89. *First period in training the young horse.*

1. Simplicity should be the prominent feature in this stage of the training; it must be remembered that the horse not only

has to learn the meaning of the bridle and the leg, but must also adjust his balance to carrying a weight on his back.

2. All work in this period should be carried out on a bridoon.

3. The first day or two of the training should be spent by the trainer in getting thoroughly acquainted with his pupil. A snaffle having been put in the horse's mouth, the trainer will lead him about, giving him confidence, and making him acquainted with his voice. He may then handle him about the head and forehand, and lead him up to strange objects. To prevent injuries to the mouth at this early stage the horse may be led by reins attached to the head-collar, the snaffle being left to hang loosely in his mouth. During these lessons the horse should be given a handful of corn or green food from time to time.

4. When the horse is thoroughly handy at being led about or on the long reins he should be saddled; if he has had experience with the driving pad there is not likely to be any trouble, but in any case he should be accustomed to the feeling of the saddle on his back, before he is mounted for the first time.

An assistant should stand in front of the horse, holding a rein of the snaffle in each hand; the man saddling him should then place the saddle quickly and quietly on the horse's back, slide it firmly back, let the girths down, and tighten them gradually.

In backing a horse for the first time the help of two assistants is advisable, one on the off side, who will hold the head collar in his right hand and the off stirrup in his left, the other on the near side holding the snaffle rein in his left hand. The man who is to mount should stand close to his horse on the near side, grasping the back arch of the saddle in his right and the front arch in his left hand; he should then raise his left foot up behind him by bending his knee, and the assistant, grasping his leg just above the ankle, should raise him quietly into the saddle on his stomach. This should be repeated several times until the horse is accustomed to the weight. The assistant will then place the rider's left foot in the stirrup ; the latter will then raise himself in the stirrup, throw his right leg over the horse's quarters and drop quietly into the saddle. The horse should then be led a pace or two forward by the assistant in order to accustom him to the weight whilst moving, the rider avoiding too strong a pressure with the legs.

After two or three lessons, if the horse is quiet, the trainer may mount with the stirrup in the usual way, care being taken to avoid touching the horse with the toe.

In dismounting the first few times an assistant should stand in front of the horse, whilst the rider after throwing his right leg over to the near side should remain lying across the saddle as in mounting, then quit his left stirrup and slide quietly to the ground. This method will prevent any possibility of the rider pressing his toe into the horse's ribs, and thus making the horse unsteady when the rider mounts or dismounts.

From the first the young horse should be taught to stand still when being mounted or dismounted.

5. When a horse displays a determination to show fight on being backed, it may occasionally be advisable to put him down and back him whilst lying down.

To do this, first select a soft place ; then strap up one fore leg with a short strap, buckle inside, and loop a long strap round the pastern of the other fore leg. Let the horse stand for some minutes without attempting to make him lie down.

Next induce the horse to go forward by tapping him lightly under the knee, at the same time pull the long strap to make him go down on his knees. It is as well at first, with a restive horse, to hold the reins under the jowl about a foot from the snaffle ring to prevent him plunging.

As soon as the horse rests on both knees he can be induced to lie down quietly on either side by a slight pressure on the back of the saddle. The voice should be used during the whole process.

After a few lessons the horse will, as a rule, lie down on being given a light tap under the knee, and with a few more lessons even that can be dispensed with and the voice alone used.

A horse should never be made to get up on his legs from lying down with a man on his back.

6. After backing the horse the trainer should devote his time to riding him about at a free walk and slow trot in a straight line, and teach him to stand still for mounting or dismounting and whenever required, and to lead readily. The rider should hold his reins long and use his legs in order to teach the horse to move forward freely at the walk.

To teach the horse to stand still, constant practice and the use of an assistant when necessary are required; the trainer should mount and dismount from either side, time after time, not allowing the horse to move forward immediately after mounting.

The horse should also be taught to make large circles to either hand, be practised over very small jumps, and be ridden frequently outside barracks.

This stage must not be hurried, as it is most important in moulding the horse's future disposition, and in building up his physical strength and preparing him for harder work later on.

The raising or lowering of the horse's head must be done gradually, and as much as possible oh the move, for if done at the halt his freedom of action may be endangered.

It should be carried out by the combined action of the legs and hands. The legs compel the horse to move forward, and drive and keep him up to the bit; the hands through the reins and snaffle regulate the position of the horse's head and neck. If the horse's head requires raising, the rider should hold his hands high. If the head requires lowering, the hands are depressed, but without jerking the reins. In both cases the rider should use strong leg pressure. To ensure the pressure on the mouth remaining light, the trainer must ride with a sympathetic hand; he must relax the pressure as soon as the horse places his head in the required position, only retaining sufficient feeling on the mouth to maintain the head in that position.

90. *Second period in training the young horse.*

1. All work in this period should be carried out on the bit.

2. The horse must be taught to give to the bridle by bending his neck at the poll and slightly yielding his lower jaw, care being taken that in yielding the head is not lowered.

The trainer must not attempt much at one time. The longer a continuous pressure on the reins is maintained, the less inclined is the horse to yield, for the mouth loses its sensitiveness. The application of the legs must often be strong to make the horse yield.

3. A natural law of leverage governs the position of the horse's head. As the head and neck are moved forward and downwards the centre of gravity of the whole horse is brought forward and he becomes heavier in the forehand and freer or lighter behind. At a trot or canter the horse naturally draws his head up to lighten the weight on his fore legs and to give them free and equal play with the hind legs.

The young horse should be trained to carry his head fairly high at the trot and canter, and at such angle with the neck as will allow the bit to have the best bearing on the bars of the mouth. As a horse cannot put his fore feet down on the ground beyond his nose, he extends his neck when galloping, in order to lengthen his stride. By thus moving his centre of gravity forward he lightens the weight on his quarters and obtains the full propelling power of his hind legs.

The extended gallop is, however, not the normal pace of cavalry.

A horse when jumping makes use of his neck both as an assistance in taking off and to adjust his weight on landing; his head therefore should remain perfectly free during every phase of the jump.

4. Reining back is a useful exercise to collect the young horse and teach him to get his haunches under him, but it should not be practised for more than a few minutes at a time, nor should

it be attempted until the horse will go up to the bit both at the trot and canter.

To teach a horse to rein back the instructor should first be on foot; later he must continue the training mounted with the help of an assistant on foot. The man on foot should stand in front of the horse and endeavour to make him go back quietly one pace at a time. He should feel the bit gently, but without a dead continuous pressure; he may give a light tap to the horse's leading fore leg, should he decline to move backwards.

When mounted collect the horse by leg pressure, and bring the weight of the body slightly forward; feel one side (say the right) of the horse's mouth by the least movement of the wrist, at the same time by the pressure of the left leg prevent the horse from moving his hindquarters to the left; lean the body a little to the right, and feel both reins. As soon as the horse draws back the off fore leg, reverse the aids until he draws back the near fore leg and so on. The ultimate object is to teach him to go backwards with his head carried as high as when going forward. The horse must not be allowed to run back, but must be kept up to the bit by leg pressure.

5. The bending lesson (*see* Sec. **71**) is useful for balancing and collecting the young horse and for teaching him to obey the rider's legs. During the first few lessons the horse's head should be turned towards the wall.

'6. The young horse should be taught to canter correctly, and later to change at the canter.

The figure of 8 (*see* Sec. **73**) is a useful exercise to teach the horse to change his legs, provided he is first made to go quietly and collectedly on the larger circle before being turned in to make the figure of 8.

7. In order that the horse may retain his full freedom of movement he should frequently be made to walk out fast and canter with a loose rein. To make a horse walk out, ease the reins and close the legs alternately, not both legs together as in the trot.

91. *Training the young horse to jump.*

1. There should be one outdoor jumping course with small and another with larger jumps, all as much like natural fences as possible, and laid out on sand or cinder-tracks with soft landing so as to be available all the year round.

Jumps should be made to represent breadth as well as height, for the horse should be practised in jumping out as well as up, in order that his action may not become cramped.

The training in jumping, like the whole training of the remount, should be gradual and systematic; even if a horse shows great promise when first jumped his education should in no way be hurried.

2. If the young horse is fit and will answer to the hand and leg he may be ridden over low and simple fences at once. To avoid all chance of failure it will, however, generally be found advisable to lead, lunge, or drive him over the jump with long reins. In a school or confined space the best method is first to lead the horse over a bar laid on the ground, and afterwards to lead him up to it and let him go, a man with a basket of corn standing beyond the bar to catch him. The obstacle should be raised gradually, and should always be put up firmly. In a short time most horses will jump a fence 3 feet 6 inches high with enjoyment. The nature of the obstacle should be varied as much as possible as time goes on. In this manner the remount may be taught to jump rails, gates, wire, etc., all of which should be fixed up so that they will not give or break.

The long whip should not be used, as it will make the horse excited and prevent him from measuring his distance from the jump.

If the single lungeing-rein and cavesson are used, the rein may be attached to the front of the cavesson and the animal led over the jump, or it may be fastened to a side " D," when he should be made to take the fence on the circle. If done in this way it is a good plan to have a wing made to the jump, which will

carry the rein over and prevent it from catching in the obstacle
and checking the horse in the mouth.

3. After a sufficient schooling following any of the above
methods, the remount should be sent down a jumping-lane, an
old horse acting as pilot on the first occasion, or if there is no
lane he may be ridden over small fences in the open. The first
jumping lessons should be given at a trot. At this pace horses
learn where to take off and jump from their hocks without
chancing a fence.

When a young, but not impetuous, horse is being ridden at a
fence, he should be allowed to go his own pace; in this way
he learns to adopt the pace most suited to the obstacle and to
throw his weight back on his hocks for a high one.

92. *Third period in training the young horse.*

1. When the young horse is fairly well balanced and collected
will rein back, do the bending lesson and figure of 8 correctly,
and when his physical powers have developed satisfactorily, the
third period of his training should commence. Most of it
should be done out of doors and with arms.

Any bad tendencies should be carefully corrected and his
manners improved.

The horse should now be taught to canter very slowly. He
should be constantly practised in breaking smoothly from a walk
and trot into a canter and gallop, and back again to the slower
paces, and made to travel at the regulation paces in company
with other horses.

2. Cantering a horse in small circles is useful for calming
excitable horses. Other horses should require but little circling.

3. The young horse in this period should also be given a certain
amount of careful training in mounted combat. He should also
be taken occasionally for quiet rides of some hours duration away
from barracks.

All the exercises and aids laid down in the instruction of
the recruit can be taught the young horse by his trainer, but

these exercises are only given as a general guide, and are not intended to comprise all that a good trainer may teach his horse. An intelligent and experienced man will think of many other exercises for himself and be guided by the temperament of his pupil, which, as in the case of men, varies with each individual.

4. No remount, whether troop horse or charger, can be considered perfectly trained until the following qualifications are fulfilled.   He must:—

i. Stand still to be mounted or dismounted and lead well.

ii. Be as well balanced as his make and shape will allow.

iii. Be able to do a figure of 8 correctly, passage, rein back, halt collectedly; change his legs when turning, so as to lead with the correct fore and hind leg, and when turned about do so actively on his hocks and not on his fore hand

iv. Be a good jumper over all kinds of obstacles, and a safe and comfortable conveyance over every description of rough country.

v. Be steady on parade and accustomed to traffic, to gun fire and to unusual sights and sounds.

vi. Be immediately obedient to the correct aids.

vii. And lastly, the perfectly trained horse must go, alone or in company, at any pace required of him without pulling, and shorten his stride, or pull up when required.

A thoroughly trained charger or troop horse will obey a very slight indication, and the rider should be able to make him turn right or left, and change his legs at the canter, by the pressure of his legs and of the reins on the neck, without any further aids. He should stop at the word of command, and, if standing still, be ready to rein back at the slightest indication.

5. Young horses should not be placed in the ranks of the troop until they have been prepared for troop drill by preliminary work in pairs or sections and by work in extended order with gradually reduced intervals.

93. *Teaching a horse to stand still without being held.*

Substitute a strong piece of rope for the rein, throw the rope rein over the animal's head, and fasten a sack to the end of it. If the horse then moves forward he will tread on the sack and give himself a severe jerk in the mouth. After a few lessons it will be found that the horse will not move when the reins are thrown over his head.

RETRAINING AWKWARD AND BADLY TRAINED HORSES.

94. *General instructions.*

1. Remounts unbacked or unspoilt on joining the army should not need retraining. A horse properly trained in the first instance will only develop faults through subsequent bad riding or ill-treatment.

The results of bad handling are shown in defective carriage and paces; in a nervous, sulky, or irritable temperament; or in a combination of the two.

2. The work of retraining a spoilt horse is much more difficult than that of training a young and untrained one; riders should therefore be specially selected.

3. The trainer should first make himself acquainted with the animal's special faults, and then set to work systematically and patiently to eradicate them. It will, in some cases, be found best to treat the horse as untrained and begin his education afresh.

4. As the work will generally be of a corrective character the horse's corn and exercise should be carefully regulated according to his amenability to discipline.

5. When the animal is put back into the ranks, he should always be ridden by a good horseman. Horses rarely forget bad habits, and quickly relapse into them.

95. *Long rein driving.*

(*See* Sec. 88, 10.)

1. A course of long rein driving will as a rule be found beneficial in retraining awkward horses. None but selected and experienced men, who have been carefully taught their use, should be allowed to use long reins.

2. To keep the horse's head fairly high an overhead check may be used.

If the horse persists in carrying his head much too high, a standing martingale fitted rather long and fastened to a broad nose band may be used.

The trainer's object, however, should be to induce the horse to carry his head correctly, rather than to force it into the proper position, and therefore plenty of play should be allowed between the martingale and overhead check.

3. The course of training will be divided into two stages as under. The lessons should be short, from fifteen to twenty minutes being sufficient at one time. Much cantering is inadvisable. Throughout the work the trainer should look out carefully for any signs of chafes or other injuries, and at the first symptoms of these should cease work till the injury is cured or its cause removed.

4. *First stage.*—The horse should first be accustomed to the feeling of the driving pad and long reins, become acquainted with his trainer and learn to obey his voice.

The work should be conducted in an enclosed place, and if possible away from objects or other horses which may distract the animal's attention. If no enclosed space is available, it will be advisable at first for the trainer to have an assistant who can help if the horse fights or gets mixed up in the reins.

The reins at this stage should not be placed through the rings on the driving pad.

The trainer, holding one rein in each hand, should stand just opposite or a little behind the horse's girth ; and should keep the shoulder of the hand holding the outward rein well forward, and this hand slightly in advance of the other. He must never stand still, but should follow the horse round on a small circle.

In a very short time it will be found possible to drop the outward rein over the quarters, though except with specially quiet horses it is best to have an assistant at hand when first doing this. The horse having been driven for a short time to one hand should be stopped so that the reins may be changed and that he may be worked for a time on the other rein.

Nearly all the work at this stage should be at a walk, the horse being induced to go forward freely and well into his bridle at that pace.

5. *Second stage.*—As soon as the horse will go forward freely and is accustomed to feeling the long reins round his quarters they should be run through the rings on the driving pad, and the second or disciplinary stage of the training should commence.

The horse should now be made to walk and to halt when required by using the reins and voice. The training should be continued by teaching the horse to walk, trot, halt and turn as required, constant care being taken that he carries his head at the proper height.

Before attempting to change the horse on the move from one rein to the other he should first be halted, then turned and sent forward again. This should be repeated until he obeys readily.

Horses when being driven in long reins should never be changed on the move at any pace. They should always be halted and turned on their haunches. To do this, the driver should be standing behind the horse and whilst leading him round with one rein he will check any movement of the haunches by holding the other rein against his flank and haunches.

Used in this way the inner rein becomes an aid similar to the drawn back outward leg applied by the rider to prevent his horse from turning on his forehand.

As soon as the horse walks, trots, halts, and turns as required, cantering should commence. He should be made to canter correctly to either hand, and to halt in the same way as at the walk and trot.

The next important lesson is to make the horse rein back collectedly.

To effect this, the trainer must stand behind the horse and keep his hands low. He will touch that side of the mouth on which the fore leg is advanced more strongly than the other, and will make the horse rein back by feeling the reins alternately; after a lesson or two the horse will rein back on feeling a short pressure on both reins.

96. *The treatment of pullers.*

1. The usual causes of pulling are :—

    i. Excitability.
    ii. Pain.
    iii. Fear.
    iv. Freshness and want of work.
    v. Hard mouth.
    vi. Bad training.

The great object in curing a puller is to get him to go collectedly; for, when he is going in a well-balanced manner, he will not pull; but when he is allowed to get his neck out at full length and to go on his forehand, he is able to pull hard.

If a horse throws his head up and pulls in that position, the standing martingale, properly applied, should stop him.

2. *Excitability.*—Some horses, naturally of a nervous, highly-strung disposition, become excited by unaccustomed sights and

sounds, by the sight of galloping horses, or by moving fast in the company of other horses. No special bit will cure this kind of puller; the only remedy is plenty of work commencing at slow paces. Only the best horsemen possessing patience and good hands should be allowed to ride them. Harness work sometimes improves them.

3. *Pain.*—A horse's mouth is most sensitive, and many animals pull on account of the pain caused by the bit, or because their grinder teeth are long and sharp and cut the sides of their cheeks. Horses' mouths, especially those who have taken to pulling suddenly, should therefore be examined, particular attention being paid to the bars and the tongue. A neglected wound in the mouth of a young horse may spoil him for ever by making him pull or render his mouth one-sided through forcing him to hold the bit on one side to protect the injured part. If an injury of this nature is found, the horse should be given a rest, being exercised if necessary on a cavesson, and when the wound is healed ridden for a time in a snaffle. If the grinders are long and sharp, the sharp points and edges should be rasped.

The corners of the lips also may be sore owing to the bit being too narrow, or through being chafed by the bit; the curb chain may also injure the chin groove, in which case the wound should first be healed and then a guard should be used.

If a horse gets his tongue over the bit and then pulls, the tongue should be tied down.

4. *Fear.*—The only method of preventing pulling caused by fear is to accustom the horse to the cause of his alarm. He should be treated kindly and only ridden by careful patient men.

The voice will often be of assistance in calming a horse which in his early training has been taught to obey it.

5. *Freshness.*—The remedy for a horse which pulls from this cause is to give him more slow steady work and less corn.

6. *Hard mouth, bad training.*—These two causes of pulling are practically the same; no horse which has been properly broken ought to have such a hard mouth that he becomes unmanageable,

though some horses will pull more than others, however well they may have been trained.

In some cases the best way to hold a horse that is not excitable, but only pulls through having a hard mouth, is to put a severe bit on him. If he pulls with his mouth open, he should have it closed with a tight noseband.

He should be retrained by a good horseman or driven with the long reins, and given plenty of school work.

97. *The treatment of refusers.*

1. To cure a refuser the first step is to discover the cause. Refusals may be due to any one, or to a combination, of the following reasons :—

    i. From the horse having been jerked in the mouth or unintentionally spurred when jumping, thus receiving severe punishment for obeying the rider's wishes.

    ii. Insufficient elementary schooling.

    iii. Want of heart or nerve in the rider.

    iv. Sickened by too much jumping, especially on hard ground.

    v. Seeing other horses refuse.

    vi. Lameness, sore shins, or illness.

    vii. Ill-fitting or too severe bit.

    viii. Sore back or badly fitting saddle.

    ix. Want of heart or nerve in the horse.

    x. Vice.

2. In many cases it is advisable to work for a time on foot leading and driving the horse over low fences. As soon as obedience is assured he should be mounted again.

3. The best way to cure a horse whose mouth has been ill-treated is to remove the curb-chain if he has one, and to jump him over low obstacles without reins.

4. A horse may sometimes refuse because he has lost his nerve temporarily. In such a case, if the horse is taken three or four times over quite a small fence, he will probably jump the fence he originally refused. Or the fence that the horse refused may be lowered or laid on the ground, and the horse made to jump it a few times.

5. Sharp rowels may be necessary on a lazy or obstinate horse, but they entail the disadvantage that in the ranks at close interval, or when jumping certain kinds of fences, the rider may unintentionally spur his mount.

6. Both the faint-hearted and the vicious horse should be treated with great resolution, and allowed no liberty of rein until he actually takes off. Punishment may often make a coward do what he fears, but gentleness and unwearying patience are more likely to succeed with vicious animals.

98. *Horses that rush at their fences.*

A horse that rushes at his fences and gets excited when jumping is best cured by steady quiet practice. He should be walked up to the fence, halted, then turned away without being allowed to jump. This should be repeated several times alone or in the company of a quiet horse until he walks up to the fence quietly; he may then be allowed to jump it. He should not be jumped when very fresh.

99. *Horses that decline to leave the ranks and horses that fret when alone.*

Horses that decline to leave the ranks or fret when alone should be ridden by good riders. They may be greatly improved by being kept stabled alone and constantly ridden alone for some months. If possible they should not be worked in the ranks until cured; when it is necessary to take them on parade before they are quite cured, they should be ridden by officers, serrefiles or trumpeters. They may be improved by being worked in single harness.

100. *Declining to stand still when being mounted.*

1. As a rule these horses will yield to constant practice. They should be mounted and dismounted on both sides slowly, time after time every day.

2. If the horse refuses to stand still after a course of this treatment the following method may be tried.

Put a loop under the horse's upper lip and over the poll with a slip knot, and when he becomes restive give it a slight jerk and say "STEADY." The horse will soon connect the sound of the voice with the discomfort caused by the twitch, and will learn to remain still on the word "Steady" without the twitch. The twitch must never be used except in conjunction with the voice.

After doing this a few times the trainer, when mounting the horse, should dispense with the twitch. With the left hand holding the reins and the cheek piece of the bridle, he should say the word "STEADY" and swing himself into the saddle, not leaving go of the cheek piece till he is firmly seated. The horse connects the word "Steady" and the pressure of the hand on the cheek piece with the twitch, and will as a rule stand just as steadily as he would with the twitch still on him.

3. A restive horse that has not been trained to stand steady will usually circle round on his forehand so as to edge away from the man trying to mount.

The rider, when mounting on the near side, should pull the horse's head round to the right by tightening up the off bridoon rein and holding it tight in the left hand ; *vice versâ* if mounting from the off side. The horse cannot now circle on his forehand away from the rider, but if he moves at all, must circle his hind quarters towards the man, thus permitting him to put his foot in the stirrup and mount with ease.

101. *General vice and bad temper.*

Such horses are most likely to be improved by a careful regulation of work and feeding, by being stabled by themselves, and by gentle treatment both in the stable and outside.

NOTES ON DRIVING.

102. *General instructions.*

1. All officers and at least one or two men in each troop should possess a knowledge of the principles of driving, of fitting harness, and of training horses to draught. Ten per cent. of the riding horses in a regiment should be trained to draught.

A riding horse if carefully broken to harness will probably not be damaged for riding purposes. A short spell of regular work in harness may be useful to put condition on a thin bad constitutioned horse, and also for inducing a fretting horse to settle down and work quietly.

2. Temperament should be the first consideration when putting together either a pair or a team. A lazy horse should never be matched with a quick excitable horse.

3. When driven from the box, horses will neither work comfortably nor be under perfect control, unless so coupled that their heads are straight when they are on the move and there is an even bearing on the reins. The bearing of the bits on their mouths should be light but constant, and the reins should never be allowed to slip through the driver's fingers.

4. Even and steady draught is a matter of importance. The weights behind teams are calculated on the assumption that every horse will do his fair share of work; this is impossible if the driving is not correct.

When draught is even and steady, every trace in the team is taut, and the horses' heads are facing straight to the front. If for example an off-horse's head is pulled inwards, his draught power is reduced and he is liable to become galled.

5. The positions of horses should be changed frequently to prevent the acquirement of bad habits, such as pulling away from the pole or shouldering the pole.

6. Wagon loads must be carefully checked and even on good roads should not exceed 700 lbs. per horse in draught. The maximum load for a 4-horsed wagon must therefore never amount to more than 2,800 lbs.

103.   *Care of wagons.*

1. It is only by giving constant attention to the vehicles that transport service can be efficient.

2. The axles and the pipe-boxes of wheels should be frequently greased and should be kept free from dust, grit and old grease, which contains small particles of metal and sand.

To grease the axle, remove the wheel and carefully clean the axle and inside of the pipe-box. Then smear the inside of the pipe-box and the outside of the axle with fresh grease and replace the wheel.

3. Wheels, showing too much play on the axle-tree arm, should have a leather or steel washer placed on the arm at the outer end of the pipe-box, between it and the linch-pin washer.

In very dry climates it may be necessary at times to keep the wheels constantly wetted to prevent the woodwork warping, cracking and shrinking.

104.   *Fitting of harness.*

1. The *breast collar* should hang horizontally, the lower edge about one inch above the point of the shoulder. The higher it is, in reason, the less chance there is of the horse galling.

2. The *loin strap* should be so fitted that the traces are in a straight line when the horse is in draught.

Traces should be of equal length, otherwise collar galls will occur. Their length must, in a great measure, depend on the size of the horses. The wheelers' traces should be of such a length that when they are in their collars their quarters are about 18 inches clear of the splinter bar.

The distance between horses in a team should not be less than one yard from nose to croup.

Breeching.—The breeching should lie horizontally about a foot to a foot and a half below the upper part of the dock and have from 4 to 6 inches play when the harness is in draught. When put back in the breeching, the horse should be at least a foot from the footboard.

3. *Pole chains.*—When wheel horses are standing in their breast collars in draught, there should be no pull on the pole chains.

4. *Kicking strap.*—This should be so fitted as to give the play of a hand's breadth between it and the horse's croup, when he is standing in his collar.

5. *Coupling.*—The correct adjustment of the coupling reins requires great care. The outer reins having a number of holes punched in them, up and down which the buckles of the coupling reins can be shifted, can be shortened or lengthened to suit each particular horse. For instance, if the near horse carries his head to the near side, the coupling rein on the off side should be taken up; when his head will be straightened, and *vice versâ.*

6. *To put to.*—The horses should be led up alongside the pole by the noseband (not by the bit), the chain should then be passed through the kidney link in the harness, the outer trace should be fastened first and then the inner, then pole up and couple the horses together. In unhooking the action is reversed.

105. *Driving from the box.*

1. *How to hold the reins and whip.*—The near rein passes over the forefinger, the off rein between the middle and third fingers of the left hand; both reins then fall through the palm of the hand and hang loose on the left side of the driver's knees. The reins are kept in position in the hand by the pressure of the third and fourth fingers assisted by the second; the thumb and forefinger should not be used for this purpose. The wrist should be rounded.

The whip should be held between the lower part of the thumb and the base of the forefinger of the right hand, thus leaving the fingers free. The whip should be carried point upwards, the stick inclined across the body and to the front. The position of the whip should not be changed when the right hand manipulates the reins. When required the right hand should be placed on the reins in front of the left, the first and second fingers on the top of the near rein and the other two between the reins. When necessary the former grip the near rein and the latter the off rein.

Reins always should be shortened or lengthened from the front; *i.e.*, either pushed back through the left hand or pulled out through the left hand.

2. The driver should sit square to his front on the box, which should be low enough to allow of his legs being well bent at the knee. If the box seat is too high the driver is liable to be pulled off when a horse stumbles.

3. To turn or incline to the right, the right hand grasps the right rein in the full of the hand, knuckles up and inclined to the front. This gives the firmest hold and at the same time allows of the position of the whip being maintained. To turn to the left, the left rein is grasped in the same manner.

4. An even and steady walk should be maintained when travelling up a steep hill; if the load is exceptionally heavy and circumstances permit, the team should be allowed to incline from one side of the road to the other as the wagon ascends.

5. The pace cannot be too slow in descending a hill, and the brake should not be applied until the horses take the breeching. When the shoe is used the wheel to which it is applied should be chained to the carriage; this prevents all chance of accident should the shoe become unshipped when travelling over rough ground.

6. Horses jib from various causes, such as sore shoulders, a too heavy load, bad driving, sore mouth, lameness, and vice.

When a horse jibs the wheels should be manned; the whip should not be used. It will often be effective to place a handful of gravel in the horse's mouth just as the power is applied to the wheels.

106. *Driving postillion.*

1. The lead driver is responsible for direction, distance, and pace; it is the duty of the wheel driver to keep the traces taut and cover him.

2. The whip is chiefly used to control the off horse, to start him, to keep him in the collar, and to guide him when turning. It should be applied lightly on the off side of the withers, fingers closed on stock and thong.

On rare occasions the whip may be used to punish a horse, when the thong should be applied once on the shoulder. This procedure is seldom justified, and is liable to upset the other horses in the team.

At all other times the thong should be held close against the stock with the end of the lash hanging down.

The driver salutes with his whip when at a walk, in the following manner. He brings it to the recover as with a sword, passes it over the withers of the off horse, right arm extended but with the elbow raised and slightly bent, hand in a line with the waist, back of the hand up and inclined to the front, fingers closed on the stock and thong. The driver should hold his body erect with his shoulders square to the front, and look the officer full in the face. When the salute is finished, the whip is brought to the recover and then down to the position of attention. The salute commences four paces from the officer, and finishes four paces beyond him. A driver when halted, or at the trot, salutes by coming to attention and looking the officer full in the face.

3. On the command "MARCH" the drivers ease the reins and close their legs to the riding horse, laying the whip over the neck and just in front of the withers of the off horse, to ensure both horses starting together.

In all alterations to a quicker pace the drivers use their legs on the riding horse and the whip on their off horse.

4. On the command " HALT " the lead driver raises the whip hand as high as the head, the whip horizontal across the front, as a signal to the wheel driver.

Both drivers feel their reins and take their horses out of the collar. The wheel driver, with his right hand on the leading rein, puts his horses back in the breeching.

As soon as the vehicle stops, every horse is again put into the collar.

When halting from any pace but the walk, the lead driver must allow the wheel driver sufficient time to stop the vehicle before he comes to the halt.

5. In wheeling to the right the lead driver wheels his riding horse by leaning his body to the right and feeling the right rein; he brings his off horse round at the same time by feeling the leading rein with his right hand.

The wheel driver follows the track of the lead driver, laying his whip over his hand horse's withers to prevent it from flying out or hanging back.

On a horse that is not properly trained the lead driver may have to apply his right leg as an additional aid. No application of the left leg is necessary, as the traces prevent the horse's quarters from flying out.

6. In wheeling to the left the lead driver wheels his riding horse by leaning his body to the left and feeling the left rein; he brings his off horse round at the same time by placing the whip over his withers.

The lead driver may have to apply his left leg on an untrained horse.

The wheel driver follows the track of the lead driver, applying the same aids at the point of wheel.

Riding horses must not be allowed to hang back.

7. In wheeling about the drivers lean their bodies slightly back, and to whichever side they are turning. In going to the

right about the wheel driver should take the leading rein in his right hand instead of placing his whip over the withers of the off horse. In wheeling to the left about it may be necessary for him to use both hands on the riding horse to keep him from turning too soon. Otherwise the aids are the same as for wheeling to the right or left, but are continued longer.

In order to prevent the vehicle from locking, the wheel driver must be careful to keep up his hand, or riding horse, as the case may be, and the lead driver must on no account make the circle too small.

Vehicles should be advanced one yard before being wheeled about from the halt.

8. To exert his strength to his utmost when pulling up hill, the draught horse must get as much weight as possible forward and into the collar. By assuming a lower and more advanced carriage of the head and neck than he would do if moving balanced and out of draught, he is able to add considerably to his power. He should therefore be allowed full liberty of rein when ascending a steep hill.

When a steep hill is met on the march, it is advisable to halt the vehicles at the foot and to send them up by twos or threes with about ten yards distance between each.

Should a check occur when the column is closed up, the lead drivers in rear must be prepared to throw off their horses to the right or left.

The pace should be a steady walk during the whole ascent, by which the top will be reached more easily and surely than if an attempt is made to "spring" the hill.

After going up a steep hill the horses should be halted, but when this cannot be done, they should be allowed to move slowly to recover their wind.

9. In driving down hill, the lead driver should hold his horses back to allow the wheel driver the management of the carriage, but the traces must be kept up; the wheel driver with his right hand on the leading rein keeps his horses steadily in the breeching, taking care not to throw them on their haunches, and in the

case of shaft draught harness, not to let too much work fall on the off horse.

For moderately steep descents the brake can be used. Should a descent be so steep that the brake is not sufficient, dismounted men must be used to hold on with the drag ropes hooked into the drag washers.

10. The brake should be applied sufficiently hard to check but not to skid the wheel. In crossing a valley the man in charge of the brake must begin taking it off soon enough for the wheels to be quite free before the beginning of the rise on the other side is reached, or in fording a river before the carriage gets into the water.

107. *Training horses to harness.*

Before being put to, the horse should be led about until he gets thoroughly accustomed to the harness. He should then be hooked into an empty wagon, at the side of a reliable old horse, who will start the wagon by himself. The horse under training should not be made to face either his bit or his collar until he has become accustomed to his surroundings. When a trained team of horses and drivers is available, the young horse should first of all be put into the off lead. Care should be taken that the other horses are standing in their collars before a start is attempted.

108. *Loading a wagon or cart.*

1. The squadron commander or transport officer should have an inventory of what each wagon is to carry made out the day previous to a march, unless they are G.S. wagons horsed and loaded according to the official tables in the "Field Service Manual." Bulk as well as weight must be taken into consideration in assessing the loads; this is necessary to secure good packing and efficient transport service. The weights of the various articles are given in the "Field Service Manual."

The load which is to be carried in each wagon should be placed beside it before the packing begins. An experienced man should then get up into the wagon and name the articles in the order in which he wishes them to be handed up to him. When the packing is complete the tarpaulin should be roped carefully over the wagon to ensure against wet and loss.

2. Care should be taken that a two-wheeled cart when loaded is properly balanced. There should be a weight of about 10 lbs on the tugs.

CHAPTER IV.

MOUNTED DRILL.

GENERAL INSTRUCTIONS FOR DRILL.

109. *Drill compared with manœuvre.*

1. Drill is the method by which troops are trained to manœuvre against an enemy with ease, rapidity, and precision.

Although drill alone can never ensure victory, a highly developed manœuvring power, essential to the success of cavalry, is impossible without it. Moreover, the rapid movement of large bodies in good order and with the minimum fatigue to the horses depends on the accurate drill of small units. Drill, therefore, is a means to the end, and, though a necessary means, it must never be looked on as the end itself.

Only the simplest formations are required, but cavalry must be capable of executing them in good order and with thorough cohesion at the fastest paces.

2. In all exercises commanders must keep clearly in their minds the difference between drill and manœuvre.

In drill the commander has no enemy to consider; he can devote most of his attention, therefore, to perfecting his command in the movements which he is practising. In manœuvre the main considerations are the tactical idea or general plan of attack and the various forms of attack.

3. In drill the commander should place himself where he can best superintend the movements of his troops, whilst when manœuvring, he should ride as a rule well ahead, where he can see the ground and the dispositions of the enemy, and thus gain time to make up his plan of attack.

110. *The instruction and the duties of leaders and guides.*

1. All leaders and guides must be thoroughly grounded in the general principles of drill and instructed in their duties— firstly theoretically in quarters, then on foot, and finally mounted.

Much elementary instruction in squadron and regimental drill may be given by means of rope drill on foot. A rope about 5 or 6 yards long can be used to represent the front of a troop, the end being held by two men who act as flank guides.

2. The squadron commander should always ride near enough to his squadron when working in a regiment or a brigade to retain absolute control over its pace and direction.

Steadiness of pace and of direction are essential for the rapid and smooth movements of large bodies of cavalry. These can only be ensured by the thorough independence of the squadron, no attention being paid to the momentary fluctuations of neighbouring squadrons.

3. Troop leaders must maintain a steady direction and pace. They must always maintain the cohesion of their own squadron, keeping the correct distance from the directing troop leader of their own squadron and never inclining away towards another squadron, even though that squadron may be the directing one of the regiment or brigade. The correction of all intervals between squadrons is the duty of the squadron commander, aided by his directing troop leader.

4. The centre guide will follow his troop leader at the proper distance, and ensure, by word of command if necessary, that the troop keeps in proper cohesion behind the troop leader.

5. The flank guides prevent the troops opening out to beyond the correct interval from their centres. They must be particular, especially on the completion of a wheel, to take up quickly a point to lead on in the same direction as their troop leader, and lead at once on it, thus preventing any tendency to over-wheel. They must remember that their duty consists

entirely in ensuring the cohesion of their own troops. **Any**
intervals between troops in a squadron must be corrected by
the troop leaders concerned; flank guides should not attempt
to do so.

111. *Pace.*

1. Correctness and evenness of pace are essential, both in
order to preserve cohesion and to maintain calmness among the
horses. All sudden changes of pace in the endeavour to maintain an accurate alignment must be carefully avoided, and any
necessary alterations of position should be carried out gradually
and quietly.

In line, care must be taken not to diminish the pace, and in
column, not to increase it.

After a change of pace has been ordered a distance of three
horse-lengths will be passed over at the original pace before
the new pace is taken up.

In formations to the front from column when at the gallop,
the leading unit must check the pace slightly to enable the
rear to come up. The commanders of the rear units, if they
find the pace too great to bring their units up into *line* in good
order should lead them opposite their proper places in *line* and
follow in *échelon* until they are able to come up in good order.

Men and horses will be trained to maintain the regular rate
of trot and gallop for considerable distances.

2. No officer or non-commissioned officer is fit to act as
troop leader until he can ride at the regulated rates of
manœuvre. (*See* Sec. **52.**)

112. *Direction.*

1. The centre or right centre troop leader of a squadron will
be the directing troop leader of the squadron. The same
principle applies to higher formations, for instance the centre,
or right centre squadron of a regiment is the directing squadron.
When two units are working together, the right-hand one will
direct.

2. Every troop leader, after seeing which is the exact direction his squadron commander wishes his squadron to take, takes up his own point and leads straight on it. The squadron commander gives the exact direction to his directing troop leader. Troop leaders, other than the directing troop leader, must glance their eyes only occasionally to the directing troop leader to ensure that they are maintaining the right direction. For the most part, they must keep their eyes steadily fixed on the point on which they are leading.

3. Every man in the ranks, after glancing to see the direction in which his troop leader is moving, takes up his own point in the same direction and leads straight on it. The men must not keep their eyes fixed towards the centre or flanks of their troops, or even on their troop leader. Having taken their direction from their troop leader they must look straight to their front, with but an occasional glance towards the troop leader.

4. All errors of direction must be noticed in good time, and must be corrected gradually and quietly.

When men are being squeezed out of the ranks, they must not struggle to maintain their places, for such action only creates disorder and upsets the horses. They must ride on quietly, and be ready to move into their places as soon as any opening-out takes place.

It must be remembered that it is essential to keep the front rank close.

113. *Changes of direction and formation.*

Each unit moves to its place in a new formation by the shortest available route, and in the simplest manner. As a rule, the formation only is indicated by the commander; the movements and pace of smaller units depend on the ground and their relative positions, and will be left to the initiative of subordinate leaders.

Any formation or movement ordered will be performed on the move (*i.e.*, troops will continue in movement after it is completed), unless the order is preceded by the words " TO THE HALT."

114. *Dressing.*

1. At the halt every man should take the correct distance in rear of his troop leader, or from the front rank ; he should take the same direction as his troop leader and should make his horse stand square facing in that direction. He should also maintain the correct interval towards the centre of his troop.

2. On the move he should ride smoothly and quietly at the pace ordered, or at that set by his troop leader, keep his proper distance from his troop leader, and maintain the correct interval towards the centre of his troop.

3. Men should give way to pressure from the point of direction but should resist pressure towards it.

4. Only when at the halt on ceremonial occasions may troops be dressed from a flank.

115. *Alignment.*

In the attack on cavalry, order and cohesion are the principal factors of success ; in its actual execution, therefore, the maintenance of a steady direction is of greater importance than the accuracy of the alignment, for order and cohesion depend largely on steadiness of direction.

If squadrons, or even troops, are a little in front of, or behind, the alignment it is a matter of little importance. But it is of great importance that the attacking line should present to the enemy the appearance of a solid and unbroken body.

All advances in line should therefore be inspected from the front or rear and not from a flank.

116. *Wheeling and shouldering.*

1. All wheels from the halt or at a walk are made on a fixed pivot, except when a column changes direction. All other wheels are made on a moving pivot.

FIG. 17.—*A troop of 17 files wheeling on a moving pivot.*

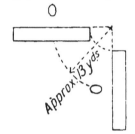

In the case of a troop wheeling on a fixed pivot the troop leader and centre guide move on an arc equal to half the frontage of the troop. In wheeling on a moving pivot they move on an arc equal to three-quarters of the frontage. Other bodies wheel in a similar manner.

Shouldering is used instead of wheeling when a body has a frontage greater than that of a squadron. The following are the words of command for the different degrees of wheel :—

"HALF RIGHT" (or "LEFT,") "RIGHT (or LEFT) WHEEL," "THREE-QUARTERS RIGHT (or LEFT) ABOUT," "RIGHT (or LEFT) ABOUT WHEEL."

When the new direction is not exactly a half, or full wheel the command "RIGHT OR LEFT" will be given. The troops will then wheel in the direction ordered until they receive the command "FORWARD."

2. *Shouldering.*—When *shouldering*, the directing troop leader, still maintaining the original pace, moves on an arc of such a size that the outer flank men can always keep in line. Subject to this limitation the arc should be as small as possible. The outer flank will thus increase the pace and the inner flank decrease it.

Shouldering should not be used with bodies of the frontage of a troop or less.

The words of command are :—" RIGHT (or LEFT) SHOULDERS " and " FORWARD," when the desired direction is reached.

117. *Increasing and diminishing the front.*

1. Unless a flank is especially named, the front will be increased or diminished as follows :—

> *When increasing the front* the rear units form on the leading unit, the second unit inclining to the left, the remainder inclining to the right and left in succession ; thus :—

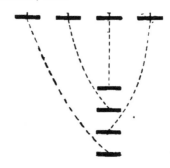

ii. *When diminishing the front* the centre or right centre
unit advances first, followed by the unit on its left;
after these, the units on the right and left will follow
in succession, thus :—

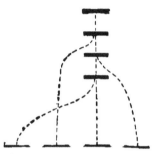

Hence the men in a section, the sections in a troop, the troops
in a squadron, the squadrons in a regiment, or the regiments in
a brigade may change their relative positions from time to time
as the drill progresses.

3. When the front is increased or diminished from or to the
halt, the whole of the men move at the pace ordered, or continue
at the pace at which they are moving ; but when the change of
formation is to be made on the move, the units in rear must
take up the next faster or slower pace, as the case may be, to the
one at which they are moving, unless another pace is specially
ordered.

4. No fault requires to be corrected with more care than the
hurrying up of the rear during a change of formation. The
men must not move up faster than the pace ordered. They
should, however, be accustomed to forming squadron and troop in
any direction at the gallop while the head is at the walk, so as to
be prepared for any sudden emergency.

118. *Commands.*

1. The leader's intentions cannot be instantly and completely understood unless there is a thorough understanding between himself and his subordinate commanders. This understanding can only be attained by practice together under varying conditions.

It is essential to rapidity and certainty of movement that the commands of a cavalry leader should be conveyed to his subordinates by the simplest means.

The following methods may be used either separately or in combination as required. Leaders of subordinate units must pass on commands to those next to them, when necessary.

2. *Following a leader.*—The commander of any body of cavalry may lead it personally by placing himself at its head and ordering it to conform to his movements.

More often he will detail another officer to act as directing guide, giving him general instructions as to pace and direction, while he himself rides to the front. The directing guide is responsible for utilising the ground to the best advantage in guiding the formation to the point indicated. In a brigade the officer so employed is usually the brigade major or the staff captain; in a regiment, the senior major or the adjutant. With bodies larger than a regiment it is advisable for the directing guide to carry a small guide flag or other distinguishing mark.

3. *By signal.*—Officers using signals (*see* pages 8–11) should, as far as possible, face the same way as those to whom the signals are made, and should use whichever arm will be most clearly visible.

Before giving a signal, commanders above the rank of troop leader may blow their whistles to attract attention; excessive whistling, however, especially when working in large bodies, is undesirable. Cavalry should be moved as silently as possible.

Troop leaders, on hearing their squadron commander's whistle, will look for his signals (not for those of the regimental commander or brigadier); squadron commanders in their turn

PLATE I.   *To face p. 171.*

TROOP IN LINE

θ

N.° 4 SECTION   N.° 3 SECTION   N.° 2 SECTION   N.° 1 SECTION

TROOP IN COLUMN OF SECTIONS

Troop of 4 Sections.   Troop of 3 Sections.

θ   θ

θ — Troop Leader

— Centre Guide

— Centre Guide Coverer

will look towards the regimental leader. The same principles apply to the leading of brigades working in a division.

The men should glance at their troop leaders for signals.

4. *By trumpet sound.*—When the commander cannot be seen or heard his commands may be conveyed by the field calls given on page 11. But it must be remembered that the sounding of field calls may serve to advertise the intentions of the commander to the enemy. Signals should be employed therefore instead of field calls whenever possible.

5. *By gallopers.*—Gallopers should be made to repeat their messages before leaving.

6. *By word of command.*—Words of command must be pronounced distinctly and loud enough to be heard by all concerned, and leaders should accompany their commands with the corresponding signals.

When in *squadron*, troop leaders, as a rule, give no words of command unless their troops are unable to distinguish their signals; in that event they give the necessary word, but no louder than is necessary to enable their own troop to hear it.

A squadron forming part of a regiment moves at the command of the squadron commander, but he should repeat the regimental commander's orders, when they have not been heard by the troop leaders of the squadron or by the other squadron commanders.

DRILL OF THE TROOP.

119. *Formation of the troop.* (*Plate I.*)

1. The troop will be formed up with 3 or 4 sections in line, in two ranks.

Commanders of sections will ride in the front rank, scouts, signallers and shoeing-smiths will ride in the rear rank.

The senior N.C.O. in the troop will be posted as centre guide in the centre of the front rank of the troop. He will take the place of the troop leader if the latter is disabled, and in this case his coverer, who should be a selected N.C.O. or man, will replace him.

The flank men of the front rank are termed *Flank Guides*.

The rule regarding the leaving of *Blank Files* in the rear rank is that No. 2 will first be left without a coverer, then No. 3, and then No. 4.

The troop will usually fall in in two ranks. Each man must know his number and place in his section, and fall in accordingly. When in *line* the distance between ranks is one horse-length; in *column* or *half-column*, half a horse-length. The front rank of the troop will be at one horse-length distance in rear of the troop leader, except when the troops are of thirteen front and are in *column* or *half-column*; the distance will then be half a horse-length.

2. *Proving a Troop.*—The men of No. 1 Section number off "From the 1, 2, 3, 4. No. 2 Section does the same when Right tell off No. 1 Section has finished, and so on. by Sections."

"Flanks of   The flank men of each section prove.
Sections—
Prove."

"As you were."

"Even Numbers   The even numbers prove.
—Prove."

"As you were."

120. *The march in line.*

1. Before moving off every horse should be standing collected and square to the front, as stated in Sec. **114.**

2. On the command or the signal of the troop leader to advance the whole troop moves off together at the pace taken by him.

3. Correct direction and strict uniformity of pace must be maintained.

4. All should ride with correct intervals and distances, and should look and march straight in the direction set by the troop leader.

The centre guide conforms to any change of direction by the troop leader by turning his horse the same degree when he arrives at the point where the troop leader made the change; the front rank men will gradually place their horses in the same direction and keep the front of the troop square to the leader's front. Rear rank men cover their front rank men as accurately as they are able.

5. If, owing to the restiveness of his horse or from other causes, the troop leader's pace should at any time be very irregular, the centre guide will regulate the pace, so as to ensure the advance of the troop being smooth and uniform.

6. Men stopped by an obstacle will drop back behind the troop without waiting for orders, until the obstacle is passed, when they will at once resume their places in the ranks at an increased but smooth pace. All rushing and hurry must be avoided.

7. Should the troop encounter a passage narrower than its front, the defile may be passed in the following manner :— On the command "BREAK," the centre and flank guides move up on the same alignment as the leader ; the front rank men nearest the centre for whom there is room, place themselves between the leader and the flank guides ; the remainder drop back, rapidly ranging themselves in three or four ranks as may be necessary, with sufficient intervals from knee to knee, but closed up nose to croup, and with their horses' heads opposite the intervals in front. As soon as the defile is passed, the leader gives the command "FORM RANKS," when the centre and flank guides drop back, and the men resume their original places.

121. *Inclining.*

1. The incline of a troop is executed as follows :—On the command "RIGHT (or LEFT) INCLINE," the troop leader makes the signal, turns his horse and marches on a point in the

required direction. Each man turns his horse and takes up his points in the same direction as that set by his troop leader, so that his knee comes, and is maintained, behind the knee of the next man on the flank towards which the incline is made.

The movements of the rear rank men are regulated by those of the front rank, each horse being so placed that it would cover the corresponding front rank horse if both were turned to the front.

2. The flank guide on the directing flank, having ascertained his new direction by glancing at his troop leader, will make the necessary turn and march steadily forward; he must be careful to avoid inclining too sharply, thereby causing the troop to open out and lose cohesion. The remainder will move parallel to him, each man preserving his position with regard to the next man on the hand towards which the incline is being made.

3. The centre guide must be particular to keep the troop moving in the direction set by the troop leader and to keep it at the proper distance from and exactly behind him.

4. On the command or signal "FORWARD," each man at the same instant will turn his horse to the former front.

5. The incline should be employed only for short distances, and in carrying it out the deviation from the original direction should be about 20°. If the deviation is more than this the ranks will become unduly spread out.

122. *Troop wheels.* *(See* also Sec. **116.)*

1. On the command "TROOP—RIGHT (or LEFT) WHEEL" the leader selects some point in the new direction on which to lead, makes the signal, and (if from the halt) moves off in the required direction on the word "MARCH." On completion of the wheel he makes the signal for "HALT" or "FORWARD" as required. He must move at an even pace throughout the wheel.

2. The front rank moves up the distance it has from the troop leader and then begins to wheel.

3. The centre guide rides in the track of the troop leader and maintains his distance.

4. The flank guides glance in the direction in which they have been ordered to wheel so as to fix on points on which to lead as soon as the wheel is completed. They move round in conformity with the movements of the troop leader, the outer flank guide being careful to keep the flank of the troop well closed in.

5. Each front rank man looks to the troop leader and increases or decreases his pace so as to be correctly placed in rear of him.

6. As soon as the front rank begins to wheel, rear rank men gain ground towards the outer flank by inclining and passaging. In the case of a section the rear rank first moves up to the ground from which the front rank commenced the wheel. During the wheel each rear rank man directs his horse on the next man but one on the outer flank of his own front rank man.

The change of distance between front and rear ranks, necessary when moving from *column* into *line* or *line* into *column,* must be made during the wheel.

123. *Diminishing the front.*

1. When the change of formation is to be made *from the halt* the word of command given below will be followed in each case by the executive command " WALK MARCH " (" MARCH," or " GALLOP MARCH ").

2. If, as in the paragraphs given below, no flank is named in the word of command, the change of formation will be made from the centre. Similar movements can, however, be made from the flank, in which case the flank must be specified in the word of command, *e.g.,* " ADVANCE IN HALF SECTIONS FROM THE RIGHT."

3. When forming sections the troop leader places himself half a horse-length in front of the leading section, the centre guide and his coverer on the left of the front and rear ranks of the leading section.

With a troop of three sections, the centre guide and coverer remain in the centre of the leading section.

In *column of half-sections* the centre guide and his coverer are half a horse-length in front of the leading half-section, and the troop leader is half a horse-length in front of them. In *single files* the troop leader, centre guide, and centre guide's coverer are in front of the troop at half a horse-length distance from each other, the centre guide's coverer being half a horse-length in front of the leading file.

If it is inconvenient to move on a broader frontage than four men abreast, the centre guide will march on the left of the troop leader, with his coverer on his left again.

4. In the following instructions the front rank men only are referred to; in every case the rear rank men follow and cover their front rank men.

When the centre section is referred to, it should be taken as meaning the right centre section in the case of troops containing four sections.

5. *From troop to sections.*

"ADVANCE IN SECTIONS" (or "FORM TROOP COLUMN".)   The centre section advances; the remaining sections, as it comes to their turn, incline inwards, follow, and cover at the proper distance.

6. *From troop to half-sections.*

"ADVANCE IN HALF-SECTIONS."   Nos. 1 and 2 of the centre section advance, followed by Nos. 3 and 4, the sections on the left and right conforming.

7. *From troop to single file.*

No. 2 of the centre section advances. Nos. 3, 1, and 4 conform in the order named. The sections on the left and right act similarly in their turn.

8. *From sections to half-sections.*

"ADVANCE IN HALF SECTIONS."   Nos. 1 and 2 of the leading section advance, Nos. 3 and 4, when they have room, incline to the right, follow, and cover, the remainder move in succession in the same manner, keeping their proper distances.

9. *From sections to single files.*

"ADVANCE IN SINGLE FILES."   No. 2 of the leading section advances, Nos. 3, 1, and 4 incline inwards when they have room, follow, and cover; the remaining sections move in succession in the same manner.

10. *From half-sections to single files.*

"ADVANCE IN SINGLE FILES."   No. 1 of the leading half section advances. No 2 inclines to the right and follows, No. 3 marches straight forward as it comes to his turn and follows No. 2, No. 4 inclines to the right and follows No. 3, the remainder move off in succession in the same manner.

124. *Increasing the front.*

1. The rear rank men in each movement follow and cover their front rank men.

2. *From single file to half-sections.*

"To the Halt.
Form Half
Sections."

No. 1 of the leading section advances **3** horse-lengths and halts. No. 2 inclines to the left and forms on the left of No. 1; No. 4 inclines to the left and forms on the left of No. 3; the remainder move in the same manner in their turn, forming half-sections first and then closing to their proper distance.

3. *From single file to sections.*

"To the Halt.
Form
Sections."

No. 1 of the leading section advances 3 horse-lengths and halts; Nos. 2 and 4 incline to the left and No. 3 to the right, forming up in line with No. 1; the remaining sections move in the same manner, forming sections first and then closing to their proper distance.

4. *From half-sections to sections.*

"To the Halt.
Form
Sections."

Nos. 1 and 2 of the leading section advance 3 horse-lengths and halt; 3 and 4 incline to the left and form on the left of 1 and 2; the remainder move in the same manner forming sections first and then closing to their proper distance.

5. *From sections to form troop.*

"To the Halt.
Form
Troop."

The leading section advances 3 horse-lengths and halts; the second and fourth sections incline to the left and the third section to the right until opposite their places in line, when they move forward and form up in line with the first section.

6. *From half-sections or single files, to form troop.*

1. *To the halt.*

" To the Halt— First each section will form as in paras. 3
Form Troop." and 4; then the troop will form as in para. 5.

2. *When on the move.*

" Form Troop." Sections continue at the original pace until
formed, then incline and move up at an increased
pace into their places in the troop.

125. *Formations and movements to a flank and rear.*

1. *Forming troop to a flank from single file, half-sections
or sections.*

" Sections, The leading body will at once wheel to the
Right (Left)," flank named; those in rear advance until
" Half-sections, nearly opposite their places in line, then wheel
Right (Left) " or and come up into the alignment on the right
" Single Files, (left) of those already formed.
Right (Left)."

2. *Moving to a flank.*—A troop may be moved to a flank
in column of *sections, half-sections,* or *single files,* by the
command :—

" Sections, In each case, the right (left) section, half-
Right (Left)," section, or single file wheels in the required
" Half-sections, direction, and moves off. The remaining
Right (Left)," or sections, &c. of the troop wheel and follow in
" Single Files, succession.
Right (Left)."   If the order to move to a flank in sections
is given when the troop is moving, the section

N 2

on the flank named wheels at once, continuing to move at the original pace; the other sections halt until it is their turn to move; they then wheel and follow in column. Half-sections and single files move to the flank in the same manner.

A troop may be moved a short distance to a flank by the command " RIGHT (or LEFT) PAST."

3. *Formations to the Rear.*—Formations to the rear can be made when in single files, half-sections, or sections by wheeling about (" SECTIONS (HALF-SECTIONS or FILES) ABOUT "), or when in line either by wheeling the troop about, or by moving to a flank in column and then changing the direction of the head of the column.

126. *Filing to the front by sections.*

This formation may sometimes be useful, especially in crossing rough ground :—

" BY SECTIONS No. 1 of each section advances, followed by
TO THE FRONT his rear rank man, the files on the left follow
FILE."   in succession. On the command " FORM
           RANKS," the leading file moves straight on,
           the remainder resume their places at an
           increased pace.

127. *The march in column of sections, half-sections or single files.*

1. When marching in column care should be taken that each man keeps the prescribed distance from, and covers exactly, the man in front. Each man should look ahead along the column, in order that he may become aware of any slight change of pace in good time. By careful riding he will be able not only to avoid increasing any irregularity of pace, but to assist in rectifying it.

2. Exact covering and dressing will be maintained when marching at ease.

3. Should it be necessary to reduce the depth of a column without altering the formation, the command " CLOSE INTO THE INTERVALS " may be given. The rear rank men then ride into the intervals on the left of their front rank men, who ride close up to the rank in front of them.

128. *Extending and closing.*

1. When a troop receives the order to extend, the men will extend to an interval of four yards between files unless another interval is ordered, the rear rank men forming on the left of their front rank men.

2. When the troop is extended the centre guide should be one horse-length behind the leader. Under no circumstances should this distance be reduced as it is of importance that every man in the troop should be able to see his leader.

3. Those men who have to change their positions when the order to extend or close is given move at the next pace faster than that at which they were marching before receipt of the order, and resume the original pace on arrival at their new positions.

4. *Extending from line :—*

i. *To both flanks.*

"EXTEND" or "To — YARDS EXTEND."   The centre guide continues to advance, and the remaining files incline outwards. Each man, on obtaining the correct interval from the man next to him towards the centre of the troop, turns to the front and takes up his dressing from the centre.

ii. *To one flank.*

"To THE RIGHT —EXTEND" or "TO THE RIGHT TO — YARDS EXTEND."   The left flank guide continues to advance and the remainder incline to the right. Each man on obtaining the correct interval from the man on his left turns to the front and takes up his dressing from the left. The left flank guide maintains the original direction until the troop leader has taken up his new position, when all dress by the centre.

Extending to the left is carried out on the same principle.

5. *Closing from extended line.*—Closing is carried out on the same principle as extending. If it is desired to close on the centre the word of command is "CLOSE." To close to a flank the command is "ON THE RIGHT (LEFT) CLOSE." To reduce the extension by drawing both flanks closer to the centre without closing completely the words of command are "TO — YARDS CLOSE."

If the signal "*For action—dismount*" is given when the troop is in extended order, each section will close on its section leader before dismounting.

6. *Extending from column of sections, half sections, or single files.*—When extending from column the troop will assume extended line formation; that is to say, the rear sections, half sections, or single files will form on the right and left of the leading body.

The troop leader moves at once to his new position in extended line.

"EXTEND" or
"TO — PACES
—EXTEND."

In the case of a *column of sections* or *half sections* the leading section or half section extends; the remaining sections or half sections move direct to the places they are to occupy when in extended line, extending as they advance.

In case of *column of single files*, the rear files move direct to their places in extended line.

DRILL OF THE SQUADRON.

129. *Posts and duties of officers, &c.*

1. *Squadron commander.*—On parade, when the squadron is in line, the commander's place is one horse-length in front of the

line of troop leaders, and opposite the centre of the squadron. In squadron column, one horse-length in front of the leading troop leader.

When manœuvring great independence must be allowed to the squadron commander with regard to his position.

When drilling his squadron he must ride where he can best superintend his squadron during each particular movement. At regimental and higher drill he is best placed where he can most quickly receive the orders of the regimental commander and can retain complete control over his squadron.

In column of route he should usually be at the head of the squadron.

2. *Squadron second in command.*—He will usually ride close to the squadron leader, so as to be able to carry out his directions at once. When not required elsewhere, his position on parade is :—

    i. In *line*, in front of the right file, in line with the troop leaders.

    ii. In *column*, half a horse-length from the outer flank, in line with the front rank of the leading troop.

    iii. In *column of sections*, on the outer flank in rear of the squadron.

    iv. In *column of route*, in rear of the squadron.

3. *Troop leaders.*—When the troops are in *line*, in *column*, or in *half-column*, troop leaders ride one horse-length in front of the centre of their troops, except when the troops are of thirteen front and in *column* or *half-column*; the distance between the troop leader and his troop will then be half a horse-length.

4. *Serrefiles.*—i. *Officers.*—In *line*, one horse-length in rear of the centre of the squadron; in *column of troops*, on the outer flank, opposite the centre, and one horse-length from the flank; *in column of sections,* &c., in rear of the squadron.

    ii. *Non-commissioned officers.*—(Squadron serjeant-major and squadron quartermaster-serjeant only). In *line*, one horse-length in rear of the flanks; in *column of troops* they move up in line at 6 inches interval on the flank of the rear rank man behind whom they were when in *line*; in *column of sections,* &c., in rear of the squadron and in front of the officer serrefiles.

5. *Trumpeters.*—The trumpeter, if with the squadron commander, will be half a horse-length in rear of him, and on his left. If not, he will be in the serrefile rank unless there is room in the rear rank.

130. *Formations of a squadron. (Plate II.)*

The following are the formations of a squadron:—

Line.—The troops, each in line, side by side without intervals. The troops are numbered from the right.

Squadron column.—The troops, each in *line*, are one behind the other at such a distance that, if they wheeled to either hand, the squadron would be in *line*.

Squadron half-column.—The squadron is in half-column when a half-wheel of troops is made from *line* or *squadron column.*

Column of half-squadrons.—Half-squadrons in *column* at a distance equal to troop frontage.

Line of troop columns.—Each troop in *column of sections,* at deploying interval, unless another interval is ordered. A useful formation for working over rough or broken ground, especially when *line* may have to be formed rapidly.

131. *Line.*

1. The squadron should be practised in making long advances at the trot and gallop with changes of direction and pace.

2. *The march in line.*—On the squadron leader's command or signal "MARCH," the whole squadron moves off together, each

PLATE II. *To face p.* 184·

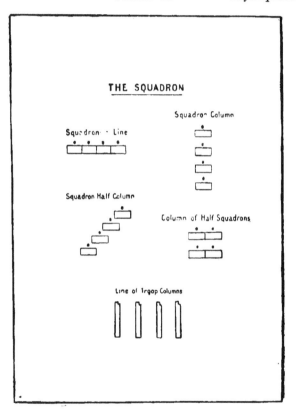

THE SQUADRON

Squadron Column

Squadron Line

Squadron Half Column

Column of Half Squadrons

Line of Troop Columns

troop acting in every respect as laid down for the advance of a single troop, the general alingment and cohesion of the squadron being secured by the troop leaders riding at the same pace and keeping the proper intervals by moving straight and smoothly in the required direction.

The right centre troop leader being the directing troop leader is responsible to the squadron commander for direction and pace, the squadron commander indicating to him on what object or in which direction he is to ride. All troop leaders, while looking principally to the front, are to be attentive to any indication the squadron commander may make for their guidance.

Obstacles are passed always on as broad a front as possible; by files breaking off from the flanks or dropping back; by advancing in extended order; by forming *squadron* or *troop columns*; or by filing to the front by sections.

If an obstacle presents itself before the front of a whole troop, the troop leader will halt and lead by the incline in rear of one of the other troops of the squadron, resuming his place in *line* when the obstacle is passed.

Extension is usually made from the centre of the squadron. During and after the extension each troop will continue to dress by its troop leader, and the squadron by the directing troop leader.

Similarly, when the *close* or *rally* from an extended formation is ordered, the movement will be made to the centre of the squadron unless a flank is specially named.

3. *Change of direction.*—The squadron commander can make a slight change of direction by ordering the directing troop leader to alter the direction gradually, or by giving the command "RIGHT (LEFT) SHOULDERS."

A change of direction to the half-right or left, or to a greater angle will be made either by wheeling the troops in the required direction, and then forming squadron, or by wheeling the whole squadron.

4. *Formation of squadron column :—*

i. *To a flank.*

"TROOPS, RIGHT   Each troop wheels accordingly.
(or LEFT)
WHEEL."

ii. *To the front.—*

"FORM SQUADRON   The centre troop advances, followed by the
COLUMN."   left and right troops in succession. This can
                  also be formed from a flank by the command
                  "FROM THE RIGHT (or LEFT) FORM SQUADRON
                  COLUMN."

iii. *To the rear.—*

The squadron first wheels troops about on the command
"TROOPS RIGHT ABOUT WHEEL," and then advances in *column
of troops.*

5. *Formation of squadron half-column.—*

"TROOPS, HALF-
RIGHT."

6. *Formation of column of half-squadrons.—*

"FORM COLUMN   The 2nd and 3rd troops advance, the 1st and
OF HALF-   4th incline inwards until they reach their
SQUADRONS."   respective positions in half-squadron, when
                 they will receive the signal *"forward"* from
                 their troop leaders.

7. *Formation of troop columns.—*

"LINE of TROOP   Each troop forms column of sections, and
COLUMNS."   the leading section of each troop places itself
                 in rear of the troop leader, who does not
                 deviate from the line on which he is moving.

132. *Squadron column.*

1. *The march in squadron column.—*The march of each
troop is conducted on the same principles as when in *line,* the
leading troop leader being responsible for the pace and direction.

2. *Change of direction.*—Change of direction can be effected by changing the direction of the head, by wheeling troops into *half-column* or *line* to either flank, or by inclining.

Wheeling the head of the column.—

"HEAD OF SQUADRON, RIGHT (or LEFT) WHEEL" (or 'HALF-RIGHT (or HALF-LEFT')—
    The leading troop wheels; the remainder wheel in succession on arriving at the point where the leading troop wheeled.

3. *Formation of line :*—
    i. *Line to the front.*—

"FORM SQUADRON."
    The leading troop advances; the rear troops incline, at an increased pace. They are fronted when opposite their places in line, and take the pace of the directing troop on arriving in line with it.

    The squadron will always be formed in the above manner on the trumpet sound "FORM LINE."

    If a line is required on the right or left of the leading troop, the command will be "ON THE RIGHT (or LEFT), FORM SQUADRON."

    ii. *Line to a flank.*—

"RIGHT or LEFT WHEEL INTO LINE."
    The troops wheel to the right together and on coming into line move forward.

    iii. *Line to the half front.*—

    An oblique line to the right (or left) front can be formed by wheeling troops half-right (or left), and giving the command "FORM SQUADRON," or by giving the command "FORM

Squadron" and then altering the direction of the leading troops during the formation. In this way line in any oblique direction can be formed.

4. *Formation of half-column :—*

i. "Troops,   Each troop wheels half-right.
   Half-right
(or Half Left)."

ii. "Troops   Each troop wheels three-quarters about.
   Three-
   Quarters,"
   "Right (or Left)
   About."

5. *Formation of column of half-squadrons.—*

"Form Column   No. 3 troop moves up to troop distance
or Half-   from No. 1. Nos. 2 and 4 form on the left
Squadrons."   of Nos. 1 and 3.

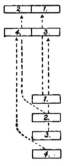

6. *Formation of line of troop columns :—*

"FORM LINE   The leading troop forms troop column. The
OF TROOP   other troops form *troop columns* to the flank and
COLUMNS."   move into their places in *line of troop columns.*

133.   *Column of half-squadrons.*

1. "FORM SQUADRON." The rear troops incline outwards,
at an increased pace, and form up in line with the leading
troops.

2. *To form column of half-squadrons to the right (or left).—*
" TROOPS RIGHT (or LEFT) WHEEL."

3. *To form squadron column.*—" FORM SQUADRON COLUMN."
The two troops on the right (if from the right) advance,
the two troops on the left incline, when their flank is
clear, cover and follow.

134.   *Line of troop columns.*

1. *Taking ground to a flank.*—Ground may be taken to a
flank by wheeling sections to the right on the command
" SECTIONS RIGHT."

2. *Formation of line :—*
    i. *Line to the front.*—" FORM SQUADRON." Each troop
      forms to its front in the usual manner.
    ii. *Line in any oblique direction.*—The squadron com-
      mander *shoulders* the squadron until the right
      direction is obtained ; he then gives the order for
      the formation of line.

135.   *Column of sections, half-sections and files.*

1. " FORM SQUADRON " (1st, 2nd, 3rd, and 4th Troops " FORM
TROOP " ordered by the troop leaders). Each troop at once
forms troop and is led at an increased pace to its position in
. line.

2. Line in any direction can be formed by altering the direction of the head of the column as desired and giving the command " FORM SQUADRON " when the rear troops form as above on the head.

136.   *Extending and closing a squadron.*

1. *Extending from line.*

" EXTEND " or   The directing troop extends from its centre
" TO — YARDS   (*see* Sec. **128**).   The troop on the right wheels
EXTEND."   half right and as soon as the left flank guide
of the troop comes opposite his place in extended line, the troop leader extends the troop
to the right (*see* Sec. **128**, 4, ii).   The two
troops on the left wheel half left and move to
the flank, each troop extending to the left as
soon as its right flank guide comes opposite
his place in line.

" TO THE RIGHT   The left troop extends to the right.   The
EXTEND " or   other troops wheel half right, and, when the
" TO THE RIGHT   left flank guide of each troop has obtained
TO — YARDS—   the necessary interval from the right flank
EXTEND."   guide of the troop on his left, the troop leader
will extend the troop to the right.   Extending
the squadron to the left is carried out on the
same principle.

2. *Extending from squadron column.*

If the command or signal " EXTEND " is
given when the squadron is in *squadron column*,
each troop will extend from its centre.   If it
is desired to form extended line from *squadron
column*, the words of command will be " FORM
SQUADRON — EXTEND "; extended *line* will
then be formed on the same principle as it is
formed from *line* (*see* paragraph 1).

3. *Extending from column of sections.*

On the command "EXTEND" each troop maintaining the original pace will extend (*see* Sec. **128,** 6).

If it is desired to form extended *line,* the command will be " FORM SQUADRON—EXTEND." Each troop will first form line; then the squadron will be formed in extended line in the same manner as it is formed from line.

4. *Closing from extended line.*

i. *Closing on the centre.*

" CLOSE." The directing troop closes on its centre.

The right troop closes to its left; then wheels half left and takes up its position on the right of the directing troop.

The left centre troop and the left troop each close to their right, wheel half right, and form on the left of the directing troop.

ii. *Closing to a flank.*

" TO THE RIGHT —CLOSE." Each troop closes to its right, the right troop advances, the remainder wheel half right and take up their places in line.

Closing to the left is carried out on the same principle.

DRILL OF THE REGIMENT.

137. *Post and duties of officers, &c.*

1. *The regimental commander, senior major, and adjutant.*— At drill the regimental commander should ride where he can best superintend the movements of his regiment, make his words of command heard, and his signals seen by the squadron commanders.

At manœuvre and in the field the system of command must ensure that it is possible for the commander to form his

regiment from any formation (whether of march, of manœuvre,
of assembly, or from the mêlée) into a suitable formation for
attack in any direction against any arm, as rapidly and with as
few commands or signals as possible. With this end in view
the regimental commander will be accompanied in the field by
the senior major and the adjutant, who will act as his assistants.
Previous to a change of direction one of the two should usually
be detached and ready in position at once to point out, or lead
on, the new direction, rejoining the regimental commander as
soon as this special duty is completed.

When the regimental commander is for any reason at a
distance from the regiment, the senior major may be given
executive command.

2. If an officer is specially detailed as directing guide, he
will place himself where he can be easily seen in front of the
directing troop leader, the latter being responsible for the
maintenance of an even pace.

3. *Squadron commanders.*—Although each squadron commander must be in a position to hear the orders, and receive
the directions of the regimental commander, he must not be so
far from his squadron that his power of leading it is diminished.
Squadron leaders are responsible at all times for the position of
their squadrons. The second in command of a squadron assists
the squadron leader and takes the executive direction when the
latter is any distance from the squadron.

4. *Troop leaders.*—When the regiment is following a directing
guide, the directing troop leader of each squadron regulates his
pace and direction in accordance with that of the officer leading.

When there is no guide specially detailed, pace and direction
are taken from the directing troop leader of the directing
squadron. In *line of squadron columns* the leading troop leaders
maintain the general alignment and the proper interval between
squadrons by preserving steadiness of pace and direction. In
column or *half column* they preserve the distances of their
squadrons.

PLATE III. *To face p.* 193.

THE REGIMENT

In Line

5. *Regimental serjeant-major.*—The regimental serjeant-major must be ready to assist the senior major and adjutant in changes of direction and pace. When the regiment is in *line* or *line of squadron columns*, he will ride in rear of the squadron of direction. When in *column of troops*, on the outer flank of the leading troop.

138. *Formations of a regiment.*

(*Plate III.*)

Line.—The squadrons each in *line* are side by side with an interval of 8 yards between them.

Line of squadron columns.—The squadrons each in *squadron column* are side by side at such interval that when each squadron forms *line* the regiment is in *line*.

Mass.—The squadrons, each in *squadron column*, are side by side at 5 yards interval. This formation is generally used as a formation of assembly or for the preliminary phases of manœuvre.

Column of troops.—The squadrons, each in *column of troops*, are in column at such distance that a wheel of troops to either hand would bring the regiment into *line*. A marching formation which is also useful at various stages of manœuvre, for advancing on a narrow front, for gaining a flank prior to wheeling into line to attack, &c.

Quarter column.—A regiment is in *quarter column* when troops are wheeled to the right or left from *mass*.

Column of squadrons.—The squadrons, each in *line*, are in column at such distance that, if the troops are wheeled to the right or left, the regiment is in *line of squadron columns*. This formation is useful for moving to a flank with the idea of advancing later in *line of squadron columns*.

Line of troop columns.—The squadrons, each in *line of troop columns*, are side by side at such interval that, if each squadron forms *line*, the regiment is in *line*. This formation is useful when passing over rough ground and for manœuvre. *Line* can be formed rapidly.

139. *Line.*

1. *The march in line.*—In the march in *line*, which should be constantly practised at a smooth and even pace, each squadron acts in the same manner as when marching singly, except that the leaders select such points in their front to lead upon as will ensure the close cohesion of the regiment.

If an obstacle presents itself before the front of a squadron, it may be turned or passed over by the squadron commander adopting some of the formations mentioned in squadron drill, or leading his squadron in rear of the next squadron until clear of the obstacle. If two squadrons have to pass through a narrow opening, the one nearer to it, or, if the distance is about the same, the one nearer the centre of the regiment, has precedence.

2. *Change of direction.*—A change of direction can be effected by the officer guiding the regiment gradually circling into the direction indicated; or the command or signal "RIGHT (or LEFT) SHOULDERS" can be given.

A change of direction to the half right or left may be carried out by giving the command

"CHANGE DIRECTION HALF-RIGHT (LEFT)." Squadron leaders give the commands "TROOPS HALF-RIGHT FORM SQUADRON," and conduct their squadrons to their places in *line.*

3. *Advance and retirement in échelon.*

    i. "ADVANCE IN ECHELON OF SQUADRONS FROM THE RIGHT."

        The 1st squadron advances; the remainder advance in succession as soon as the preceding squadron has moved a distance equal to the frontage of a squadron and the interval between squadrons when in line.

    ii. "ADVANCE IN ECHELON OF WINGS FROM THE RIGHT." The rear wing is held back to a distance equal to its frontage and the interval between wings.

iii. "Retire in Echelon of Squadrons (or Wings) from the Right."

This movement is executed on the same principle as an advance, each squadron wheels its troops right-about if the retirement is from the right or left-about if from the left, when it comes to its turn to retire.

iv. "Advance in Double Echelon."

The centre squadron (or squadrons) advances, the flank squadrons following at open column distance, unless any other distance is ordered.

In all échelon movements the leading body directs.

4. *Formation of line of Squadron columns.*—"Line of Squadron Columns." Each squadron forms *squadron column*.

5. *Formation of mass.*—"Form Mass." The centre squadron forms *squadron column*; each flank squadron forms *squadron columns* from the flank nearest the centre, changes the direction of its head and moves at an increased pace into its position in *mass*.

If executed to the halt the centre squadron forms *squadron column*, moves up the depth of the column and halts. Flank squadrons wheel troops inwards; then wheel heads to the right and left respectively and form up in *mass* by inclining.

6. *Formation of line of troop columns.*—"Line of Troop Columns." Each squadron forms *line of troop columns*.

140. *Line of squadron columns.*

1. The march in line of squadron columns is conducted on the same principles as the march in line (*see* Sec. **139**).

2. *Change of direction.*

Any slight change of direction can be made by *shouldering* or by instructing the directing guide or the directing squadron leader to make the change, the remainder conforming at once.

The regiment should be practised in changing direction to the extent of the quarter circle, the rear troops of squadrons covering as rapidly as possible.

A change of position to the rear is executed in a similar manner, the front being first reversed by the wheel-about of troops, and the squadrons being again fronted on reaching the new alignment.

"CHANGE DIRECTION HALF-RIGHT (LEFT)."— Squadron leaders wheel the heads of their squadrons half right and lead them into their places in line at an increased speed.

3. *Advance and retirement in échelon.*—Advances and retirements in any échelon of squadron columns are executed as from line (*see* Sec. **139**).

4. *Formation of line.*

i. "FORM LINE."—Each squadron forms squadron on both flanks, as in squadron drill.

ii. *Line* can be formed to the half-front by shouldering or changing direction in *line of squadron columns,* and forming *line* when required.

iii. *Line* can be formed to the flank by changing direction to the right or left and forming *line.*

The following method may also be employed :—

"LINE TO THE RIGHT."—The 1st squadron wheels into *line* to the right; the remainder wheel their troops half-right and when opposite their places in line wheel their troops half-right again and move up in line with the first squadron.

5. *Formation of mass.* "FORM MASS."—The 2nd squadron advances; the remainder are moved into their places in *mass* at an increased pace by changing the direction of their heads. *Mass* can be formed on any squadron (*e.g.,* "MASS ON THE 1ST SQUADRON ").

If *mass* is to be formed from and to the halt, the directing squadron advances the depth of the column, the remainder wheel into *line* inwards, and wheel troops to the front when they have their proper interval. If the directing squadron is not to advance, the remainder may move into position by wheeling troops.

Mass to the half-front, or to a flank, can be formed by the command " MASS TO THE HALF-RIGHT," or " MASS TO THE RIGHT." The 1st squadron takes the required direction and the remainder form *mass* on its left by changing the direction of their heads.

6. *Formation of column of troops.*—" FORM COLUMN OF TROOPS " (or " COLUMN OF TROOPS FROM THE RIGHT (LEFT) "). The directing squadron advances; the remainder wheel heads half-right and half-left, and take the shortest route into their places in column.

" COLUMN OF TROOPS TO THE HALF-RIGHT (LEFT)."—All squadrons wheel their heads half-right; the 1st squadron continues to advance, and the remainder move into column by the shortest route.

" COLUMN OF TROOPS TO THE RIGHT (LEFT)."—All squadrons wheel their heads to the right.

141. *Mass.*

1. *March in mass.*—This is conducted on the same principles as the march in line (*see* Sec. **139**).

2. *Change of direction.*—This is effected by altering the direction of the officer of direction or by giving the command " RIGHT (or LEFT) SHOULDERS." The regiment should be practised in changing direction to the extent of the quarter circle, the rear troops of squadrons covering as rapidly as possible. Changes of position to the rear are executed in a similar manner, the front being first reversed by the wheel about of troops.

3. *Formation of squadron column to the flank.*—" SQUADRON COLUMN TO THE RIGHT (LEFT, HALF-RIGHT, HALF-LEFT)."

The squadron on the flank named changes the direction of its head, the remainder form on its left by wheeling or shouldering the heads.

4. *Formation of line to the front.*—Line of squadron columns
will first be formed in the required direction, and squadrons
deployed. In case of urgent necessity, as when manœuvring to
gain the flank of an enemy's line, the following method may be
adopted:—The direction being first changed, if necessary, by
shouldering, the command "FORM LINE" may be given, when
the two flank squadrons will wheel heads outwards, gallop away
to each flank to allow the centre squadrons to deploy and then
deploy themselves.

5. *Formation of line to a flank.*—"*Line to the Right.*" The
first squadron wheels troops to the right at once; the other
squadrons advance and gain their places in line by the half
wheel of troops.

6. *Formation of line of squadron columns.* — "LINE OF
SQUADRON COLUMNS." The directing squadron advances; the
other squadrons wheel their heads outwards, and when opposite
their places in line wheel heads to the front and move up in line
with the directing squadron.

7. *Formation of column of troops.*—As from *line of squadron
columns* (*see* Sec. **140**).

142. *Column of troops.*

1. *The march in column of troops.*—When marching in
column, attention should be paid to the preservation of the
proper distances between troops. The leading troop leader of
each squadron is responsible for the distance and covering of his
squadron.

When the regiment is to move off, the commanding officer
gives the caution "THE COLUMN WILL ADVANCE," and the
squadrons are put in motion and the direction indicated as in
the march in line, care being taken that the movement from
head to rear of the column is simultaneous.

When the *halt* is ordered, rear bodies must halt simultaneously with the head.

2. *Change of direction.*—The direction of the column is changed by the command "HEAD OF THE COLUMN, RIGHT WHEEL (HALF-RIGHT OR RIGHT)."

3. *Formation of mass :*—
 i. *To the front.*—"FORM MASS" or "ON THE LEFT (or RIGHT) FORM MASS." These movements are executed as in formation of *line* except that the squadrons remain in *squadron column* and form at close interval.
 ii. *To a flank or half-flank.*—"MASS TO THE LEFT (RIGHT, HALF-LEFT, or HALF-RIGHT)." The first squadron wheels its head in the required direction; the remainder move into their places in mass by changing the direction of their heads.
  If executed to the halt, the leading squadron after wheeling moves up the depth of a *squadron column* and halts; rear squadrons advance until nearly opposite their places in *mass* before changing direction.

4. *Formation of line of squadron columns.*—Squadron columns can be formed in any direction exactly as formations of *line*, except that the squadrons remain in *squadron column.*

5. *Formation of line.*—"FORM LINE." The 1st squadron forms *squadron* on both flanks, the 2nd squadron wheels its head half-left, the 3rd wheels its head half-right, and as soon as they have got their proper intervals, wheel heads half-right and half-left respectively, form squadrons in the same manner as the 1st, and move up into the alignment.

When the rear squadrons are required to form on a flank the command will be—"ON THE RIGHT (or LEFT), FORM LINE."

In any of these movements an oblique line can be formed by indicating the required direction to the leader of the leading squadron, or by adding the words "LEFT (or RIGHT)

FORWARD (or BACK)," to the caution FORM LINE.   The head of the leading squadron is at once placed in the required direction, and the heads of rear squadrons, after getting the proper interval, are wheeled parallel to it before squadron is formed.

Line to the half-front can be formed by the command " TROOPS HALF-RIGHT," followed by " FORM SQUADRONS," and " FORM LINE."

Line to a flank is formed by the command " RIGHT (or LEFT) WHEEL INTO LINE."

If, after the head of a column of troops has begun to change direction (e.g., to the right), it be desired to form line to the left on the new alignment, the caution can be given " LINE TO THE LEFT ON THE NEW ALIGNMENT."   The squadrons ready on the new alignment wheel into line to the left; the remainder form in line on their left.

DRILL OF THE BRIGADE.

143. *Posts and duties of officers.*

1. The brigade commander will ride wherever he can best super-intend and direct the movements of his command.   When the brigade is halted on parade, his post in all orders of formation is ten horse-lengths in front of the leading officer or officers, and opposite the centre of the brigade; his staff officers are two horse-lengths in rear of him, and at one horse-length interval from each other.

2. The duties of the brigade major are to assist the brigadier. He may act as directing guide to the brigade himself or he may detail another officer of the staff for the purpose. The brigade guide may carry a small guide flag to unfurl when he is guiding the brigade so that he can be readily distinguished.

PLATE IV. *To face p. 201.*

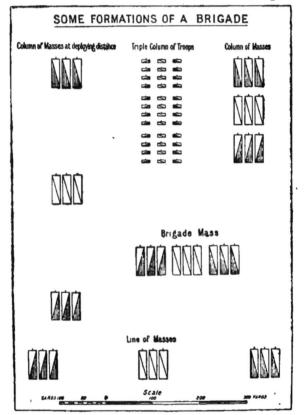

SOME FORMATIONS OF A BRIGADE

Column of Masses at deploying distance

Triple Column of Troops

Column of Masses

Brigade Mass

Line of Masses

Scale
YARDS 100   50   0   100   200   300 YARDS

144. *Formations of a brigade.*

The following are the orders of formation of a brigade:—

> *Brigade mass.*
> *Column of masses.*
> *Column of masses at deploying distance.*
> *Line of masses.*
> *Column of troops.*
> *Double or triple column of troops.*
> *Column of squadrons.*
> *Quarter column.*
> *Echelon of regiments* (in any formation).
> *Line of squadron columns.*
> *Line of troop columns.*
> *Line.*

The orders of formation are the same in principle as in the case of the regiment.

145. *Movements and changes of formation to be practised.*

1. *From brigade mass:*—
   The march in *mass.*
   Formation of *line* or *line of squadron columns.*
   "   *column of troops.*
   "   *line of masses.*
   "   *column of masses.*
   "   *double échelon of masses* at close or deploying interval.

2. *From column of masses:*—
   March in *column of masses.*
   Changes of direction and formation of *column of masses at deploying distance.*
   Formation of *squadron columns and line.*
   "   *brigade mass* to the front or flank.
   "   *double échelon of masses.*

3 *From column of troops* :—

The march in *column of troops*.
Changes of direction.
Formation of *line* and *line of squadron columns*.
      „   *brigade mass*.
      „   *line of masses*.
      „   *column of masses*.

4. *From double échelon* :—
Changes of front and direction.

5. *From line of squadron columns* :—
The march in *line of squadron columns*.
Changes of direction and position.
Formation of *line*.
Advances and retirements in *échelon* or by the succession of
    regiments or wings.

Formation of *brigade mass*.
      „   *line of masses*.
      „   *column of masses*.
      „   *column of troops*.

6. *From line of troop columns* :—
Formation of *line* and *échelons*.

7. *From line* :—
The march in *line*.
Changes of direction.
Advances and retirements in *échelon*.
Formation of *squadron and troop column*.
Movements in *double échelon*.

146. *Brigade drill instructions*.

1. Brigade movements are designed to make the brigade
supple and capable of assuming a suitable attack formation
in any direction with the least possible delay.

2. In the formation of *line, line of squadron columns,* or *line of masses* from *échelon,* it is a general rule that regiments will be formed first, and afterwards brought up into the alignment. From *column,* regiments will be formed as soon as they have got their interval, and then be brought up into the alignment.

3. In brigade movements, regimental commanders must move their regiments into the required position with rapidity, and must not devote their attention to details of regimental drill.

4. When regiments move independently, the regimental commanders must name their regiments before giving the executive word of command.

5. Regimental commanders will repeat the brigadier's field calls only when absolutely necessary to show that they have been understood, and will, as a rule, give the orders for the movement of their own regiments either by word of mouth or by signal.

When the brigadier's order is given by signal only, regimental commanders will give the executive signal for their squadrons to move into the new formation.

When the order of the brigadier is not distinctly heard, or is not understood, each regimental commander, when the intention is obvious, will conform as quickly as possible to the movement executed by the other regiment or regiments.

6. The sound " FORM LINE," " SQUADRON COLUMN," or " MASS," indicates that each regiment will assume that formation. If repeated, *brigade line, brigade line of squadron columns* or *brigade mass* is required after regimental *line, line of squadron columns,* or *mass* has been formed.

7. The exact movement to be performed by each regiment in brigade drill must often be decided by the features of the ground, and great latitude must be given to regimental commanders in this respect. The movements described in the following sections must be looked upon as guides rather than as hard and fast forms to be adhered to under all circumstances.

147. *Brigade mass.*

1. *To form line of squadron columns to the right.*

> On the Brigade commander's order "SQUADRON COLUMNS
> TO THE RIGHT," the first regiment forms *line of
> squadron columns* to the right at once.

> The commander of the second regiment moves his regi-
> ment forward, and, when by use of the *shoulder* he has
> brought his right squadron opposite its place in line,
> he gives the commands " FORWARD "—" SQUADRON
> COLUMNS FROM THE RIGHT " or " SQUADRON COLUMN
> TO THE HALF-RIGHT."   The actual word of command
> depends upon the amount he has shouldered.

> The commander of the third regiment does the same,
> forming on the left of the second regiment.

2. *Change direction.*

> The brigade commander will either give the command
> "RIGHT (LEFT) SHOULDERS," when the whole brigade
> will shoulder, or will employ a directing guide to lead
> the brigade round as required.

3. *Double échelon.*

> Advance and retirement in *double échelon.*

148. *Column of masses.*

To form *line of squadron columns.*

> The leading regiment opens out from its second
> squadron.

> The commanders of rear regiments move their squadrons
> forward by the use of the *shoulder* until their inner
> flank squadrons are opposite their places in *line of
> squadron column.*   Each then forms *squadron column*
> on the outer flank.

PLATE V.   *To face p. 205*

SOME FORMATIONS OF A DIVISION

Column of Brigade Masses at deploying distance	Column of Brigade Masses	Column of Regimental Masses	Column of Regimental Masses at deploying distance

Divisional Mass

Line of Brigade Masses

Line of Regimental Masses

Scale

0   ¼   ½   ¾   1 MILE

149. *Line of squadron columns.*

1. *To form brigade mass to the right.*

On the brigade commander's order " BRIGADE MASS TO THE RIGHT," the right regiment forms *mass* to the right at once, and the remaining regiments form *mass* on its left.

2. *To form column of masses to the right.*

On the brigade commander's order " COLUMN OF MASSES TO THE RIGHT," each regiment forms *mass* to the right at once, and the rear regiments then draw up to their correct distance at an increased pace.

DRILL OF THE DIVISION.

150. *Posts and duties of officers.*

The divisional commander will ride where he can best super-intend and direct the movements of his command. On parade his post is ten horse-lengths in front of the brigadiers and opposite the centre of the division ; his staff officers are two horse-lengths in rear of him, and at one horse-length interval from each other. Divisional staff officers will arrange to guide the division with flags on the principles laid down for a brigade. Whilst working in division the brigade staff may continue to use guide flags, provided that brigade guide flags are not likely to be confused with divisional guide flags.

151. *Formations.* (*Plate V.*)

The following are some of the formations which a division can assume :—

Divisional mass.—The brigades each in *brigade mass* are placed side by side on the same alignment at intervals of 16 yards.

Line of brigade masses.—The brigades, each in *brigade mass*, are on the same alignment and at deploying intervals plus 16 yards.

Line of regimental masses.—The brigades, each in *line of masses*, on the same alignment and at deploying intervals plus 16 yards.

Column of brigade masses.—The brigades, each in *brigade mass*, are in column at wheeling distance plus the interval between brigades in *line* (about 230 yards distance when troops are of 17 front).

Column of brigade masses at deploying distance.—The brigades, each in *brigade mass*, are in *column* at a distance equal to a brigade in *line* plus 16 yards.

Column of regimental masses.—The brigades, each in *column of masses*, are in *column* at wheeling distance plus the interval between brigades in *line*. (Distance—about 90 yards with 17 front troops.)

Column of regimental masses at deploying distance.—The brigades, each in *column of regimental masses at deploying distance*, are in *column* at a distance equal to a regiment in *line* plus 16 yards.

Column of squadrons.—The brigades, each in *column of squadrons*, are in *column* at a distance equal to the length of a squadron in *line* plus the interval between the brigades in *line*.

Echelon or double échelon of brigades in any formation.

Line of squadron columns.—The brigades in *line of squadron columns* are placed side by side in the same alignment at intervals of 16 yards plus the frontage of a squadron in *line*.

Line.—The brigades in *line* are placed side by side in the same alignment at intervals of 16 yards.

152.   *Changes in direction and formation.*

Changes in direction and formation are made on the same principle as in squadron, regimental, and brigade drill.

CHAPTER V.

FURTHER PRELIMINARY INSTRUCTION.

153. *Methods of dismounting for fire action.*

1. Each troop will usually be in close order when ordered to dismount for action. If, however, it is desired to dismount when extended, the signal for dismount will be given and each section will close on its centre and dismount independently.

2. The following methods will be used as the situation demands.

i. *First method—*

"FOR ACTION— FRONT (RIGHT OR LEFT)— DISMOUNT." The troop leader advances two horse-lengths, the front rank one, and then the odd numbers of both ranks one horse-length. All except the Nos. 3 then dismount independently and as rapidly as possible, handing over the reins of their horses to the No. 3 of their section, who remains mounted. When the force is in column of sections, the necessary room for dismounting is obtained by Nos. 1, 2 and 4 passaging their horses outwards.

ii. *Second method—*

"RIGHT (or LEFT) or ODD (or EVEN) NUMBERS— FOR ACTION FRONT (RIGHT or LEFT)— DISMOUNT." The men ordered to dismount advance one horse-length and dismount. The numbers not ordered to dismount then move up into the intervals and take the reins of the men who have dismounted. The reins should not be passed over the horses' heads. If the troops are in column of sections the necessary space for dismounting is obtained by passaging outwards. If they are in *columns of half sections* and the right files are ordered to dismount, the latter will either dismount on the off side, or passage to the flank in order to obtain space to dismount on the near side.

iii. *Third method*—

" WITH LINKED   The whole dismount as in the first method,
  HORSES FOR   the even numbers then bring their horses up
  ACTION FRONT   into line, closing in towards the right; the men
  (RIGHT or LEFT)   take one pace to the front, and turn about and
  —DISMOUNT."   link their horses as described in Sec. **76**, 4.

The horses of troop officers and supernumeraries will be linked on the right of their troops.

One or two men per troop should be left to look after the horses.

iv. *Fourth method*—

" WITH COUPLED   The whole dismount as above and the
  (OR RINGED)   horses are coupled or ringed as described in
  HORSES, FOR   Sec. **76**, 5.
  ACTION FRONT
  (RIGHT or LEFT)
  —DISMOUNT."

2. After giving the command to dismount troop leaders move at once to the flank ordered, so that the dismounted men may see immediately where to fall in.

The dismounted men, as soon as they have handed over their horses, double out as quickly as possible and without any noise, forming up in single rank behind their troop leaders each rear rank man on the left of his front rank man.

When forming to the front the squadron will form up in line, that was the formation of the squadron when the order to dismount was given, or in column of troops if column was the previous formation. When forming to a flank the squadron will form up in the line.

3. On the command " MOUNT " the men will run as rapidly as possible towards their horses, walking when they get near to avoid frightening them; each man will take his horse, and if the horses are coupled undo his own reins. If the horses are in line the odd numbers will lead their horses forward one horse-length to give the even numbers room to mount; all then mount independently, and take their places in the ranks. Nos. 3 if already mounted will assist the men of their sections to mount any horses that are restive.

If the troop is formed in sections or files, the men on arriving at their horses passage them so as to get sufficient room to mount; in this case they must not move them up, as they might thereby delay the mounting of the men in front.

If the command " STAND TO YOUR HORSES " is given to men on dismounted duty, they double to their horses and stand to their heads.

154. *Picketing horses.*

1. A horse, when picketed, requires a frontage of about 5 feet and a distance of about 12 feet. When horses are fresh from stables they may at first be allowed a greater frontage.

2. Except in very hot weather horses will be picketed in lines facing away from the prevailing wind, with intervals of 5 yards between the heel pegs of one line and the head pegs of the next line, to allow of a gangway. When sufficient space is available this interval may be increased to 9 yards; 4 yards being allowed to admit of the horse being swung round on his heel peg on to new ground facing in the opposite direction, and 5 yards as a gangway. When the additional 4 yards interval is available and the ground is to be occupied for more than one night, half the head pegs should be used to secure the built-up rope, and the other half to mark its alternative position. When on bad-holding ground, all the head pegs should be used to secure the built-up rope.

Five yards should be maintained between a horse line and the nearest tent peg, building, or wall.

3. Saddlery and harness will, as a rule, be placed in gangways; forage at the rear ends of the horse lines.

If horses are unaccustomed to picketing, an adequate number of line guards should be posted to prevent stampedes.

4. Before the force reaches the ground where it is intended to camp or bivouac a party should be sent on to allot the ground to the various units and to mark it out. The ends of the horse lines of each troop should be marked, so that no time is wasted

when the troops arrive. The ends may be marked by small flags or sticks pushed into the ground, or by small heaps of stones.

5. On the arrival of the force each squadron should be halted in any convenient formation on the ground just outside that marked out for its horse lines. Each troop, acting independently, should lay its lines down in a methodical manner. The following procedure is suggested:—

i. Dismount and ground arms clear of horses. The Nos. 3 may hold the horses, their arms being placed with the remainder, or the horses may be coupled.

ii. Return to the horses, remove picketing gear from the saddles, the Nos. 2 taking that of the Nos. 3, and move to the ground marked out for the horse lines.

iii. Drive in a double peg at the flag, stick, or stones marking one end of the troop line, and put the built-up rope together, passing it through all the other head peg loops.

iv. Fasten the rope to the double peg at the end of the line, and stretch it out in the direction of the other flank flag, then drive in the pegs at equal intervals along the line.

v. Lay down the heel pegs and heel ropes, Nos. 2 being responsible for those of Nos. 3.

vi. Return to the horses and lead them in single file on to the lines; each man halts opposite the ring of his own piece of built-up rope, unfastens the head-rope and ties it to the line with a *clove-hitch* and a *draw loop*, first passing it through the ring of the built-up rope.

vii. Fasten shackles round the horse's hind leg above the fetlock with buckles outside (change the leg frequently). Drive in the heel peg (they must not be dressed), so that the horse will stand as directed below with the heel rope taut, and then secure the end of the heel rope to the loops of the pegs with two half-hitches. When the horse is picketed, the head-rope should he sufficiently long to allow the horse's head to be in its natural position when the horse is standing perpendicular to the picket line, but no longer. (*See rope galls below.*)

Fig. 18.

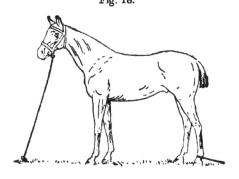

Fig. 19.

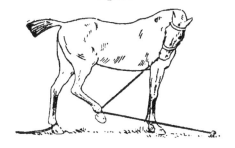

6. *Rope galls.*—In Fig. 18 the horse is shown tied up correctly, the head brought over the picket line, and sufficient length of head-rope allowed to enable the animal to look freely about.

In Fig. 19 the effect of a long head-rope is seen, the animal in moving about has managed to get his heel over it. In this position the animal works its leg up and down on a taut rope, and in a few seconds may cut through the skin and inflict an injury requiring a considerable time to heal.

155. *Swimming and crossing rivers.*

1. To enable cavalry to cross unfordable rivers every man in the ranks should be taught to swim, for a man who is not confident of himself in the water may render useless the efforts of a horse that can swim well. Good swimmers will be found in every body of troops, and these should be used as instructors of the men who cannot swim.

2. All horses should be taught to cross a running stream. Those which at first refuse must be either led beside a horse that swims boldly or towed across from a boat or raft.

In the latter case, a tow rope should usually be employed, as oars will often frighten a nervous horse.

When teaching horses to cross a river, every care must be taken that they are not frightened. All horses swim naturally, and it is only through fear that they sometimes become unmanageable.

3. When all the horses of a squadron have learnt to cross, the whole squadron may be sent across in a mob, led by a few steady horses with their riders.

Instead of moving all the horses away immediately they land, it is generally advisable to keep a few horses at the landing place to attract those that are to cross later.

4. For the passage of rivers large rafts can be constructed (*see* "Manual of Field Engineering") to carry a few horses each, but it is rarely worth the labour, time, or materials to do so. It

is preferable to use small rafts or boats to carry the men, their arms, equipment, and saddlery, and to make the horses swim; or to carry the arms, equipment, and saddlery only, the men swimming with their horses.

5. Before a squadron crosses a river, a party should, if necessary, be detailed to prepare the banks. When the current is swift a supplementary landing-place should usually be prepared about 200 yards down stream, in case any horse gets carried down and is unable to climb the bank.

6. All saddlery except the head collar and bridoon reins is removed and secured in the saddle blanket with the head rope. Indifferent swimmers or men who cannot swim load and man boats, or make rafts if required, and ferry them across. All the remainder strip, packing their clothing with their saddlery.

7. Prior to entering the water, the reins should be knotted, and a lock of the mane pulled through the knot to prevent the reins slipping over the head and becoming entangled with the fore legs.

8. All the horses, led by four selected for steadiness, cross in fours, extended, and at 10 yards distance. As the horses get into deep water, the men should slip off on the down stream side and hold on to the horses by the mane.

The men should lie along the top of the water, as much as possible, guiding the horses by splashing or by pulling the near or off rein as required. Against a strong current, horses should be kept at an angle of about 45 degrees against the direction of the stream, to avoid being carried too far down.

If a horse shows no disinclination to cross, the rider should leave him perfectly free, catching hold of his tail. On reaching the landing place any loose horses should be caught by men specially detailed for the purpose.

9. In practising cavalry horses in crossing temporary bridges the horses should first be ridden across in single file at a horse-length distance from each other, care being taken to keep them

at a slow walk and to prevent all hurrying towards the front or trotting. Horses that are unsteady should fall out and be ridden across by themselves, backwards and forwards several times in succession, a lead being given to them by a steady horse. When the horses go with perfect steadiness across the bridge in single file, they should be ridden across in half-sections.

A sprinkling of sand or some straw laid on the planks deadens noise and prevents slipping.

156. *Field engineering.*

1. It is necessary that cavalry should be trained to carry out unassisted the following duties :—

   i. Crossing rivers, by means of improvised bridges and rafts.

   ii. Demolition of railways, bridges, etc.

   iii. Demolition and repairs of telegraph lines.

   iv. Construction of simple defence works, entrenching, loop-holing, &c.

Details of instruction are given in the "Manual of Field Engineering."

2. In addition to the instruction in elementary field engineering, such as entrenching and loopholing, which every cavalryman will receive, a proportion of non-commissioned officers and men in each regiment will be specially trained in hasty demolitions, light bridging, &c. They will be known as "cavalry pioneers." The percentage of pioneers should be as follows: 12 per squadron in regiments of the line and 9 per squadron in the Household Cavalry.

A course of instruction in the duties of pioneers will be carried out annually by the cavalry at all stations at home. Every subaltern officer will be put through the course. The instruction will be carried out in regimental or brigade classes, the former superintended by an officer who has qualified at the Cavalry School, or who has received certificates from the School of Military Engineering, at Chatham, or from one of the schools in India, the latter by an officer of a field troop if one is available.

157. *Reconnaissance and inter-communication.*

1. Every cavalryman must be trained in reconnaissance, and those who show special ability should be further trained as scouts or despatch riders.

2. In every regiment the following should be the minimum number of trained scouts :—

    1 officer, scout leader.
    1 serjeant scout.
    8 regimental or 1st class scouts.
    16 squadron or 2nd class scouts.

Scouts will be classified annually as 1st and 2nd class, and badges will be awarded for one year.

Every second-lieutenant will be instructed in the details of the work of a scout and should qualify as a 1st class scout before he can be considered fit for promotion.

3. In addition to the above there will be at least four trained despatch riders in each squadron who will be trained to find their way across country with verbal and written messages, and instructed in such details as are necessary for carrying out the duties of orderlies. For instance, they should know by name and be able to recognize the commanders of units other than their own in the brigade, and the commanders and staff officers of their own brigade and division.

4. Although every man in the squadron should be instructed in the duties of ground scouts, a sufficient number of men, selected for their superior intelligence and good horsemanship, should be specially trained as the ground scouts of the squadron.

5. The following are the subjects in which scouts should receive special instruction. As far as time permits these subjects should also be included in the training of all cavalry soldiers :—

    i. *Ability to find the way.*—The scout must be taught to find his way in a strange country, by the use of an ordinary map or rough diagram ; by memory of the map ; by the stars, sun, and compass ; by landmarks ;

by questioning natives of the country. As maps may not always be available on service, he should be practised in working without their aid. After having seen a map and having had the opportunity of making some notes from it, he should be able to work without it.

In all circumstances he should cultivate the habit of observation of roads, features, direction of march, etc.

ii. *Use of eye and ear.*—He should be practised in observing the same distant object both with and without glasses; in noting small signs or details, both far away and underfoot; in interpreting various sounds; and in the use of all his senses at night.

iii. *Concealment.*—The importance of taking cover and of selecting a background to suit the colour of his clothing should be emphasized; of remaining perfectly still; of concealing his horse by keeping his head towards the enemy; of avoiding the sky line; the use of trees; selecting look-out points when on the move, and getting from one to another quickly and unseen.

As a rule the scout should make observations when halted behind cover. Ground between the various halting places should be crossed at a rapid pace, and scouts should be taught not to loiter in the open.

iv. *Getting across country.*—Instruction should be given in practical cross country riding, in the crossing of such obstacles as railway embankments, dykes, wire fences, rivers, and canals, and in riding from point to point.

v. *Reporting.*—As the result of a scout's work depends on his ability to furnish a useful report, he should receive special instruction in this subject. (*See* Sec. **189.**)

vi. *Sketching.*—When the man has learnt to read a map, elementary instruction should be given in enlarging maps. He should learn judging distances, both long and short, by time or by eye and by night as well as by day; making simple approximate scales; finding approximate north point; drawing a rough map from memory; reading foreign maps.

vii. *Horsemastership.*—A scout should know how to save his horse on a long reconnaissance; how to water, feed, and rest his horse; how to detect and how to treat lameness; how to prevent and how to treat galls and minor wounds. Practice in knee haltering, linking, rounding up horses, &c.

viii. *Tracking.*—Tracking is an aid to scouting and can only be learnt by constant practice. Elementary instruction may be given by specimen tracks.

6. After receiving elementary instruction in the foregoing, the men should be practised in scouting individually, in pairs, and also in larger patrols. Special instruction should be given in the selection of look-out points and in moving quickly from one point to another without being seen; reading signs; detecting and reporting ambuscades; scouting by night.

Experience in these details can only be gained by practice. Instructors, therefore, must exercise their ingenuity in devising schemes.

7. Every scout should occasionally be sent out on special missions for distances of fifty miles or more in order to develop his powers of finding his way, to teach him to save and look after himself and his horse, to give him practice in reporting, and to develop generally his intelligence and self-reliance.

Trained scouts as a rule should work in pairs, but young soldiers and less intelligent men should be sent out alone on definite missions, with a view to developing their initiative and self-confidence.

8. Instruction in the transmission of information will usually be practised in connection with reconnaissance schemes and scouting exercises.

9. Despatch riders will be practised in forming connecting posts between detachments and the main body both on the move

and at the halt, passing messages, verbal as well as written, from one to the other and registering the despatches as they go through.

10. All ranks should understand generally the use of other means of transmitting messages, such as the telegraph, telephone, wireless, signal, &c. The signal units should be practised as frequently as possible in co-operation with other troops during field exercises and manœuvres.

11. The transmission of verbal orders and messages should be practised regularly; opportunities for such practice occur frequently during work in barracks and in the field.

158. *Instruction in night operations.*

(*See* also Sec. 238.)

1. The success of night operations in war depends to a large extent on practice and training in peace. Much of the instruction can be carried out during winter afternoons and evenings. It will often be unnecessary to use horses during this training.

2. The elementary training should consist in explanations followed by practical work. The following may be taken as a general guide as to the methods to be adopted in carrying out the elementary instruction :—

i. *Visual training.*—One man of a section should march away and be stopped by voice or pre-arranged signal as soon as he is out of sight. He should call out the number of paces he has taken. The same man should then advance towards the section from some distance further off, and be stopped as soon as he becomes visible, later counting his paces to the section.

It should be explained that :—

    (a) Ability to see in the dark increases with practice.

    (b) Objects are more visible when the moon is behind the observer than when it is in front of him.

    (c) An observer may stand up when he has a definite background and should lie down when he has not.

When the men have been practised in observing a man approaching at a walk they should be similarly practised in observing a man who is endeavouring to approach unseen.

ii. *Training in hearing.*—Instruction will be carried out on similar lines to visual training. At first the advance of a single man should be listened for, gradually the number should be increased so that facility may be acquired in judging the strength of a party approaching. It is easier to hear sounds on soft ground standing and on hard ground lying.

3, The following are some of the chief points to bear in mind :—

i. Men must be accustomed to find their way by night and to note by day land marks, which they will be able to recognize again by night.

ii. In war troops are always liable to be called upon to saddle up and march in the dark. Every man should be taught when in camp or bivouac to arrange his saddlery and kit every evening in such a manner that he can saddle up in the night without confusion or delay.

iii. Intercommunication and the passing of orders by night must be practised.

iv. Men should be taught to capture small hostile posts silently; to lay traps to catch despatch riders, and other tasks of this nature which are likely to fall to their lot by night in war.

Special parades for the purpose of instruction in marching should rarely be necessary except for transport, but advantage should be taken of every opportunity, such as is offered when troops march to and from the manœuvre ground, of giving instruction in marching both by day and by night.

CHAPTER VI.

TRAINING IN FIELD OPERATIONS.

(*See* also " Training and Manœuvre Regulations.")

159. *General principles.*

1. Instruction in fighting, protection, &c., will usually be given in the form of schemes, or problems, which may be set by the commander himself or by an officer acting as director.

The instruction will be progressive and will usually be carried out in two stages.

i. *Tactical exercises*, i.e., Operations against a skeleton force where the enemy is limited to fixed directions or movements. They may be carried out first slowly with occasional halts for explanations, and later at the pace at which they would be carried out in war time.

ii. *Manœuvres*, i.e., Operations against a skeleton or real force under a separate commander who, within the limits of the scheme, is free to adopt any formations and make any movements he chooses.

2. Good results can seldom be obtained unless each scheme has been thought out on the ground beforehand. The problems whether set verbally or in writing should usually consist of two portions :—

i. A clearly defined tactical situation.

ii. A definite task to be performed by the commander.

Each scheme should be arranged to illustrate a principle laid down in the instructions for handling cavalry in war.

3. It is important to teach cavalry leaders to come to rapid decisions. When therefore the problem is set by a director, the

space of time allowed to elapse between the explanation or issue of a problem by him and the issue of the executive orders by the commander should be shortened as the training progresses.

Before the troops move every man should be made to understand the scheme and, when secrecy is not essential, the method in which the commander proposes to act, so far as it may be possible to decide on it at that stage.

4. At the conclusion of a scheme the director will call up the subordinate commanders and briefly sum up the exercise, commenting on the way it has been carried out, pointing out mistakes, and emphasizing the lessons to be learnt. If he has acted as commander as well as director, he should also give his reasons for his plan of action. He may if he thinks fit, call on subordinates to state their views and reasons.

To stimulate the interests of the men as well as to increase their knowledge the commander should make certain that every man knows how the scheme was carried out, and hears any criticism which may be useful to him.

5. It must be impressed on all ranks that in fighting, whether mounted or dismounted, decisive success can be gained only by the offensive, and that a bold attack even by inferior numbers will usually be more effective than defensive action.

160. *Skeleton enemy.*

1. A skeleton enemy is useful when a commander wishes to exercise his command as a whole and cannot arrange to be opposed by another unit. It is also useful when practising the mounted attack and it is desired to charge home.

2. The smallest skeleton unit is a troop. Each troop will keep two men detailed for duty as skeleton enemy when required. When acting as such they will represent the flanks of a troop.

Scouts, signallers and leaders, all of whom should wear a distinguishing mark, will usually be required with a skeleton force.

It should be remembered that the scouts attached to a skeleton enemy receive valuable instruction, as they are employed against troops. Their numbers, therefore, should not be restricted.

Leaders of skeleton squadrons should, if possible, be officers, and leaders of skeleton troops should be non-commissioned officers.

Flagmen should be practised occasionally in squadron and regimental drill.

3. As a rule the skeleton force should not be allowed to move faster than a trot, otherwise operations, such as deployments and the passage of defiles, will be carried out quicker than would be possible with real troops. Care should also be taken to prevent a flag force from occupying a smaller space than would the force it represents.

4. Infantry can be represented by men with red flags, but a few extra dismounted men should usually be added to fire blank ammunition.

5. The representation of guns and machine guns by flags, though generally useful for tactical exercises, is often unsatisfactory when practising manœuvres.

For manœuvres it is generally preferable to use real guns and machine guns, even if one gun has to represent a whole battery.

161. *Provisions for safety during training in field operations.*

1. Cavalry commanded by an officer, when working in daylight against other bodies of troops, will draw swords on the occasions when they would do so in war. Lances, however, will not be brought to the engage.

2. When making mounted attacks against other bodies of troops, the attacking line will commence to slacken the pace when about 150 yards distant from its target and must halt at 50 yards distance. The command " CHARGE " must not be given.

3. When working against a skeleton enemy, on the other hand, the command "CHARGE" should usually be given, and the attack delivered as it would be in war. The skeleton force must give way and gallop off at the moment when the troops approaching them break into the actual charge; if they retire sooner it will be impossible to judge the proper moment for the charge.

The men of the skeleton force when making a flank attack against an attacking line must act with care and quickness to avoid accidents.

4. Troops engaged in practising fire tactics with blank ammunition will not approach nearer than 50 yards from their enemy.

162. *General remarks in training in mounted action.*

1. Careful training in fighting formations is essential, for only those formations which have been constantly practised in peace are useful in war.

2. The instruction is to be based on the principles laid down in Chapter XI., and must be methodically carried out.

The squadron is the best school for teaching these principles, but instruction should commence during troop training and be continued during the training of the larger bodies.

3. The charge should be the culminating point of the mounted instruction of cavalry. Units must be taught to move to the attack in good order in any direction and from any formation; they must be trained to assume immediately after a mêlée a double rank line formation, which, though irregular, may still be capable of manœuvring.

4. As it will often be necessary to pass over long distances at a fast pace before the actual attack is delivered, units must be trained, by means of progressive exercises, to move fast for considerable periods without loss of order and without distressing the horses.

5. A leader should be able to direct the attack with certainty upon the particular part of the enemy's line which he wishes to strike. The unit must therefore be trained to control accurately the direction of its attack.

All attacks should be made upon some definite target, at first stationary and later, as the training progresses, in movement. In order to develop a judgment of pace and direction charges should be practised against an enemy moving diagonally across the front.

6. In practising the mounted attack, after covering 50 yards at the most rapid pace that the unit can bear in good order, the commands "Trot" and "Walk" will be successively given; the pace will be gradually decreased before the final halt. No attempt should be made to halt abruptly after practising the charge.

On the command "Trot" swords are sloped and lances carried.

7. The attack, short of the delivery of the charge, should be practised frequently so that the men and horses do not get excited when an attack is made. Should the horses become excited and out of hand when the charge is to be made, it may be advisable for the commander to give the command "Trot" after he has given the command "Line will Attack."

8. Units should be taught to rally rapidly to the front or to either flank. Opportunity for this may be arranged in either of the following methods :—

 i. In simulation of the *mêlée*; when after the trot has been ordered subsequent to a charge, the command "Break up" will be given. The unit will then break up into disorder, the men circling round each other for a few minutes at the walk, pointing with their swords or lances, without reference to their proper places in the ranks. In this exercise the men should gain ground gradually to the front as they would endeavour to do during the actual hand-to-hand fight.

ii. By advancing into rough or broken ground, such as a wood, where good order cannot be maintained.

In either case on the command "RALLY" the men must rally with the utmost rapidity. As soon as the majority of the men have rallied, the commander will advance at the gallop for 200 or 300 yards and execute another attack, preferably in a new direction, and again break up and rally. The rally will be always executed on the move.

Though the men should be given frequent practice in "breaking up" they are not to be taught to look on the *mêlée* as the natural result of a charge; for if after charging an enemy, it is possible to maintain the ranks in good order and not break up into a *mêlée* the enemy's overthrow will be all the more complete.

9. In training for the mounted attack all units should be practised in the following:—

i. Deploying into line to the front and half front rapidly from column.

ii. Forming line to either flank by wheels of troops or squadrons from column of troops or columns of squadrons.

iii. Changing the direction of the advance up to a quarter of the circle after having deployed.

iv. Parrying flank attacks and the use of supporting lines generally.

v. Delivery of flank attacks in conjunction with the main attack.

vi. Rapid formation of an attacking line from a long column or immediately after passing through a defile.

vii. Long gallops in column and changes of direction of the head with the object of wheeling into line in a given direction should be practised by brigades; formation of column to a flank from mass should also be practised.

viii. Rapid deployments into three or four successive lines for attacks against infantry and artillery.

ix. A vigorous pursuit.

x. Retirement with the object of rallying on the first favourable opportunity.

10. In practising mounted action ground scouts should be used and thoroughly instructed in their duties.

163. *Instructions of squadrons in the mounted attack.*

1. The attack should be practised over a space of three quarters of a mile to a mile, of which about a third should be passed over at the trot and the remainder at a gallop, except the last fifty yards, which may be at the charge. First, single men, next sections, then the troop, and lastly the squadron will be exercised in this manner. When the ground is not sufficiently extensive to admit of these distances being passed over, the space allotted to the trot should be shortened, as it is important to accustom the men to riding in perfect order at the gallop.

2. The enemy should be represented by two mounted men at a sufficient distance apart to allow of the squadron passing between them. At first these men will be directed to remain halted, but, as the troops become more mobile, an officer or N.C. officer will be placed in command of the skeleton force and ordered to move in accordance with a definite plan.

3. After a series of tactical exercises the squadron commander should manoeuvre his squadron against a flagged enemy under a separate commander with power to move as he likes; and later one squadron should manoeuvre against another.

4. The principles to be observed when attacking infantry and artillery, and for combining fire action with a mounted attack, will be taught in a similar manner.

Each troop should be exercised in passing over distances up to two miles in extended order at the gallop, checking or halting on the way in the hollows or behind cover to gain breath.

164. *Instruction of regiments and brigades in the mounted attack.*

1. Regiments will be taught mounted tactics in the same manner as squadrons, but more scope will be afforded to practise attacks in échelon, parrying flank attacks and the combination of fire with shock tactics, &c.

In order, however, to fit the regiment to take its place as a portion of a larger attacking line it should be given a considerable amount of practice in attacking wholly deployed in one line.

2. When practising the attack against cavalry, the regiments should usually be employed in line side by side, the flank regiments, if necessary, dropping back squadrons in échelon for flank protection. The rapid delivery of attacks from approach formations should be practised.

165. *Training in fire tactics.*

1. It must be impressed on the men that ability to hit the target on the range, to judge distance accurately and to make intelligent use of cover, are by themselves insufficient to insure success when fighting dismounted.

In addition, the principles laid down for the fire tactics of cavalry must be understood and constantly applied, and men must be trained to work rapidly under the direction of their leaders, and to support each other.

2. To train troops effectively in dismounted fighting it is necessary to make free use of both ball ammunition for field firing, and blank ammunition in tactical exercises and manœuvres.

Ball firing as compared with blank has the advantages of providing practice in aiming and in judging distance; it teaches the difficulties of shooting accurately over unknown ranges, and the importance of observing fire. On the other hand, the danger entailed by the use of ball ammunition precludes the use of opposing forces; is apt to curtail the initiative of subordinates; and further tends to limit the possibilities of teaching the employment of flanking or converging fire and of combining fire action with shock action. Field firing is of more value for small than for large forces.

The use of blank ammunition avoids the disadvantages of ball mentioned above, and, though it affords no instruction in accurate shooting, it is a valuable means of teaching tactics.

Commanders must make use of both methods, each of which supplements the other, in teaching their commands. In both cases the schemes must be pre-arranged with care after a thorough study of the ground.

3. Leaders must be taught to give their men sufficient time to see the target and to adjust their sights, and the men must be made to realize the disadvantages of opening fire prematurely.

4. Special attention should be paid to the protection of the flanks of a dismounted force.

5. Machine guns and horse artillery should be practised in supporting cavalry dismounted action whenever opportunities can be made.

6. As far as possible the supply of ammunition (Sec. **219**) should be practised during exercises in the field.

166. *The training of the machine gun section.*

1. The tactical instruction of the machine gun section will commence as soon as the second period of the training of the section (*see* Sec. **11**) has been completed.

The instruction must be based on the general principles laid down (*see* Sec. **225** to Sec. **236**) and should be carried out away from barracks.

2. The main features of this training will be :—
    i. Instruction in the selection of fire positions and in bringing the machine guns into action rapidly, both from limbered wagons and pack equipment.
    ii. Instruction in fire control, in the various methods of fire, and in the use of combined sights.
    iii. To practise the combination of machine gun fire with the shock action of cavalry.
    iv. To practise the co-operation of machine guns with dismounted cavalry.

PART II.—WAR.

CHAPTER VII.

GENERAL PRINCIPLES OF THE EMPLOYMENT OF CAVALRY IN WAR.

167. *The functions and characteristics of the arm.*

1. An efficient cavalry is of incalculable value to an army. The wide fronts on which armies operate and the large number of troops employed make it more difficult than formerly to change dispositions that have once been made. Early and accurate information is therefore of greater importance than ever to a commander, and cavalry is one of the chief means at his disposal for obtaining it. Without cavalry the other arms are hampered by ignorance of the enemy's movements, cannot move in security, are unable to reap effectually the fruits of victory, and have great difficulty in extricating themselves in case of failure.

Frequent opportunities will also occur for successful cavalry action in co-operation with the other arms in a general engagement, where the absorption of the contest, the extended formations adopted by the infantry, and the exhaustion entailed by the continued strain of battle combine to render artillery and infantry peculiarly susceptible to sudden and unforeseen attacks by mounted men.

Furthermore the possible results to be attained by successful
raids against an enemy's communications have always been
great, and have not been decreased by the dependence of modern
armies upon railways.

2. The principal characteristics of cavalry are the power to
move with rapidity, to fight when moving, to seize fleeting
opportunities, and to cover long distances in a short time.

168. *The command and leading of cavalry.*

1. The system of command must always be methodical, and
the necessary arrangements and orders for any operation must
be as clearly and carefully issued as circumstances will permit.

2. The characteristics of the arm often allow but little time
for consideration. Rapid decisions must often be made under
most unfavourable conditions, and executed at once without
detailed instructions or explanations.

In many cases it will be impossible for the cavalry commander to gauge, with any degree of accuracy, the strength and
dispositions of his adversary, and his orders can then be based
only on a general consideration of the circumstances.

3. A force once scattered is most difficult to concentrate.
Detachments, therefore, must be kept down to a minimum, and
it is the duty of the commander of any detachment, the moment
his special mission has been accomplished, to move on his own
initiative to rejoin the main body, subject to the general
principle that, in reconnaissance, touch with an enemy when
once obtained should not be lost without orders from superior
authority. This latter principle, however, is one which cannot
always be observed in the case of troops, especially patrols,
charged with a special mission. It may then be impossible to
keep under observation hostile forces, encountered on the way,
without endangering the success of the special mission.

4. Though cavalry is often able by its own fire power to create opportunities for a charge, on the battlefield it is the fire of the other arms that will usually make the opportunity for the charge, except in case of complete surprise. Cavalry officers must therefore understand the principles which govern the movements and action of the other arms in the field.

5. Every commander is responsible for the protection of his command against surprise. The principles of protection are given in " F.S. Regs., Part I.," Chapter V.

169. *Economy of horseflesh in the field.*

1. All ranks should appreciate the power that the horse confers on the arm. They must understand how to use his power to the utmost when occasion requires, and how to spare it in every possible way at other times.

In normal conditions, demands must not be made upon cavalry which would only be justified in moments of crisis. The exceptional demands which either pursuit or retreat may make upon the endurance of the horses must never be forgotten by the cavalry commander. The employment of troops on operations of secondary importance must not be allowed to use up the means of action at decisive moments.

Opportunities to feed, water, and rest should if possible be given to men and horses even during the progress of the battle.

Except in warm climates commanders should endeavour to make use of billets to shelter their horses instead of bivouacs.

2. In order to avoid weakening a body of cavalry, a wise economy with regard to the performance of protective and orderly duties is essential. Whenever possible, messengers should be mounted on bicycles or other mechanical means of transport rather than upon horses. A rational system of communication towards the rear, whereby horseflesh is saved, is important in the case of cavalry acting in advance of an army.

3. The power of operating depends largely on suitable arrangements for subsistence. It is therefore one of the most important tasks of a cavalry commander either to ensure the timely arrival of supply columns or to use systematically the resources of the district in which he is operating; for it is on the latter system that a force of cavalry will often have to rely when at a distance from its main body. (*See* Sec. **240.**)

170.   *The sub-division of the duties of cavalry.*

1. The commander-in-chief in order to gain full value from that arm must clearly determine what he requires from it, and group his units accordingly in a suitable manner and in sufficient strength.

2. When cavalry is employed in the service of protection, it is to a certain extent bound to the force it covers. When, on the other hand it is employed for any purpose requiring a considerable degree of independence, it is usually inadvisable to hamper its freedom of action by imposing upon it any responsibility for the protection of its own army, for it is not possible for a body of troops to carry out an independent rôle while its commander at the same time is compelled to subordinate his plans to the movements of another force.

3. Mounted troops when detailed to carry out general protective duties are called for the time being " protective mounted troops "; while those employed on work necessitating their release from protective duties are designated " independent cavalry."

4. It will depend mainly upon the general situation and upon the strategical object in view, whether the greater part of the cavalry is employed in the first instance upon protective or other duties. When the first consideration is to obtain accurate information as to the dispositions and strength of the hostile army, the commander-in-chief will usually send

forward as strong a body of cavalry as possible upon a mission of reconnaissance. When, on the other hand, the first consideration is to cover a concentration or to conceal movements and intentions from the enemy, the greater part of the force will be employed on the protective mission.

5. One of the factors which govern the question as to whether a body of cavalry should be sent forward on a reconnoitring mission or not, and at the same time regulates generally the distance from the main army at which it should operate, is that information is likely to be of little value unless the main army is in a position to profit by it before the situation has changed materially. For example, an extended reconnaissance by a large force of cavalry undertaken at a time when the main army was engaged in concentrating and could not modify its movements in consequence of information received, might entail efforts out of proportion to the probable results, and, unless special reasons existed to justify the expenditure of energy involved, it would probably be wiser, under such conditions, to hold the mass of cavalry in hand until a more favourable opportunity for its action arose.

6. At any time circumstances may arise which make it necessary for the cavalry to be regrouped ; for the cavalry which has been acting independently to assume a protective rôle and *vice versâ*, or for either body to reinforce or merge into the other. Even without orders from superior authority the respective commanders of the independent cavalry and protective mounted troops should always seize any opportunities that may offer of co-operating in furtherance of the commander-in-chief's plan, but with due regard to the special responsibilities allotted to each.

7. In a force composed of one or more divisions it is usual to allot a proportion of the mounted troops to divisional duties. These troops are known as the divisional mounted troops and generally form a permanent part of the division (Sec. **173**),

x 25119 B

171. *The independent cavalry.*

1. When the independent cavalry has been allotted a mission of reconnaissance by the commander-in-chief, it will push forward into, or, according to circumstances, on the flank of, the zone separating the two armies according to the direction in which it is desired to reconnoitre. Such reconnoitring patrols and detachments will be despatched as may be considered necessary for the object in view.

The number and strength of these detachments, which must be as few as is compatible with the attainment of the object in view, will vary with the circumstances of each case. (*See* Sec. **184.**)

2. In carrying out its special mission the independent cavalry is likely to find itself opposed by the hostile cavalry in strength, or so threatened by the proximity of the latter that it cannot venture to ignore it. In such circumstances it will usually be advisable, or perhaps necessary, to concentrate every effort, for the moment, on defeating the hostile cavalry. If this can be accomplished, the power of carrying out the special mission allotted will be increased and a considerable moral advantage will be gained. It must always be remembered, however, that, when carrying out a special mission, the defeat of the hostile cavalry is merely a means to an end, and that it is not justifiable to turn aside from the primary object to seek an encounter which, even if successful, cannot appreciably further the attainment of that object.

3. When the enemy's cavalry is met in such superior force as to render a victory over it very doubtful the wisest course may be to endeavour to attain the object in view by refusing a decisive encounter; or, while manœuvring to attract its attention, to entrust the special mission to patrols or detachments.

4. When it is judged expedient, as a means to an end, to undertake the defeat of the hostile cavalry, every endeavour should be made to find or create a favourable opportunity for a vigorous attack with as little delay as possible. Dismounted action may often be usefully employed in connection with the plan of ultimate vigorous mounted attack, but it is from the

latter that the most rapid, decisive, and far-reaching results are to be expected.

5. Besides reconnaissance other special tasks may be assigned to cavalry acting independently, such as intercepting the enemy's movements, raiding his communications, seizing important points, operating so as to deceive and delay the enemy. It is rarely possible, however, for the same body of cavalry to carry out effectively more than one task at a time.

6. From what has been said above it is clear that the circumstances affecting the execution of duties other than that of protection are likely to be so varied, so difficult to foresee, and so liable to change that the commander of an army should normally content himself with giving definite instructions as to the particular task the cavalry commander is to perform, and leaving him such freedom of action in accomplishing it as is possible with due regard to other considerations. Clear instructions must always be given to the cavalry commander, however, as to any special considerations to be borne in mind in addition to the execution of the particular task allotted, e.g., instructions as to the probable time and place of a general action and as to whether the need for the cavalry to be present thereat is to override the necessity for the execution of the task allotted.

7. Only the most general principles regarding the dispositions of a force of independent cavalry can be enunciated. The service of reconnaissance requires a certain measure of dispersion, whereas tactical success demands concentration. A commander has to decide, according to the particular circumstances of the operations, how far it is desirable for him to scatter and how far to concentrate his command to achieve his object. In coming to a decision he should bear in mind the necessity for employing as few men as possible on detached duties.

172. *The protective rôle of cavalry.*

1. An army may be covered either by a general advanced guard, by a body of protective mounted troops operating in front of the tactical advanced guards of the various columns, or by both. The strength and composition of a general advanced guard will

be determined by the commander-in-chief, according to the purposes for which it is required. It will usually be composed of all arms, and will include either the whole or part of the protective mounted troops. When no general advanced guard is formed, the protective mounted troops will usually be under the direct orders of the commander of the force it covers.

2. The following are among the duties which may be allotted to the protective mounted troops :—

    i. To afford the commander of the force it may be covering timely information regarding the enemy's movements and the front which he is covering.

    ii. To furnish information regarding tactical features, resources, and roads of the country in advance of the main body.

    iii. To oppose hostile enterprises and prevent the enemy obtaining information regarding the movements of the columns in rear.

      The protective mounted troops may also be employed to seize and hold positions in front of the slower moving infantry, and deny their occupation to the enemy until the main body arrives.

3. As the duty of the protective mounted troops is to secure tactical liberty of action for the force they are covering. they must be sufficiently far ahead to give the commander of the latter time to form his plan of action and to deploy his force for battle.

4. Whilst the opposing armies are at a distance from one another, the commander of a general advanced guard in disposing his force will usually employ his cavalry for reconnaissance, and his infantry as supports; he must, however, always ensure intimate co-operation between all portions of his force so as to utilize his whole available strength when necessary.

Similarly the protective mounted troops, when operating by themselves, should be so disposed as to make effective action, as a whole, possible, should circumstances require it; that is to say, a large portion should as a rule be kept as concentrated as the nature of its duties will admit, and patrols, suitably supported, should be pushed along all the approaches by which hostile bodies might advance.

5. Protective mounted troops will generally move in bounds from one favourable position to another on the principle described in Sec. **196.** Occasionally, however, it may be advisable to maintain a line of observation on one line until the new line of observation is taken up, but before adopting this method of advance the commander should consider fully the possible danger of defeat in detail that may be incurred by such procedure.

6. When the heads of the opposing armies are drawing near each other, it becomes the duty of cavalry, assisted by the other arms to clear up the tactical situation by driving in the enemy's protective troops. This will involve offensive action and will usually be the work of all the mounted troops available.

173.   *Divisional mounted troops.*

1. On the line of march the duties of the divisional mounted troops are to assist the infantry in the immediate protection of the division by supplying mounted men for patrolling in connection with advanced guards, flank guards, rear guards, and outposts; to maintain connection with the protective mounted troops or general advanced guard and with neighbouring columns; to furnish escorts, orderlies, despatch riders, and to facilitate intercommunication generally.

2. The divisional mounted troops will be of great assistance when employed with advanced, flank, or rear guards, for their mobility enables them to examine a wide extent of ground and thus save the infantry much exhausting work. When attached to infantry outposts they may be employed for reconnaissance or as protective patrols. When communication within the outposts cannot be maintained by signalling or the use of cyclists, the divisional cavalry will furnish sufficient mounted men with the supports and the reserves for the purpose.

3. When a division is in action, the duties of its divisional mounted troops are to watch carefully and patrol the flanks and rear; to reconnoitre localities which may be held by the enemy;

and when necessary to assist the signal company in maintaining communication with neighbouring forces.

4. In order to spare the horses of the divisional mounted troops great economy must be exercised in the employment of mounted orderlies and despatch riders. Orderlies must be returned punctually to their units and should not be employed for duties other than those for which they were detailed. Cyclists should be used instead of mounted messengers whenever the situation and the ground permit.

5. In detailing divisional mounted troops for the various duties described above, the advantages of retaining a portion of these troops under the hand of the divisional commander as a mobile reserve must not be overlooked.

174. *Cavalry during the preliminary phases of a general engagement.*

1. As opposing armies get into close touch with each other, each commander will require as definite information as is possible regarding his opponents' strength and dispositions before he commits his main army to battle. In order to ensure complete and timely information of the enemy's dispositions, a carefully organized and extensive system of reconnoitring detachments will be necessary at this stage on the part of the cavalry. If the hostile cavalry is still formidable, the number of these reconnoitring detachments will be limited by the necessity of maintaining a concentrated group of cavalry and horse artillery in readiness to meet it.

2. At this stage the sphere of action of the independent cavalry and of the protective mounted troops will to some extent coincide, and some regrouping in accordance with the commander-in-chief's plan will be necessary. As the opposing main forces gain touch, the cavalry will be compelled to clear the front and concentrate on one or both flanks. The timing of this movement and the selection of the areas within which the cavalry is to operate may have great effect upon the subsequent development of the battle. In choosing these areas the commander-in-chief must consider both his general plan of action and the configuration of the

ground. The larger masses of cavalry should usually be concentrated in such a position that they can assist to the full in the decisive phase of the battle. In choosing this position the commander should bear in mind that close and intersected ground is less suitable than more open country for the action of cavalry in masses.

It is important therefore that these factors should be weighed, both in any regrouping of the cavalry which may be ordered, and in the arrangements for the close reconnaissance of the enemy.

3. In carrying out this reconnaissance, it may be necessary for a portion of the cavalry to anticipate the enemy by occupying positions of importance; whilst other portions manœuvre to delay his advance. Thus part of the cavalry may be engaged in supporting scouts and patrols, and part may be holding tactical points, and in this manner forming a screen, behind which the commander-in-chief will be able to conceive and develop his plan of action in accordance with information obtained.

175. *The co-operation of cavalry with the other arms in battle.*

1. When the preparation for the engagement has developed, and the main body of infantry closes with the enemy, the cavalry will be compelled to clear the front. The groups of cavalry in the front line will be replaced by infantry, each group rallying to its own main body, so as to be prepared for action when opportunity offers.

In these circumstances it is the duty of the commanders of cavalry units, directly they are relieved, to withdraw their commands to concentration points without delay or confusion To this end they should anticipate relief by withdrawing men who can be spared from the firing line to the supports, by reconnoitring routes, and by warning subordinates to be ready to vacate their positions.

They should also collect and pass on to the officers who relieve them as much information as they can concerning the local situation, the enemy's dispositions, and the ground in the vicinity. When possible this information should be conveyed by a personal interview.

2. The rôle of the cavalry after being relieved by the infantry will depend on circumstances. It may be used to operate against the enemy's flanks and so incidentally protect the flanks of its own army; to assist in enveloping movements; to delay the approach of hostile columns; or to deceive the enemy as to the commander's plan of action. In all circumstances it must be at hand when wanted, and available to act at the point which offers the best tactical chances and the prospect of decisive results.

3. The conditions which favour the mounted action of cavalry upon the battlefield have been described in Sec. **167**. Cavalry can seldom hope to reduce an enemy to a state of moral and physical degeneration. This condition must be produced by the attacks of the other arms. Cavalry must therefore keep in the closest touch with the other arms and take advantage of their progress, offering them such help as it can from its guns and rifles, and supplementing their decisive attack by sweeping the battlefield with its squadrons. Any success gained by the guns and infantry is thus extended far beyond the actual position captured; and the fruits of victory can be reaped.

4. The position of the cavalry commander is important, for he must be able to seize an opportunity for effective action when it occurs. In the absence of orders from higher authority, it rests with him to recognize the right moment to take part in the combat, and he must therefore be so placed that he can watch carefully the course of the battle, if necessary taking up his position at a considerable distance from his command. In his endeavour to act without delay he must be careful that his command is not committed prematurely or in confusion. He must arrange to reconnoitre beforehand all ground over which the cavalry may have to act, and to take such steps as may be possible to make it more suitable for the movement of cavalry, *e.g.* by opening gates, cutting wire fences, ramping ditches and so forth. His orders must be clearly given, objectives clearly pointed out to subordinates, his force duly detailed in accord-

ance with these objectives, and moved and deployed as far as possible under cover, before he launches his attack. His point of observation must be connected with the commander of the main force and other divisional commanders by field telegraph, telephone, signalling, or despatch riders. At times it will be desirable for him to detach one of his own staff to the headquarters of the main force or, if necessary, to the headquarters of the neighbouring divisions in order to keep him in touch with the course of the operations as a whole, and to ensure that someone with headquarters is conversant with the cavalry situation.

In order that the cavalry commander may be kept informed of all that is going on in his sphere of action, officers (in addition to the necessary patrols) should be sent out into those sections of ground which he cannot overlook himself.

5. Surprise by large masses of cavalry may seldom be feasible ; but small bodies which, by taking advantage of the ground and of the absorption of the enemy's attention in the battle, can remain in the close vicinity of the troops engaged, will often be able to take the opposing troops unawares, and if employed vigorously on a favourable opportunity, may effect results out of all proportion to their numbers. Masses of cavalry should be able, however, to achieve great results against troops which are worn out, demoralized, and obliged to leave their fighting positions.

In all hard-fought battles critical periods will supervene when a determined effort by one side or the other will result in victory. Such periods offer excellent opportunities for cavalry action, but they can only be seized if cavalry are employed in concentrated force. To bring about the defeat of an army, to reap the fruits of a great victory, or to cover a retreat, numbers are necessary.

Every cavalry officer should know how an infantry fight is conducted, be able to estimate the general course of an engagement, and recognize the consumption of the enemy's reserves and the gradual exhaustion, both moral and physical, of his troops.

Whilst opportunities must be seized without a moment's delay and exploited with the utmost determination, the temptation to undertake a charge must be resisted when it is likely to achieve no important results.

Distant action by the cavalry against the flank or rear of an enemy will very rarely influence the final issue, and will often result in wasting time and strength on petty combats with small protective detachments.

176. *Cavalry in pursuit.*

1. The pursuit is the special duty of cavalry, and the demands which it will make upon the horses must be kept in mind by the commander of the army as well as by the cavalry commander during the earlier phases of the action.

An energetic pursuit is the only means by which the full fruits of victory can be gathered; it must be undertaken with every available man, and must be continued until the enemy is completely scattered.

2. Whether the cavalry should break through gaps in the hostile line, or operate on one or both flanks, will depend entirely on the circumstances of the fight. In most cases, however, direct pursuit will be undertaken by the infantry; pursuit on lines parallel to the enemy's retreat is usually most effective for mounted troops, who, on account of their mobility, may repeatedly attack the flanks of the enemy, with the ultimate intention of anticipating him at some point on his line of retreat.

3. When pressing a retreating enemy, cavalry should as a rule move by several parallel or converging routes, so that if the enemy makes a stand and succeeds in checking one portion of the pursuers, other portions will be available at once to turn and attack his flanks.

4. It is important that the cavalry should gain and retain touch with the enemy's main columns, and keep the commander informed of their movements.

177. *Cavalry in retreat.*

1. If a withdrawal becomes necessary, cavalry must act energetically to gain time, and must endeavour to delay the enemy's advance by every means possible (*see* " Field Service Regulations, Part I.," Sec. 72).

2. The commander will determine, in accordance with the features of the ground, whether delay is best brought about by the occupation of positions blocking or flanking the enemy's line of advance, and whether the employment of fire action only, a combination of fire and mounted action, or a vigorous and timely mounted attack will be the most effective.

3. The power of combining fire action with mobility gives cavalry great delaying power. It enables cavalry to deceive the enemy as to the nature of the force by which it is opposed and to act swiftly from any direction. An enemy whose flanks are threatened by a force of cavalry acting in this manner may be forced to make detachments and hesitate in his advance.

The offensive is nearly always more effective than the defensive; it will often be better to attack the enemy than to rely solely on passive defence in a succession of rear guard positions.

4. The enemy's advance will be greatly delayed should a portion of his leading troops be caught in an ambush and destroyed. After a lesson of this nature the pursuers for some time afterwards will advance with increased caution and the pressure on the rear guard will in consequence be relieved.

5. Special precautions should always be taken to watch and secure the flanks, and the retention of some portion of the force in hand in case of emergency is essential.

6. It is the duty of cavalry throughout a retreat to keep the commander informed of the movements of the enemy's columns, for there are few greater causes of anxiety than ignorance of a pursuing enemy's movements.

178. *Raids.*

1. Raids are only permissible when they do not interfere with the concentration of superior force at the right time and at the

right place and when the objects, if accomplished, are of sufficient importance to compensate for the consequent exhaustion of the horses' strength.

A raid which prevents a strong hostile force of the enemy from reaching the battlefield in time, or seriously impairs the efficiency of the enemy in battle by preventing the arrival of much needed ammunition or supplies may be justifiable. On the other hand a raid which may keep the cavalry from the battlefield without containing at least a corresponding force of the enemy should not be undertaken.

In no circumstances should cavalry be given a roving commission to cause damage and destruction in the rear of the hostile forces. A raid should only be undertaken for a definite and adequate purpose; the commander of a raiding force should therefore be given a definite objective.

2. As surprise and rapidity of action are the two essential factors of a successful raid, small forces will often be successful where larger ones would fail. Horses and men must be specially selected; they should be employed, however, as units under their own officers, the least suitable being picked out and left behind. Transport must be reduced to a minimum and the force must for the most part live on the country. The commander must be prepared moreover to abandon his transport should he find its presence detrimental to the accomplishment of his purpose.

3. As far as possible the proposed route should be secretly reconnoitred before the raid is begun, so that the danger of unexpected delays may be minimized.

4. When a raid on an important railway line is in question, it must be remembered that the line in all probability will be strongly guarded at all vulnerable points, such as important bridges and tunnels, and watched by patrols and armoured trains, that little damage is done by removing a few sleepers or rails and that to effect a considerable interruption of the traffic the destruction of an important bridge or tunnel is generally necessary.

CHAPTER VIII.

MOVEMENTS.

(See also "F.S. Regs. Part I." *and* " Animal Management.")

179. *Marches.*

1. The power of making long and rapid marches without loss in numbers or energy is one of the chief factors of success in war. This power is maintained by enforcing strict march discipline and by the exercise of constant care for the welfare of the horses.

2. Before commencing a march commanders of squadrons and troops should make certain that the saddlery is correct, that the shoeing has been properly attended to, and that all the horses are fit for the march.

They should see that materials such as bandages or old putties are taken to prevent or cure rope galls and for horses, whose legs require bandaging. A small supply of numnah and blanket material should be taken to make any slight alterations that may be required in the saddling of horses whose backs show signs of too much pressure in one place.

3. If it is not likely to be possible to water the horses during the first few hours of the march, a very early start should be avoided, for horses will not usually drink very early in the morning.

Even when marching at a very early hour a small feed should always be given before starting.

4. Sufficient time should be allowed each morning for the men to saddle up carefully, but on no account should horses be saddled up an unnecessarily long time before starting, and left with their saddles on.

Before starting, the men and horses should be inspected in order to make certain that the horses are properly saddled and bridled and that no unauthorised articles are carried on man or horse.

5. The length of a day's march may be reckoned at from 20 to 25 miles. If proper care is taken, a forced march of from 40 to 50 miles may be made occasionally without serious detriment to the efficiency of the horses and men; but marches of such length should not be undertaken without urgent reasons.

6. Whenever circumstances permit, the men should march on foot, leading the horses, for fifteen minutes or more in every hour.

When the horses are being led they should be kept as close to the edge of the road as possible so as to avoid blocking the traffic. The usual distance between horses from head to croup should be maintained.

7. To enable men to look round their horses and saddles, a short halt should be made about a quarter or half-an-hour after starting or as soon as day has broken. Subsequently halts of about fifteen minutes' duration should be made every two hours when circumstances permit. During a long march a halt should usually be made after four hours to water and feed the horses. Whenever a halt is made all horses should be allowed to graze as much as possible. During long halts the horses should be off-saddled and their backs hand-rubbed. During short halts girths may be loosened and the saddle eased. When troops halt, the commander should give out at once the duration of the halt, so that the men may know exactly at what mtime they ust be ready to march again. Whenever a halt is made the men should be ordered at once to dismount. When in the vicinity of the enemy, the rate of marching and the number and duration of halts will depend upon tactical considerations.

8. As a general rule the rate of march should be about five miles an hour, including short halts.

Only when the tactical situation imperatively demands it, should the rate of the trot exceed eight miles an hour.

Owing to the fact that the route will seldom be quite flat and that in the neighbourhood of the enemy the tactical situation may compel a force to move in bounds from one favourable position to another, no exact time table can be laid down, and each march will have to be arranged to suit the country and the tactical requirements.

Troops should usually trot when the ground is level and walk or lead when going up or down hill.

Except when engaged with the enemy each squadron commander should change the pace of his squadron at the same point on the road where the squadron in front changed its pace.

The last two miles or so of a day's march should always be traversed at a walk, so as to allow the horses to cool.

9. In all circumstances when marching an even pace should be maintained throughout a column, in order that the fatigue caused by repeated increases of pace and sudden checks may be avoided. The officer leading the column must proceed at a uniformly even pace. He should never, unless specially ordered, move faster than the normal rate, and if the column is of any length, he should move slightly slower.

If a good look-out is kept, everyone should be able to anticipate variations in pace when they occur, and be prepared to lessen the suddenness of them. If a sudden check is unavoidable men should usually pull out across the road, so as to avoid running into the horses in front of them, and at the same time passing the check the whole way down the column, but this should not be done if there is a risk of blocking the road.

10. When any body of mounted troops is approaching a defile, to pass which it is necessary to diminish the front, the leading body or bodies should trot on, cross the defile, and clear such a distance beyond it as will obviate any delay or obstruction, then halt if necessary, for the remainder. This applies to each successive body in rear.

11. To avoid tiring the horses the men should sit square and steady in the saddle whether sitting *at attention* or *at ease.*

No man should quit his stirrups, and when trotting each man should rise in them. The correct places in the ranks should always be maintained.

When dismounting the rifle must never be left on the saddle.

Men should notice and report the least signs of any injury to their horses. A small lump on the horses' backs, if noticed in time, can generally be relieved at once by altering the fold of the blanket or by changing the saddle or rider. Whereas, if no notice is taken, and the horse worked as before, a sore back will result in a few hours. A loose shoe should be attended to at once.

A tired horse may brush, but if at the first signs of this happening a brushing boot is fitted, and when there is time his shoeing altered, he can be kept at work.

12. Whenever possible, both when on the march or when halted, the right of the road should be left clear for other traffic. In all cases sufficient room will be left for the passage of staff officers, orderlies, &c.

Occasionally it may be advantageous to march on both sides of the road, leaving a free passage down the centre, but this method of marching should not be adopted unless the road is exceptionally wide and clear of traffic or has good grass borders, If a halt takes place on such occasions, those men on the right of the road should usually be moved over to the left before they dismount.

Horses should never be halted on a bridge, or in a gateway or ford.

When halted in narrow roads the horses' heads should be turned towards the centre of the road.

13. To ensure that each body of troops marches correctly, an officer or N.C.O. should march in rear of each unit. In rear of every force of cavalry there should be a small rear group with farriers attached, which will collect all men who have fallen out

and keep them in rear until the main body makes its next halt, when they will re-join their units.

14. Good march discipline is as important with the transport as it is with the fighting troops, for the mobility of cavalry is largely dependent upon the mobility of its transport.

No unauthorized person should be allowed to ride on the wagons. Officers' servants and all other men marching with transport should always move in formed bodies under the command of a N.C.O.

It will often fall to the lot of mounted troops to assist transport in difficulties caused by the fatigue of the draught animals or by the nature of the roads. In these circumstances it is of great importance not to let a wagon or cart stop while crossing a bad place. Squads of men should be placed at the specially bad places to assist in turn the teams which show signs of stopping.

180. *Entraining and detraining.*

1. The floors of trucks used for the conveyance of horses should be at least 1½ inches thick. Cinders, sand or gravel should be sprinkled on them to prevent the horses slipping; on no account should straw or any inflammable material be used for this purpose.

2. The force to be entrained should be told off in groups according to the number of horses to be entrained in each truck. When there is sufficient room, each group should be formed up in single rank at right angles to its allotted truck; when sufficient space is not available, each group should be formed facing its truck. The men then put down their kits. If they have formed at right angles to the train, the kits will be in front of the horses and, if facing the train, the kits will be in rear. When the horses are to be entrained saddled, sword and scabbards, bits and nose bags should be removed; in taking the sword off, the shoe case should also be removed. Bridoon reins should be taken

over the horses' heads, the end being slipped through the throat lash and again passed over the heads.

3. The entrainment should be carried out without noise or violence, so that the horses do not become excited or obstinate. The first horse to enter a truck should be the quietest available, and the man leading him should walk quietly in without looking round; the remainder should follow the leader immediately, any horse giving trouble being kept to the last. The horses should be led into the back and front ends of the truck alternately and secured by the head ropes to the truck rails. Nose bags should be secured to the truck rails in rear of the horses.

4. After the horses are loaded the men fall in by their arms and are told off in groups according to the number of men conveyed in each carriage. They are then marched to their carriages and entrain.

5. When entraining vehicles the loads should be distributed equally over the truck floors, and if any flooring planks are rotten, sleepers should be put across them under the wheels. The minimum thickness of floor should be two inches.

The wheels nearest to the ends of the trucks should be securely lashed to the false buffers or to rings. The lashing should be given a turn round the axletree of each pair of wheels on the truck to prevent the jolting of the train causing any movement. The poles of four-wheeled wagons, except limbered wagons, should be lashed to the upper part of the wagon on entrainment. All two-wheeled and limbered wagons should be entrained with their poles in position. The points of poles or shafts should not protrude far enough to strike against bridges or the sides of tunnels; the maximum height of the load above the truck floor should not exceed eight feet.

6. The men detrain with their arms and kits, and, if the unit is going to embark, they march straight on board to stow their kits before taking the horses out of the train. If not for embarkation, they place their kits in line outside their horse trucks and commence detraining at once.

181. *Embarkation by means of horse-brows.*

1. Before embarkation begins it should be ascertained that the way to the furthest stall is quite clear, and that the brows and decks offer secure foothold. The foothold may be improved by putting down coir mats, ashes or sand; the coir mats should be securely fastened, for if loose they slip under the feet.

2. The men after detraining should fall in with their arms and kits. They should be then marched on board to stow their arms and kits. They then return to the train, unbox the horses and fasten the nose bags round the horses' necks. Horses should be led along the horse-brow by the head rope, the man walking in front and holding the rope at its full length in order that the horse may have his head as free as possible.

If the brow is at a steep downward angle, the horses should be sent down with head rope undone and hanging down, and should be caught by men at the bottom of the brow.

182. *Slinging horses.*

i. *Transports alongside.*

1. When horses are to be embarked by slinging, the rifle buckets and swords must be removed; the head-rope should be fastened in the ordinary way round the neck; the ship's halter will be put on under the head-collar; the bridoon reins should be left loose (as they may be required for keeping the head in the proper position while lowering down the hatchways), but they should be knotted to prevent them getting entangled in the horse's legs, the surcingle must be moved round so that the buckle is on the seat of the saddle and not under the horse's belly. Slings should be minutely inspected before the embarkation begins. A double guy should be made fast to the horse's head, one end being held on shore and the other on board, in order to keep the head steady.

2. In slinging horses, five men are required, one at the head, one at each side, one at the breast, and one behind. One end of

the sling is passed under the horse's belly, and both ends are
brought up to meet over his back; one man passes his loop
through the other loop, and it is received by the man on the
other side, who hauls it through, hooking the tackle to it, both
men holding up the ends of the sling until it is taut. The men
at the breast and behind bring their ropes round and make them
fast to the grummets, and the man who holds the horse's head
makes fast the guys to the ship's head-collar. The breech band
and breast girth must be securely fastened. Timid or restive
horses should be blindfolded. When all is ready, the word
" HOIST AWAY " will be given, and the horse is to be rapidly run
up from the ground to the necessary height, and then carefully
lowered down to the hatchway. Two or three men should be
stationed at the hatchway and between decks to guide the horse
in being lowered. A soft bed of coir mats must be provided for
the horse to alight upon, and the men stationed in the lower
deck must be ready to receive him and take off the sling, as on
first feeling his legs he is apt to plunge and kick violently unless
firmly handled.

3. In disembarking, sand should be laid on the wharf for the
reception of the horses. Horses are apt to fall on their knees at
once unless carefully held up.

ii. *Transports not alongside.*

4. The method of embarking horses in boats or flats will vary
according to circumstances. If the boats can come alongside a
wharf, or can approach close to an open beach, the horses can
either be led on board by gangways, or be slung in the manner
described above, sheers or a derrick being erected. When the
boats cannot come sufficiently near the shore to enable horses to
be hoisted on to them, piers or platforms must be constructed.
The piers should always be provided with stout side railings
about three feet high, and the floor covered with shingle,
cinders, or sand to prevent the horses slipping.

5. When embarking in boats, the detachment should be formed up opposite them, and the same rules, so far as practicable, followed as when embarking in vessels alongside a wharf. A man must be told off to each horse, and take with him in the boat the whole of his kit, equipment, saddlery, &c. The men should take off arms, belts, and spurs. The horses should, if possible, be placed athwart the boat alternately, the head to tail. Each man must hold his horse until the vessel is reached. Sand or straw should be put in the boats to prevent the horses slipping.

6. In the absence of boats and appliances, the following method of embarking horses by swimming may be employed:—

The horses having been halted a short distance from, and out of sight of, the point of embarkation, are stripped of all appointments except the bridoon and headstall, which latter should be close fitting.

A horse having been led to the landing place, two men prepare him for the water. No. 1 holds his head. No. 2 places the sling in position and secures the straps with yarn, so as to prevent the sling opening in the water; he then fastens the breast rope and breeching securely. A rope of about eight yards in length, with an eye at one end, is next passed round the neck and fastened rather tightly by an overhand knot, so as to prevent its becoming either looser or tighter. The bridoon is then taken off, and to support the horse in the water another rope is attached to the lower ring of the headstall under the chin, or else a short rope is passed round the girth in front of the sling and close behind the elbows, the ends being brought up and fastened over the withers. The horse is controlled altogether by the neck rope.

The horse is then led into the water as far as he will walk towards the boat, in the stern of which should be a man, who receives the neck rope in his right hand, and immediately reeves it through the stern ring of the boat to secure additional power in the event of the horse plunging; the headstall or girth rope he receives in his left hand.

When once the horse is swimming, the neck rope should be hauled close up while the headstall or girth rope gently supports him in the water.

A small rowing boat with two oars will be sufficient. It should not be pulled too fast, or the horse will make no attempt to swim.

On reaching the ship's side the hook and tackle should be lowered, the hook passed through the sling's eye, and the horse hoisted up on board.

Care should be taken to arrange the tackle so that the horse, in being hoisted in, is kept clear of the ship's side.

7. Horses may, in cases of emergency only, be disembarked by swimming. When this method is adopted, the horse should be lowered in the sling over the side of the vessel without fastening the breast rope or breeching. When the tackle is unhooked the sling opens, and is at once slipped from under the horse. The neck rope should be hauled up and secured, and the horse supported, as explained above. If necessary, four horses may be made to swim ashore as a time, two on each side of the boat. It is important that horses should be kept at the point to which the others are to swim.

Horses should be cool before being put into the water.

183. *Slinging guns and vehicles.*

1. The following is a useful method of slinging limbered wagons.

Two four-inch slings are used, one round each axletree, and a hook rope hooked into the trail eye. The bights of the sling are placed on the tackle hook, to which the end of the hook rope is also made fast.

Limbered wagon will, as a rule, be embarked loaded on their wheels, the poles should not be removed before slinging. If the wheels are removed, special care must be taken that the linch pins and washers are put away.

2. G.S. wagons can be slung by four chain slings connected to a common link at the one end and provided with hooks at the other, these four hooks are then secured to all four wheels of the vehicle. The poles must be removed before slinging, and *made fast to the body of the wagons.*

If cordage only is available, two slings, each consisting of one rope 3 in. by 60 ft., knotted at a suitable length, and two lashings, 1½ in. by 30 ft., for guy ropes are required.

To adjust the front sling pass one end inside the wheels and under the futchels of the fore carriage in front of the axle. To adjust the back sling loop one end of the sling over the nave of the off hind wheel. Pass the sling over the load and loop the other end to the nave of the near hind wheel. Care must be taken to see that the drag washers are turned down to prevent the sling from slipping off.

The hook of the hoisting tackle is then passed through the end of the two ends of the front sling and under the centre of the back sling.

The pressure can be taken off the sides of the carriage by making use of loops made with polechains or ropes at the end of poles through which the slings are passed.

CHAPTER IX.

INFORMATION AND INTERCOMMUNICATION.

(*See* also " Field Service Regulations, Part I," Chapter VI.)

184. *General principles.*

1. Strategical, tactical, and protective reconnaissance is carried out by means of patrols or detachments, the movements of which depend upon whether the reconnaissance is strategical or tactical, or whether it is protective. In the former case their operations should be based on the movements of the enemy, rather than on the immediate movements of the force from which they are detached.

In the latter case their movements must be based almost entirely on those of the force whose safety it is their duty to secure.

2. Patrols are the usual means by which cavalry endeavours to obtain information. A well-arranged service of protection on the part of the enemy or the presence of hostile inhabitants will, however, often stop patrols before they have gained their object. Unless supplemented by larger bodies ready to fight and make an opening for them to advance further, they will often be able to find out but little, or, should they succeed when unsupported in penetrating a protective line, they will be unable to send back their information.

In favourable circumstances skilfully handled reconnoitring patrols and small reconnoitring detachments may obtain information of value without the employment of force; but, as a rule, to carry out an effective reconnaissance, cavalry must be prepared to fight, and to fight successfully a certain concentration of force is necessary.

3. Throughout the service of reconnaissance economy of strength should be practised. It will be impossible to use officers as leaders of all patrols, generally speaking they should be employed only to lead those of particular importance.

4. The strength of a reconnoitring patrol should be limited; for the larger it is the more difficult will it be to escape observation. It should, however, be sufficiently strong to ensure that the information gained is transmitted without delay to the superior commanding to whom reports have to be furnished.

When a reconnoitring patrol is not in itself strong enough to get into a position from which it can observe, or to transmit its information back, a larger detachment should be sent in its place. Its rôle is to throw out patrols to which it acts as a support. It opens the way for the patrols, and forms a rallying point for them if required. It collects information by taking prisoners, seizing telegraph offices, etc., and forms stations for transmitting messages from their patrols to the rear.

The size of these detachments will depend largely on the number of patrols and the number and strength of the connecting posts they have to furnish; the distance they have to go; the resistance they are likely to meet; and the attitude of the inhabitants.

It is obvious, therefore, that their size cannot be fixed by rule, but must always be considered with reference to the task they have to perform and the condition under which they have to work.

5. The number of patrols and detachments sent out to reconnoitre will depend largely on the object in view. If the enemy's cavalry is still a fighting force, the number of detachments will be limited by the necessity of maintaining a contentrated group of cavalry and horse artillery in readiness to meet it.

6. Motor cars, motor cycles and cyclists will often be a useful addition to reconnoitring detachments. They should seldom be employed for obtaining information owing to their liability to

capture, but as despatch riders they may be of great use in relieving the horses of much exhausting work.

185. *The conduct of patrols.*

1. Patrols like all other bodies of mounted troops should move in bounds, covering the distance between good positions rapidly.

2. They should adopt such formations that if surprised by the enemy they cannot all be captured. Sometimes it may be advantageous to extend laterally; at others, when for instance the patrol is marching down a road with high fences on both sides, it may be better to extend from front to rear.

3. Protection should be arranged on all sides, as is the case with all bodies of troops of whatever size. As advanced guard one or two men may be pushed ahead of the patrol. The flanks and rear may often be sufficiently protected if different men riding with the patrol are made responsible for keeping a look out on each flank and to the rear, both when the patrol is moving and when it is halted.

4. Any place likely to harbour an ambush, such as a wood, ravine, or village, if it cannot be avoided, must be approached with caution. Scouts should be sent forward and round it before the whole patrol approaches within close range. It is usually best for advanced scouts to move quickly when near such a position, and to get round its flanks and rear as rapidly as possible, so as to discover the presence of any enemy concealed in or behind the position; but occasionally, when time is pressing, the point may be directed to gallop straight through a village. By moving fast the risk of being hit by the fire from an ambush is lessened.

5. When in the vicinity of the enemy patrols should vary the direction of the march when they get under cover, so that they emerge from the cover at a place where they are not expected by the enemy. In this way they lessen the risk of capture.

186. *The despatch of a reconnoitring patrol or larger detachment on an independent mission.*

1. The instructions of the commander of a force to his cavalry leaders should be definite and precise as to the information that is required and the localities to be reconnoitred. The cavalry commander will arrange for the despatch of the reconnoitring detachments to obtain the information required, and of any other detachments or patrols which he may think necessary.

2. The leader of a reconnoitring patrol or larger detachment should, when time permits, be given clear written orders, and in addition his mission should be explained to him verbally.

He should be told :—

   i. What is known of the enemy and of country in which he is to operate.

   ii. The probable moves of neighbouring reconnoitring detachments as far as they concern him.

   iii. What information is required.

   iv. Approximately to what distance and in what direction he must go.

   v. About how long he may expect to be away.

   vi. Where reports are to be sent and by what means.

He should be given an opportunity of considering his orders and of asking questions on any point that is not clear to him. He should then be left a free hand in carrying out his mission. Scouts before being sent out should receive similar instructions.

The written instructions given to the patrol leader should be destroyed before the patrol or detachment starts.

3. When patrols or reconnoitring detachments have to march considerable distances success will to a great extent depend on the careful preparations made by the patrol or detachment leader before starting.

Such questions as the time of starting, supplies, transport, water on the march, possible positions for connecting posts, must all be weighed, and a clearly defined plan of action must be adopted.

4. After receiving his instructions and forming his plan of action the leader should explain the whole, or as much as may be desirable, to his subordinates, so that every man may know how to carry on the duty in the event of accidents.

He should warn them that if captured they should refuse to give any information beyond stating their rank and name, and tell them that by international custom they cannot be punished for this refusal.

187. *The leading of a reconnoitring patrol or larger detachment sent on an independent mission.*

1. Common sense must guide the conduct of a reconnoitring detachment or patrol. The leader may make use of mobility, deception, force, or extreme boldness in order to obtain information; safety may be sought in mobility, secrecy, and a wise choice of routes. But to obtain the required information it is essential that he must not be drawn away from his mission.

The actual reconnaissance must as a rule be carried out by the leader of a patrol, the men who accompany him being employed to provide his protection and to transmit his messages.

2. The normal method of advance in daylight is to move rapidly from one suitable position to another, each time first feeling the way forward by patrols or scouts. By advancing in this manner the patrol or detachment is less liable to surprise and the leader obtains time for observation than would be possible if the patrol moved at a regular pace throughout the journey. The general rate of advance will depend on the proximity of the enemy and the nature of the country. When there is reasonable ground for belief that the enemy is at a distance, the advance may be rapid.

3. When operating in a country where the inhabitants are hostile, towns, villages and outlying houses should be avoided as much as possible.

If a village must be traversed, a few men should be sent ahead to skirt it and block the exits on the far side, thus preventing any inhabitant leaving with news of the arrival of the detachment.

4. Information will usually be obtained in the day-time; but, when it is impossible to move forward in day-light without being discovered, it may be necessary to reconnoitre by night, or to move by night up to the neighbourhood of the enemy, and to observe him by day from a concealed position.

5. When moving by day, every precaution must be taken to avoid being seen by the enemy, or by hostile inhabitants. Should the patrol come under the observation of the enemy, every effort must be made to mislead him as to the commander's intentions. When in the near neighbourhood of the enemy it may be advisable to avoid the roads where hoof marks or dust may betray the presence of the patrol. Scouts should keep in the shadows as much as possible by day or night. The light of the sun on a bright button or on the polished seat of a saddle may disclose the presence of an otherwise hidden patrol. Small reconnoitring parties should not rest all together in one place. The commander should post a few look-out men to watch in each direction. The men should rest by their horses. Halts for the night should be made in isolated woods or lonely farms, the inhabitants of which have been seized, and which the enemy's patrols are not likely to visit. If reconnoitring parties halt before darkness sets in, they should change their position after dark; it will usually be safer to change the position even when a halt is made after dark. Only a small percentage of horses should be off-saddled at a time, and as soon as a horse has fed he should be bitted. Reconnoitring parties should be clear of their night resting-places before day-break.

6. No man should carry any written instructions or private diaries or papers, such as might give information to an enemy.

In the presence of civilians, whether friendly or otherwise, no mention should be made of the direction from which the detachment or patrol has come or of the intended advance; it is often advisable to give the inhabitants false information.

7. A patrol on finding the enemy should as a rule send in a report and then, unless such action would be contrary to instructions, should follow him up. Detailed information as to his strength, dispositions, and moves, should then be sent in.

8. If the enemy is not found where he was expected, the reconnoitrer should think for himself as to what his commander would require him to do ; as a rule, negative information should be sent back.

9. Although patrols are not sent out with the primary object of fighting and although they should seldom do so if, without fighting, they can attain their object by a careful use of the ground, it must be clearly understood that if they suddenly meet small parties of the enemy the assumption of a resolute offensive will often be their best course of action.

10. If a patrol is cut off by the enemy its members must make every effort to get away, so that at least one may arrive back with the information already gained, if necessary scattering and rallying again at the last halting place if no other place has been previously chosen. Every member of a patrol, while advancing in an enemy's country, must take notice of land marks and distances as he goes along, so as to be able to find his way back. In moving back, he should seldom adhere actually to the road by which he came, as that may lead him into ambuscades. When working in the presence of any enemy, patrols must never cease their attempts to obtain the required information. They must be both bold and cunning, and if stopped at one point they must try again at some other.

11. During reconnaissances when the opposing armies are not far distant from each other it may often be advisable for a detachment to dismount and open fire in order to engage the enemy's attention, whilst it patrols move forward to suitable points for observation from which the attention of the enemy has been diverted.

12. Patrols and detachments sent to reconnoitre the enemy should always be prepared to be out for several days.

188. *Gaining information.*

1. Information may be gained by personal observation of the enemy; by questioning the inhabitants, prisoners and others; or by tapping telegraph wires, taking letters and newspapers from post offices, by observation of tracks, dust, fires, deserted camp-grounds, uniforms, etc.

2. In questioning prisoners and hostile inhabitants, it is as well that each should be examined separately out of hearing of the others. The questioner should, as a rule, endeavour to lead them to suppose that he knows more than he really does about the subject, and give the impression that to many of his questions he already knows the answers, but is putting them to test the truth of the speaker.

3. Men not accustomed to seeing large numbers of troops are apt to exaggerate their strength, a fault which a scout should be careful to avoid.

A scout should know what are the usual formations of the enemy, and what are the normal strengths of his various units.

Troops moving along a road or defile may be timed passing a certain point. For each minute, the following numbers would approximately go past:—

Cavalry at a walk, in sections	- -	120
Cavalry at a trot, in sections	-	240
Artillery guns, or wagons, at a walk	-	5
Infantry in fours -	- - -	200

Information as to the uniforms of the enemy, number of regiment on the buttons or badges, &c., may be of great use.

189. *Reports.*

1. Reports should be drawn up in accordance with "Field Service Regulations, Part I.," Chapter II.

2. The writer should avoid giving unnecessary detail and when time permits should give a summary if the report is long.

3. Indelible pencil should not be used, because messages written with it are unreadable if exposed to moisture. The writing should be so clear that it can be read easily in a bad light.

4. It is usually advisable to keep a copy of all messages sent, so that the writer can refer to his former messages and correct or confirm information already sent.

190. *Transmission of information.*

1. However valuable the information obtained by patrols or reconnoitring parties may be, it is of little use unless it reaches the commander of the force in time for him to act upon it. Great care, therefore, must be taken to ensure that all information is transmitted to its destination safely and rapidly.

2. Skilfully placed connecting posts will facilitate the transmission of information. Their number and strength will be regulated by the nature of the country, the attitude of the inhabitants, the proximity of the enemy, and the troops available.

As a general rule, whenever a reconnoitring detachment is to proceed a considerable distance, its commander should drop his own connecting posts as he advances.

These should be carefully hidden, well away from towns and villages, and close to water; at times, however, concealment may be impossible and they will be compelled to rely on force for their protection. In such circumstances the commander who establishes the post should be careful that its strength is sufficient for the task it has to perform.

Every man in the reconnoitring detachment should, if possible, know where connecting posts are situated.

3. The despatch rider should be a man of resource capable of finding his way across country. As a reconnoitring detachment advances, the despatch riders, who should be detailed beforehand, should have their attention drawn to all roads and other routes likely to be useful in their return journey.

4. The official to whom the despatch is addressed, and the place in which he may be found, must be explained clearly to the despatch rider.

It will often be advisable for despatch riders to work in pairs, for confidence is greatly increased by company. Important despatches must be sent in duplicate by different routes, and it may be advisable to employ officers to carry them.

5. All messengers on approaching a body of troops or group of officers should call out loudly and without hesitation the rank and name of the officer to whom the despatch or messages is to be delivered.

Mounted messengers should as a rule dismount immediately after handing a message to an officer. If the latter is in an exposed position or under fire, the man should dismount, hand his horse over, and come up on foot.

A dismounted messenger, after handing over his message to an officer in an exposed position or under fire, should lie down.

Messengers should when possible be given receipts for their messages, and should usually be directed to return to their own units.

191. *Engineer reconnaissance.*

Whenever the cavalry division is moving through an area likely to be passed over by the main army, the commander of the engineers should arrange for the collection of information regarding any engineering difficulties which are likely to be met ; he will report the damage done by the enemy to bridges, railways, telegraphs, etc., and what materials are available locally for the repair of the same. This information is of importance to facilitate the march of the main army and it must be collected and sent back quickly. To assist the commander of the engineers in this matter he must be informed of the cavalry commander's plans, and should have access to all the reconnaissance reports received.

192. *Ground scouts.*

1. The duties of ground scouts are to ascertain whether the ground in the immediate vicinity is passable for cavalry, to point out obstacles and to indicate the best points of passage. Reconnaissance of ground from a broader or tactical point of view is not their function. The use of ground scouts therefore in no way dispenses with the necessity for reconnaissance of the ground by specially detailed officers as laid down in Sec. **198.**

193. *The employment of signal units.*

1. The employment of signal units will depend upon the nature of the operations, but their primary function is the provision of a system of intercommunication by means of which information collected by reconnoitring troops may be transmitted rapidly back to cavalry divisional headquarters and thence, after collation, to general headquarters or to the headquarters of other bodies of troops with which the cavalry division may be in touch.

2. No definite allotment of duties to the signal squadron and to a signal troop can be made, but as a general rule the signal squadron provides the communications of cavalry division head-quarters with :—

     i. General headquarters or headquarters of troops co-operating with the cavalry division ;

     ii. With headquarters of cavalry brigades and other component units of the division, or with reconnoitring detachments sent out under direct orders from divisional headquarters.

The signal troop provides the communications between brigade headquarters and the headquarters of regiments and other component parts of the brigade.

3. To establish an effective system of intercommunication the several means of communication available must be carefully co-ordinated and employed with due regard to the relative import-ance of the communications required. The commander of the signal unit with divisional or brigade headquarters should be given early information of contemplated operations or move-ments.

4. Subordinate commanders should render every assistance possible to complete the intercommunication system provided by the signal service, and there should be close co-operation between regimental signallers and the signal service.

5. The signal units with the cavalry division are equipped so that the telegraph and telephone systems existing in the country can be used as circumstances may permit. The circumstances in which hostile telegraph or telephone lines can be tapped with advantage are generally rare. The personnel of the signal troops, however, can be used for this purpose when required.

CHAPTER X.

GENERAL PRINCIPLES OF CAVALRY TACTICS.

194. *Shock and fire action.*

1. The rifle endows cavalry with great independence in war, and numerous situations will occur when it can be used with greater effect than the sword or lance. But a bold leader will find frequent opportunities for mounted attack which will produce more rapid and decisive results than can be gained by even the most skilful use of the rifle. It is, however, by no means necessary when an attack is made that only one of the two methods should be employed, for fire action can create favourable opportunities for shock action, and a well-executed combination of the two methods will often present the greatest chances of success.

Cavalry must be prepared, therefore, to use either the sword or the rifle, or the two in combination.

2. In combining shock with fire action the latter may be provided by horse artillery, machine guns, or rifles, or by any combination of these three.

In the mounted fight with opposing cavalry the fire action will be provided as a rule by horse artillery and machine guns. The nature of the ground or dispositions of the enemy may, however, render it desirable to dismount men to hold tactical features or to supplement the fire of the guns and machine guns.

The action of horse artillery and of machine guns in co-operation with cavalry are similar to a certain extent. Their duty is to prepare the way for the cavalry and to support it in the fight.

3. In combining fire with mounted action the chief factors of success are :—

    i. That the two attacks are correctly timed.*

    ii. That the two attacks do not interfere with each other.

In order to fulfil the first of the above conditions it will often be necessary to push the guns and machine guns boldly forward; while to fulfil the second the commander should separate the mounted attack from the fire attack, so that the latter is not masked up to the moment of collision.

This can be carried out either, by moving the mounted attack away from the fire attack; by moving the fire attack away from the mounted attack; or by moving each away from the other, as in Fig. 20 on p. 270.

4. It must depend upon the general situation when fire should be opened. To open fire prematurely may divulge the commander's intentions. On the other hand, the enemy may present so favourable a target as to make it advisable to open fire at once. Again, it may be desirable and possible to force an enemy by fire action to deploy early and in the wrong direction; or fire may be employed to occupy the enemy's attention, and thus create opportunities for mounted attacks elsewhere.

5. In cases where a cavalry commander has to depend principally on the rifle to achieve his object, the possibility of assisting or of completing the work of the dismounted attack by a mounted attack must always be kept in mind. A portion of the command, though not necessarily entirely withheld from the fire action, should be held ready to act mounted either by taking advantage of the effect produced by the fire to deliver a

---

* NOTE.—In moving to a "position of readiness" preparatory to coming into action the maximum rate of march of horse artillery may be taken as 10 miles an hour. Even in the most favourable circumstances horse artillery cannot be expected to bring an effective fire to bear on a hostile mounted force in less than one minute and a half after the order to come into action has been received.

charge, by charging the enemy as he retreats, or by cutting off
his retreat.

Similarly, subordinate commanders when employed dismounted
must be prepared to deliver a mounted attack at any moment
on their own initiative.

Fig. 20.

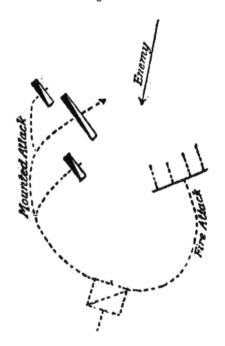

6. When small bodies of cavalry unaccompanied by horse artillery or machine guns meet similar small bodies of the enemy's cavalry, their best course will usually be to make a resolute mounted attack at once, should the ground be in any way suitable, without delaying or weakening this mounted attack by dismounting men.

If small bodies show a resolute determination to attack at once on every feasible opportunity, cavalry may establish a moral superiority over the opposing cavalry, which will prove of inestimable value throughout the campaign.

195. *Ground as affecting cavalry tactics.*

1. When in the neighbourhood of the enemy one of the first duties of a commander on halting in any position is to make himself acquainted with the ground in his immediate vicinity. He should usually carry out a personal reconnaissance, and also despatch one or more officers to reconnoitre for him. Information is usually required as to the localities specially suitable for mounted or fire action, the possibility of concealment, and the obstacles to free movement. Reconnaissance of this nature is particularly useful to a leader before making an attack, as it is most important for him to know the ground in order that he may take advantage of the facilities it offers.

2. As an additional precaution against encounter with hidden obstacles ground scouts should be used. Many obstacles, such as quarries, ditches, wire fences, bogs, which may be quite invisible from a distance, may cause disaster if unexpectedly encountered by troops moving rapidly.

3. The successful use of ground in cavalry tactics, whether mounted or dismounted, largely hinges on taking advantage of features to conceal an approach. Surprise is of primary importance to cavalry in attacking. Even if the enemy becomes aware of the threatened attack the exact direction in which it is to be delivered can still take the enemy by surprise. For this reason the attack should normally be made in a direction different from that of the approach.

196. *Movement and pace.*

1. Normally a body of cavalry, when within possible reach of an enemy, should move forward by successive advances from one favourable position, such as a ridge or river line, to the next. The intervals between such positions should be passed rapidly and at each a halt should be made whilst the next move forward is reconnoitred and arranged. This system, as a rule, should be adopted by every body of cavalry, no matter the size, when moving anywhere near an enemy.

2. When charging cavalry, the cohesion and steadiness of the ranks are of more importance than rapidity of pace. Against infantry or artillery, where it is generally necessary to cross a fire-swept zone and to make the most of surprise, rapidity of movement is of great importance.

CHAPTER XI.

MOUNTED ACTION.

197. *Approach march when within striking distance of hostile cavalry.*

1. The approach march is made with the object of getting close to the enemy in order to attack him at a disadvantage.

2. The general disposition of a force of cavalry at this stage will depend on the intentions of the commander, the nature of the country, and the size and composition of the force.

The force should, however, be well concentrated, but with sufficient intervals to give elasticity for passing over uneven ground, to enable subordinate commanders to make full use of the ground, and to permit rapid deployment should it become necessary. In open country the artillery will, as a rule, move massed on a flank of the cavalry, taking advantage of roads if any are available. The bulk of the machine guns will usually accompany the artillery. Some machine guns and on occasions some horse artillery may be detached to strengthen the advanced guard.

3. Care should be taken to keep the horses as fresh as possible for the fight and to make use of all cover, both with a view to effecting a surprise and to preventing unnecessary exposure to fire. Ground exposed to the fire or view of the enemy should be crossed rapidly.

198. *Reconnaissance and protection during the approach march.*

1. As soon as the force concentrates for the approach march additional patrols should be sent out to obtain more complete information as to the enemy's position, strength and movements.

The country must in addition be reconnoitred sufficiently far in front to enable the commander to turn its features to account in his plan of action. Specially selected officers should be entrusted with this duty.

2. It may sometimes be necessary to make small detachments to support the patrols sent out with the object of driving back hostile patrols, or to occupy positions of tactical importance near the line of advance. In order that these detachments may not be lost to the main body at the moment of collision, they must rejoin or support the attack on their own initiative the moment their task has been accomplished. (*See* Sec. **168.**)

3. When the approximate position of the enemy is known and there is a possibility of surprising him, the advanced guard may be replaced by patrols consisting as a rule only of pairs of officers accompanied by a few intelligent despatch riders to bring back information. Their messages will probably be verbal, as there will be no time for writing.

199. *Manœuvring advanced guard during the approach march.*

Occasionally the advanced guard may be given a manœuvring rôle and operate so as to deceive the enemy, cause him to draw off in one direction and thus afford an opportunity for the mass of the force to attack unexpectedly from another. The advanced guard must in such cases be sufficiently close to its main body to enable the latter to profit by the enemy's mistake.

200. *Transport during the approach march.*

1. Before beginning the approach march the commander should give directions as to the concentration of any vehicles that can be dispensed with in the approach march, in a position offering facilities for parking and for defence.

2. Those vehicles that cannot be left behind in this manner will follow the main body of the force at sufficient distance to

prevent them becoming involved in the action. The localities seized for the successive advances of the main body will in turn serve the same purpose for these vehicles. The position of these vehicles should be known to the troops so that it can form a rallying point for returning patrols, stragglers, &c.

201. *Position of leaders.*

1. Personal reconnaissance in a cavalry fight is essential. During the approach march the commander must be where he can overlook the ground across which his command may be launched in attack, where he will be free from concern about details, and where he can influence quickly and with decision the action of his command as a whole. When the leader has given general directions regarding the advance, a staff officer should supervise the direction and pace in accordance with those instructions.

2. Having launched the attack, he should be where he can observe the fight and, at the same time, keep his reserve well under his hand. He must be in a position to rally his troops and to take measures to reap the fruits of success or to ward off the consequences of defeat.

3. Leaders of subordinate units should remain close to the commander until the last possible moment, and see situations through his eye. Having been told the situation and the general plan of action, which will include the method of developing the fire attack, they should rejoin their units.

202. *General principles concerning the mounted fight against cavalry.*

1. The commander must at the right moment combine the attack of his units upon the main portion of the enemy's force in accordance with a definite but simple plan.

2. Good observation, able leading, and a sound system of transmission of orders are essential to success. Initiative must

be exercised by all subordinate leaders, who must assist their
superior commanders by acting according to their judgment
when orders fail to arrive, or when circumstances necessitate a
deviation from the letter of the order received. In practice
there will seldom be time to explain the whole plan to all subordinate leaders. From their previous training they should be
able to grasp the idea of the plan so soon as the deployment
has been completed.

3. The attacking line must be strong, well closed up, and in
good order, so that it may strike the enemy an irresistible blow.
It should present to the enemy the appearance of an unbroken
front of great cohesion.

4. The enemy should be surprised as to the time and direction
of the attack. He may then be compelled to fight with his units
unprepared for attack and in a direction which he did not expect.

5. When the ground favours the advance and conceals the
direction of the march, every effort should be directed to
throwing the whole weight of the charge against the enemy's
flank so as to compel him at the last moment to change his front
to meet the blow.

6. Once a large force has deployed, the cavalry commander is
powerless to modify his plan should he find that the enemy is
still manœuvring. It is therefore of importance in the attack by
large forces to retain a reserve to guard against the unforeseen
and to avoid premature deployment.

203. *Disposition for the mounted attack on cavalry.*

1. The tactical formations must be of the simplest and capable
of rapid alteration to suit any change of situation.

The shape of the attack, especially its breadth of front, will
usually be determined by the nature of the ground to be crossed
and the width of the enemy's front. When attacking with two
or more brigades not more than one brigade should be employed
in one line, because a longer line cannot be controlled by one

man, and because the longer the line the greater is the difficulty of avoiding disorder in the ranks.

2. When launching a mounted attack it will generally be impossible to foretell the exact strength and direction in which the enemy will meet it. The attacking force when greater than a squadron should, therefore, usually be in successive bodies, the rear or supporting bodies being in échelon on the flanks of the leading body.

When either flank of the first line is equally liable to attack, there should be supporting bodies in échelon in rear of both flanks. On the delivery of the attack the body on the flank which the enemy does not attack can become the reserve.

When the enemy is more likely to attack one flank than the other, the supporting line or lines should be placed on the flank most liable to attack and the reserve on the other flank. Only when the inner flank rests upon an impassable obstacle should the reserve be placed on the same flank as the support.

3. Though a line is supported by an échelon in rear, it may still be necessary for a flank portion of it to drop back ready to outflank any body of the enemy attempting to strike the line in flank.

4. Echelons in rear must support the leading line very closely, firstly in order to prevent the first line being overwhelmed before the succeeding lines become engaged, and secondly to increase the rigour of the charge by the confidence inspired through the proximity of supporting troops.

5. In large forces the supporting lines themselves should often adopt an échelon formation, maintaining their leading units at a short distance from the line they are supporting.

6. It may often be advisable to form an offensive flank, that is to say, to place a body of troops in échelon in front of the main attacking line, in order to take the enemy's main line in flank, or to force it to change its direction and thus become exposed to an attack in flank by the main line.

The employment of an offensive flank when working over
open ground has small chance of success against an enemy with
any capacity for manœuvre. On the other hand, in working
over ground screened from view and fire an offensive flank, if
skilfully led, often promises important advantages which justify
its employment.

7. When, owing to the proximity of the enemy, there is not
sufficient space to form to the front for attack, the force may be
moved to a flank in such a manner that, when the moment for
the delivery of the attack arrives and the troops are wheeled in
the direction of the enemy, it will be in attack formation. This
method of attack may also be used for deceiving the enemy as to
the true direction in which the final attack will be delivered.

204. *Final deployment and charge.*

1. Careful observation of the enemy, and accurate calculation
of space and time are necessary to ensure that the attack is
delivered at the right moment.

2. The several lines must retain their power of changing
direction as long as possible. The second and third lines may
often be able to retain this power longer than the first line, as
they may not have a definite objective in front of them when
the attack is first launched.

3. The intervals between units are not required in the attack;
regimental and squadron leaders should, therefore, close their
regiments and squadrons in on the directing unit as soon as the
final deployment is commenced.

4. Movements should be rapid but without haste or confusion,
and complicated manœuvres and long words of command should
be avoided.

5. In order to economise energy and retain cohesion for the
shock, the attacking troops will remain as long as possible at the
trot; they will increase the pace to a gallop in sufficient time to
permit of the charge being made with the necessary momentum,

but cohesion must not be sacrificed for pace. Should an opportunity occur of surprising the enemy, or of striking him before or during deployment, the gallop may be commenced at a considerable distance from the objective.

6. When the commander wishes to obtain the necessary momentum in anticipation of the charge (usually at about 300 to 500 yards distance from the enemy) he will give the command " LINE WILL ATTACK." The pace will then be slightly increased, swords and lances will be brought to the engage; every horse must be thoroughly in hand, the men must be riding close, and there should be two distinct and well-defined ranks; troop leaders will be careful to keep their correct distance from the directing troop leader, and on no account should they exceed this distance; flank guides will press in towards the centre of their troops; and the rear rank men will fill up any gaps which may occur in the rank in front of them.

Just prior to the charge being ordered the regimental and squadron commanders should be on, or approximately on, the same alignment as the troop leaders.

7. By his skill in choosing the right moment for the charge the leader can increase his chance of success. The shorter the distance over which the charge is made, the greater will be the cohesion and the fresher will be the horses for the actual shock.

The charge should not be ordered, therefore, until the line is about 50 yards distant from the enemy.

8. On the command " CHARGE " one cheer will be given, the front rank will bring swords to the sword in line, and every man will tighten his grip of the saddle and increase his speed with the fixed determination of riding the enemy down.

9. After the charge, the situation may develop in one of three ways :—

(i) The enemy may not meet the attack, but turn about before the collision and retreat.

(ii) The collision may be followed by a successful mêlée and a pursuit.

(iii) The collision may be followed by a mêlée in which the attack is unsuccesful and has to fall back.

205. *The pursuit.*

1. The enemy may not meet the attack, but may turn about when the collision is imminent, or he may retreat after the mêlée. In either case once he has given way he must be kept running.

2. The actual pursuit of an enemy in disorder and in full flight can only be kept up by men also in loose order and at full gallop. In such a state pursuing cavalry are at the mercy of any fresh hostile body that may appear. They must, therefore, be followed as closely as possible by formed bodies which have been retained in hand or rallied.

3. The commander directly he finds that his attack has succeeded must at once organize the pursuit, allowing some units to follow in loose order with the utmost speed and resolution while rallying the majority and bringing them on in support as quickly as possible.

4. Guns and machine guns in a pursuit are most effective and must be used with great boldness. All large masses of the enemy must be broken up, and any attempt on his part to hold a position with his reinforcements or rallied troops must be prevented.

206. *The mêlée.*

1. In a mêlée determination, horsemanship and the skilful use of the sword and lance decide the issue.

2. Individuals who are not actually engaged in the mêlée will be collected and led on in close formation to form the nucleus for rallying.

207. The rally.

1. On the command "RALLY," every officer of the units ordered to rally must collect behind him the men in his immediate neighbourhood, and men must rally behind the nearest officer as rapidly as possible. Normally squadrons should rally in line, ready to attack again immediately.

2. Should the attack fail or be beaten in the mêlée, a retirement must be made with the object of rallying on the first favourable opportunity. It will often be possible to check the enemy with rifle, machine gun, or artillery fire. Every advantage must me taken of suitable fire positions which may serve as rallying points. During the movement to the rear, officers and non-commissioned officers must endeavour to retain the troops under their control, so as to be able to counter-attack at the first available opportunity.

208. Mounted attacks against infantry and artillery.

1. The conditions which favour a mounted attack upon infantry and artillery have been described in Sec. 167. Though opportunities for attack will usually be fleeting, the preparation and the execution of the attack should be as methodical as circumstances permit.

In the explanation of the plan of attack each commander should be given a definite objective, and be told a point or points at which the troops are to rally.

Other troops in the neighbourhood should if possible be informed of the projected attack so that co-operation may be ensured. When the enemy's troops alter their dispositions to meet the cavalry attack, favourable opportunities for action will frequently be offered to those troops attacking from another direction.

2. The dispositions for the attack depend upon the ground, the position of the objective, and the time available.

Squadrons in extended order may be used to divert the enemy's attention from the main attack.

x 25119   U

If the front of the attacking cavalry be too narrow, it will not only have to face the fire of the troops immediately in its front, but it will be a focus of fire from all sides. As many attacking units therefore should be formed as there are bodies of the enemy to be charged, and whenever possible, a flank attack should be combined with a frontal one.

Against infantry the attack should be made in successive lines. The leading lines should be in extended order, but to inflict permanent damage on the enemy they must be supported by bodies in close order. In order to ensure the necessary support to the leading lines and to increase the moral effect on the enemy, successive lines should not be at a greater distance than 200 yards. The general effect of such attacks in depth should be a succession of very rapid blows, each line taking advantage of what the preceding line has effected.

The attack against artillery should be made on one or both flanks of the line of guns in extended order. A portion of the attacking force should be detailed to attack the gunners when the guns have been ridden through. Other portions should be detailed to deal with the escort, limbers and horses if these can be located before launching the attack. The limbers and horses are very important, and should be seized as soon as possible. If the horses can be captured they should not be shot, as with their assistance it may be possible to remove the guns, or they can be taken away if the guns have to be left.

3. After attacking infantry or guns it will sometimes be advisable to pass right through and rally to a flank instead of returning by the route by which the charge was made.

CHAPTER XII.
DISMOUNTED ACTION.

209. *General Principles.*

1. The principles governing the fire action of cavalry and infantry differ, firstly because cavalry by retaining the power of acting mounted at any time is much more mobile than infantry, and can combine a mounted charge with fire action, secondly because cavalry, having to detach a proportion of men to take care of the led horses has relatively less fire power than a body of infantry of the same size.

2. A guiding principle in dismounted action is that cavalry should employ its mobility to compensate for its relative lack of fire power. This mobility enables it to attack suddenly from any direction and to develop fire more quickly from close formations than infantry can. Consequently it is able to deal blows at the enemy's flanks and rear before he has time to meet them, or can overwhelm the head of his columns with fire before he can deploy.

3. It follows, then, that surprise and rapidity of action are very important factors in dismounted action, and that when surprise has been achieved, cavalry should usually develop its full strength immediately the attack commences.

In order that cavalry may obtain the full advantage of its mobility, it is necessary that the commander should possess the power of rapidly breaking off the fight and resuming it, if necessary, from some more effective direction. For this reason, as well as to ensure mutual support, a complete system of communication between the commander and all his subordinates as well as with neighbouring units must be arranged.

U 2

4. When acting dismounted, special precautions must be taken to safeguard the flanks.

Flank protection can usually be obtained by holding localities on the flanks and by using protective patrols to watch for the enemy's approach. It is the duty of commanders on the flanks of a firing line to detail special men or detachments to watch and protect the flanks. All dead ground in the vicinity of the flanks must be looked into and visual communication kept with the patrols protecting the flanks.

210. *Principles of fire action.*

1. However skilful individual men may be, the greatest effect can be produced by their fire only when it is efficiently directed and controlled. The normal cavalry fire unit is the troop, though, if the troops are much scattered, it may be the section leader. The value of a fire unit commander depends upon his ability to apply the fire of his unit at the right time and in the right volume to the right target.

2. The duties of a fire unit commander in controlling and directing fire consist in:—

    i. Carrying out such orders as he may receive from his superior commander; and using his own judgment in the absence of definite orders.

    ii. Indicating targets.

    iii. Issuing orders for sighting, and, when possible, supervising the correct adjustment of sights.

    iv. Regulating the volume of fire.

    v. Reporting when ammunition is running short.

(*See* also "Musketry Regulations, Part I," Secs. 55 to 59, and 96.)

3. The squadron leader regulates the employment and co-operation of the several troops, and exercises constant care in maintaining communication with his immediate commander. He orders the opening of fire, subject to such orders as he may receive from the regimental commander, issues general

instructions as to the targets and the distribution of the fire, and observes the effect.

In other respects he leaves fire control to the troop leaders, and interferes only when he desires to combine the fire effect of several troops at a certain moment or over a certain space, or if he observes circumstances which have escaped the troop leader's notice. During the fight he will see to the timely replenishment of ammunition.

4. A high standard of fire discipline in the men is not less important than skilful control and direction of fire by the leaders. Fire discipline means strict attention to the signals and orders of the commander, combined with intelligent observation of the enemy. It ensures the careful adjustment of the sight, deliberate aim, economy of ammunition, and prompt cessation of fire when ordered or when the target disappears.

5. Cavalry should rarely engage in a protracted fire fight, as this involves loss of mobility.* In order to develop the greatest effect from the moment when the leader decides to open fire rapid bursts and concentration of fire from as large a number of rifles as possible should usually be employed, when favourable targets present themselves, rather than a slow continuous fire distributed against the whole of the enemy's front.

6. Economy of ammunition is of importance and should be effected, not by limiting fire when needed, but by judiciously timing its use. The delivery of sudden bursts of fire will usually be found to be the most effective method of regulating the expenditure of ammunition.

Pauses of this nature, if skilfully timed, have a great moral effect, and have the advantage of deceiving and confusing the enemy.

Commanders of all units should keep themselves informed of the amount of ammunition in hand, so that shortage at critical moments may be obviated.

* For the circumstances in which a deliberate fire fight may be necessary *see* Sec. 216.

7. Every available means should be used to obtain the correct ranges. The squadron commander, when reconnoitring preparatory to dismounted action, should be accompanied by the squadron range takers. Their estimates should be communicated to the troop and section commanders, who should lose no opportunity of supplementing them by the estimates of their best judges of distance and by enquiry from other troops already engaged.

211. *The use of ground and cover.*

1. The soldier will be taught the importance of the relationship between fire and movement, and that the wise employment of every feature of the ground is of great importance in promoting fire effect and reducing losses. Reconnaissance by the commander before he commits his troops is as important in dismounted as it is in mounted action.

2. Troop and section commanders will be taught that when an advance is being made by rushes, they should endeavour to decide beforehand on the next halting place, and should point it out to their men, who must get there as quickly as possible when the signal to advance is given.

3. Practical instruction will be given in the use of ground. The soldier will be taught that the most important requirement in cover when firing is that he can use his rifle to the best advantage. In endeavouring to do so he should expose himself as little as possible to the enemy's fire, but must understand that if he merely seeks safety and neglects thereby the full use of his rifle he will be failing in his duty.

4. If an equally good view can be obtained it is better to fire round the side of cover than over it, as the firer is then less visible.

5. When firing from behind cover the soldier must keep his eyes on the target between each shot; otherwise he may lose sight of the target and this may result in his shooting without looking over the sights.

6. It will be explained that cover from view, which does not also afford cover from fire, should not provide a good aiming or ranging mark for the enemy. A hedge or bush, in country where such features are of uncommon occurrence, may become a dangerous trap if men crowd behind it and the enemy discovers they are there. Moving objects catch the eye more quickly than those that are still, and when, in default of cover, men are lying in the open, all but the necessary movements to load and fire must be avoided. Men halted in the open should not show up against the skyline.

7. Cover from hostile air-craft can best be obtained by moving through woods or along hedgerows. It will also be explained that the difficulties of observation from the air are increased if men stand still or lie down when a hostile air-craft approaches, and refrain from looking up when it passes overhead. It must be understood, however, that when once committed to the attack no attempt will be made by the firing line and supports to seek cover from the enemy's air-craft, the mission of which at this time will more probably be to locate the reserves.

8. It will be explained that even a few troops marching on a wide road are clearly visible from the air. In order to conceal a movement from hostile air-craft troops should keep to the sides of the road, and march on grass rather than the metalled portion. Narrow roads with high hedges are the most favourable for concealment.

212. *The movement mounted to the first fire position.*

1. The commander of a body of cavalry, who intends to act dismounted should decide, after personal reconnaissance if possible, on his plan of action, the place at which he intends to dismount, and the position of his led horses. He should then assemble his subordinate commanders at some point where the

ground over which he intends to act can be seen, explain his plans, and issue his orders.

It is important that the latter should be clear and complete, in order to ensure rapidity of action and to avoid confusion. Only exceptional circumstances, such as the seizing of a very favourable and fleeting opportunity, can justify the omission of these preliminary steps.

The commander of a force about to act dismounted should, whenever circumstances permit, be well ahead of his main body, in order to have time to reconnoitre.

2. To take full advantage of their mobility cavalry should advance mounted as close as possible to the position at which they are to open fire, subject to the necessity for concealment and cover for the led horses. The commander of the force will lead his men by a concealed route to the place at which he wishes to deploy; subordinate commanders will then either lead their commands to places where they are to dismount or, if necessary, will order a further deployment.

3. It may happen, however, that the mounted advance will have to be made within range of the enemy's fire and over ground where cover is limited. In these circumstances the advance will consist of a series of rushes from shelter to shelter, each as rapid as possible; advantage being taken of the positions of shelter to steady the ranks, to arrange for the next bound forward and to give the horses a momentary breathing space.

4. The formations to be adopted during the advances will usually depend on the facilities for concealment offered by the ground and the effect of the enemy's fire.

Against direct artillery fire small shallow columns, each on a narrow front, such as troop columns, are least vulnerable. These columns should be on an irregular front, so that the range from the enemy's guns to each column it different. The intervals between such columns should not normally be less than fifty yards,

and the distance between each should be greater than that
covered by the bullets of a shrapnel, that is to say it should be
over two hundred yards.

Small columns are also less vulnerable to long range infantry
fire than are lines of men in extended order at moderately close
intervals. They are also more easily controlled than extended
lines.

When advancing over fire-swept zones at effective infantry
range or when effective fire is possible, troops should usually
move in extended order.

213. *Dismounting.*
(*See* also Sec. 153.)

1. The position chosen for dismounting will usually be the
place nearest to the firing position where concealment is
possible.

2. The method of dismounting will depend upon the tactical
situation. The normal method will be that carried out on the
command FOR ACTION RIGHT (or LEFT)—DISMOUNT, as by this
method the greatest number of rifles is put into the firing line
compatible with the mobility of the led horses. Whenever the
tactical situation permits, the numbers 3 should be ordered
to dismount.

3. When great speed in mounting or dismounting is required
or when the troops are in half sections, one man out of each half
section may be dismounted.

4. When the mobility of the led horses is not essential, the
maximum number of men may be deployed in the firing line by
coupling, ringing or linking the led horses.

Linking horses takes more time than coupling them, but is
preferable if the fire position is to be occupied for a considerable
time, or when it is advisable to keep the horses close together.
Coupling horses is often suitable when the fire position is very
extended.

5. If the men have dismounted in the normal manner and it is desired to reinforce the firing line, the horseholder in every alternate section should be ordered to hand over his horses to the horseholder of the section next to his own and to join the firing line.

6. Troops should dismount and form up rapidly and without noise.

214. Led horses.

1. When a force of a squadron or more dismounts at one place for fire action, an officer should usually be specially detailed to remain in charge of the led horses. Otherwise a non-commissioned officer should be placed in charge.

If no commander is detailed, the senior present must take command of his own accord.

His duties will be :—

    i. To keep in constant touch with the commander in the firing line, so that he will know the moment the led horses are required, or, if the firing line is advancing, when he may be required to move the led horses to another position. For this reason he should if necessary detail a man to place himself where he can observe the firing line and communicate what is going on.

    ii. To safeguard the led horses from surprise. To this end he must arrange for a sharp look-out to be kept.

    iii. To ensure that none of the led horses are exposed.

2. The following are the chief considerations when deciding on the positions of the led horses :—

    i. They must be under cover.

    ii. They must be as close to the firing line as circumstances will permit.

The position should not be immediately in rear of the firing line, if in such a position the horses are liable to

losses caused by unaimed fire. It may often be necessary
therefore to move the horses as soon as the men have dismounted.
The commander of the dismounted unit will usually choose
the positions of the led horses and give orders for any change.

If however the commander of the led horses finds it advisable
to change their position without orders he will notify the
commander of the unit, so that the latter may always know
where his led horses are.

215. *Movement on foot to fire position.*

1. The commander of a unit dismounting, after giving the
necessary orders regarding the position of the led horses, the
protection of the flank, and the amount of ammunition to be taken
from the horse holders, either leads the force forward himself
or gives directions to his subordinates as to the positions that
he wishes them to take up. He should lose no time in going to
the fire position with his range takers in order to reconnoitre and
decide on the fire orders required, so that fire may be opened
with the least delay and greatest effect.

2. It will generally be necessary to occupy the fire position as
rapidly as possible, but this necessity will seldom make concealment unnecessary. The enemy should not know until the
opening of the fire that the position has been occupied; if all
movements are well concealed it will sometimes be possible to
deceive the enemy as to the actual position that has been taken
up. When the immediate occupation of a position is not
necessary, the commander, accompanied by his subordinate
leaders, may make a preliminary reconnaissance of the position.

3. The units extend as they move forward. Each section
leader, subject to the general control of the troop leader, will
determine the method of advance, and see that the general
direction is maintained and there is no crowding. Section
commanders are responsible that the troop leader's signals
and orders are quickly and correctly passed along the line, and
obeyed promptly.

216. *The attack.*

1. The power of developing fire effect rapidly from any direction enables cavalry to draw a ring of fire around an unprepared or slower moving enemy. Enveloping or converging fire has great moral and material effect, cavalry should therefore be always on the look out for opportunities for enveloping an enemy.

2. When a hostile force is encountered, one or both flanks of the firing line can be extended quickly by pushing troops or squadrons on to successive positions round the enemy's flanks. Such movements will usually take the form of a rapid advance by one or more portions of the command, mounted as long as possible, covered by the fire of some or all of the remaining squadrons.

3. In order that each advance may be covered by a timely outburst of fire from all troops in the vicinity, leaders must always be on the look out for opportunities to assist the advance of neighbouring units by fire, and commanders of units should, whenever possible, inform neighbouring units of their intention to advance.

4. Long advances on foot should be avoided. Surprise and rapidity of action can usually be best attained by galloping from fire position to fire position in such formations as will take full advantage of the ground.

5. Occasions will, however, arise when cavalry will have to drive home a determined attack on foot, *e.g.*, when a party of the enemy, behind good cover from artillery fire, holds a position which cannot conveniently be turned and denies the use of the most suitable line of advance.

6. On such occasions cavalry must be formed for dismounted attack in depth. The firing line, which may be preceded by scouts and subdivided into firing line and supports, being followed by a reserve in the hands of the commander.

The object then is to establish the firing line in a fire position as close as possible to the enemy and to obtain superiority of fire over him. This will entail the gradual reinforcement of the firing line from the rear and may necessitate a long advance on foot and a protracted fire fight.

7. The guiding principle in an attack of this nature is mutual support by fire. Fire should be employed to make movement possible and to enable the firing line to close with the enemy. The various parts of the firing line must help each other forward. Similarly supports, if formed, must seek opportuities to use covering and supporting fire to help forward the firing line.

8. The object of each advance and the method of carrying it out must be clearly determined before it is begun.

When the advance of the firing line is checked by the enemy's fire, further progress must usually take the form of rushes, which, according to circumstances, may be made by the whole line simultaneously or by portions of it alternately. No hard and fast rules can be laid down as to the conduct of such an advance, which should be governed by the following general principles.

A considerable proportion of casualties usually occurs when men are getting up to advance, and when about to lie down after an advance. Casualties should be reduced by making these movements suddenly and simultaneously.

At close infantry ranges. under heavy fire, advances should be made very rapidly and should usually be limited in duration.

The length of rushes, however, must depend primarily upon the extent to which the fire of those troops, who are not advancing, is able to keep down the enemy's fire. It will also depend upon the nature of the ground, and the physical condition of the troops. If a fire position offers good cover, behind which men can rest, it may be advisable to make a rush of some length across open ground in order to reach it. On the other hand, long rushes made without adequate object may fatigue the troops and make their fire unsteady, besides affording the enemy a relatively easy target.

9. In advancing by rushes within close infantry range, the particular portions of the line to move first and the strength of each such portion will depend on various considerations. The facilities for advance offered by the ground will rarely be the same everywhere. Where the ground favours movement parts of the firing line will be able to work forward into fire positions, whence they can help forward those parts which are less favourably placed. The extent of such fire positions and the facilities for approaching them will often determine the extent of frontage of the parts of the line to advance simultaneously. Creeping, crawling, and advancing man by man check the rate of progress very considerably and are to be regarded as exceptional methods, only to be employed when it is not possible to gain ground in other ways.

10. For the action of machine guns in support of dismounted attack *see* Sec. **229.**

217. *The defence.*

1. Cavalry, more especially small bodies, will often be called upon temporarily to occupy localities for defence. When so employed they should take full advantage of their mobility, and as a general rule by attacking the enemy at a distance cause him to deploy prematurely and delay his advance. In the defence, as in the attack, concealment and surprise are of importance, but the paramount consideration must always be to bring an effective fire to bear on the attack, chief attention being paid to securing a wide and open field of fire. Whenever time and means permit, the position should be put in a state of defence.

2. During the initial stages of a defensive engagement and before the enemy's plans are discovered the commander should deploy as few men as possible, retaining the remainder in readiness to act as circumstances may demand, when the enemy has disclosed his dispositions. He will then be able to take immediate advantage of any opportunity that the enemy may offer for a successful counter-attack.

3. The value of enfilade fire is as great when acting in defence as in the attack, and occasions will constantly occur when a small party, favourably situated on a flank, may effectively harass the enemy's advance.

4. When the object of the operation is to delay the enemy, it will usually be advisable to open fire at long range, in order that he may be forced to deploy at some distance from the position; but if the object is to effect a surprise, it may often be advisable to allow the enemy to advance to within decisive range before opening fire.

5. For the action of machine guns in defence see Sec. **229.**

218. *Leaving a position.*

1. When leaving a position to advance or to retire great care should be taken to prevent the enemy from discovering the intention of the commander. If the firing has been in bursts with intervals of silence, the fact that there is no firing will not indicate the evacuation of the position. For this reason the evacuation should follow immediately after a burst.

2. It may often be advisable to withdraw part of the force from the position, while those remaining continue the bursts of fire until it is time for them to move.

3. When men leave the firing line they will be careful to avoid any movement to attract the attention of the enemy. They should usually move in the prone position until they are well hidden from view. If there is a possibility of the enemy occupying the position as soon as it is evacuated, the last men to leave should mount and move away rapidly.

219. *Ammunition supply.*

1. The two horse artillery brigade ammunition columns forming the divisional reserve of ammunition are under the divisional

artillery commander, who, if necessary, allots them to various units, controls their movements, and is responsible that communication is maintained with them.

2. When a cavalry brigade commander wishes to form a brigade ammunition reserve, he will detach from each regiment one or more of the small arm ammunition wagons. The reserve will be commanded by an officer specially detailed and should have signallers and orderlies attached to it. It forms a link between the regimental reserve and the artillery brigade ammunition column.

When it is formed, the brigadier will detail the first position to be taken up and inform the units that are to be supplied. Subsequent changes of position should usually be made under orders from brigade headquarters and not on the initiative of the commander of the brigade reserve. But the latter must always be prepared to move on his own responsibility, for occasions may occur, such as when the brigade reserve is suddenly threatened with attack, when the brigadier will not have the opportunity of issuing the requisite orders in time. Whenever the commander of the brigade reserve finds it necessary to move without orders, he will inform brigade headquarters and the commander of each regiment as early as possible.

When a cavalry brigade commander wishes to replenish his brigade ammunition reserve, he will either apply to divisional headquarters, giving the position of his reserve, or arrange direct with the commander of the ammunition column which has been allotted to his brigade. In the former case the divisional commander will notify the brigade commander as to the locality where he must assume responsibility for the safety of the ammunition.

In the latter the brigade commander himself will arrange for the safety of the ammunition, if necessary asking the commander of the brigade next to his own to furnish an escort for the ammunition until he himself can ensure its safety with his own troops.

The commander of the brigade ammunition reserve will :—

i. Open up communication as soon as possible with the brigade ammunition column and also with the various regimental reserves.

ii. Employ the orderly sent him from the brigade ammunition column only for the purpose of communicating with that column.

iii. Take the earliest opportunity (when about half the ammunition with the brigade reserve has been issued, or sooner if necessary) to fill up empty transport from the brigade ammunition column. The request for the amount of ammunition required will be sent, in writing, to the officer in charge of the small arm ammunition section of the brigade ammunition column by the artillery orderly furnished for that purpose, who will also act as guide to the officer bringing the ammunition forward. When the ammunition is carried in S.A.A. carts, the number of full carts required will be demanded.

iv. Not send men and transport animals belonging to the brigade reserve to the brigade ammunition column, nor men and transport animals belonging to the latter further to the front than the brigade reserve, except in case of emergency.

v. Retain empty transport in the brigade reserve until reloaded or replaced.

vi. Sign receipts prepared by the officer in charge of the brigade ammunition column for the number of full carts received, if the ammunition is forwarded in S.A.A. carts, or for the number of full ammunition boxes if the ammunition is forwarded by other transport.

vii. After an action or during a pause in the engagement make good from the brigade ammunition column all deficiencies of ammunition.

X

3. The three limbered G.S. wagons which are allotted to each regiment (one per squadron) for the carriage of ammunition will normally form a regimental reserve, one or more being detached to form a squadron or brigade reserve when required. On the march the regimental reserve will usually follow in rear of the regiment, under the command of a non-commissioned officer.

In a mounted action it will remain with the rest of the first line transport.

In a dismounted action its movement is controlled and its safety ensured on the same principles as are those of a brigade ammunition reserve.

4. Whenever dismounted action involving a large expenditure of ammunition is probable, fifty extra rounds a man should be issued from the regimental reserve. When this is done, the regimental commanders should take the necessary steps to replenish their reserves as soon as possible.

CHAPTER XIII.

HORSE ARTILLERY, MACHINE GUNS, AND ENGINEERS.

HORSE ARTILLERY.

220. *General principles regarding the disposition of horse artillery in a force of cavalry.*

1. The following are the chief considerations which a cavalry commander should keep in mind in deciding on the position of his guns, when his command is on the move.

    i. When marching in column of route, the horse artillery should be near the head of the main body, normally just in rear of the leading unit. It is not as a rule advisable to attach guns to the advanced guard.

    ii. When moving across country, the guns are usually best placed on one flank and approximately level with the head of the main body, but they should be allowed a certain latitude in conforming to the pace of the latter and in selecting the most suitable ground to move over.

    iii. When moving across undulating or hilly country in the neighbourhood of the enemy, it will often be advisable to keep some guns back on one rise to cover the advance of the main body to the next.

    iv. The movement of artillery is materially affected by the surface of the ground. The cavalry commander should consider this point, and whenever possible keep it on a road.

2. When mounted action is contemplated, the guns should usually be massed so that they can operate from a flank with one line of fire, in accordance with the principle described in Sec. **194.**

3. When cavalry is fighting dismounted, it may occasionally be advisable to attach batteries or sections of horse artillery to cavalry brigades or regiments instead of keeping all the guns massed.

4. Within the limits of the general instructions received from the cavalry commander the horse artillery commander must be prepared to act on his own initiative and be ready to seize all opportunities of effective action against the enemy. When in the field he should keep near the cavalry commander until the guns are launched on a definite mission. The cavalry commander must keep the artillery commander informed as to his plans and intentions.

221. *The employment of horse artillery in co-operation with cavalry attacking mounted.*

1. The principles to be followed in the employment of fire to prepare and assist shock action are described in Sec. **194.**

2. The cavalry leader will indicate approximately the position for the guns to suit his tactical plan, but the exact place for their coming into action and the moment for opening fire or changing position must be left to the decision of the horse artillery commander in accordance with the situation.

3. During the cavalry fight the horse artillery will concentrate a rapid well-aimed fire on that portion of the enemy's cavalry on which the decisive attack is about to be delivered, so that it may be thrown into confusion.

Immediately the collision occurs the fire should be directed on any supports or reserves that the enemy may be bringing up.

As a rule it is only when the guns can no longer fire on the enemy's cavalry that their fire should be directed at hostile artillery. But occasionally circumstances may require the fire to be directed at the enemy's artillery under other conditions.

4. When mounted cavalry are attacking dismounted men or guns, the leader will usually endeavour to attack the enemy in flank, by gaining ground to a flank or by changing the direction of his advance as he approaches his objective.   On such occasions horse artillery should bring such a rapid and concentrated fire on the enemy's infantry or guns as to pin them to their ground and prevent them from changing their position in order to face the approaching cavalry.

5. If the attack succeeds, the horse artillery will act at once on its own initiative to prevent the enemy re-forming or holding positions from which he could check the pursuit.

In order to gain decisive results the pursuit must be organized, For this purpose the artillery commander must keep in touch with the cavalry commander, and it is advisable that the former should retain under his own immediate control at least some portion of his guns so that they are available to carry out the latter's orders.

6. Should the attack fail, the horse artillery must remain in action and form a rallying point for the cavalry, which in falling back must avoid masking the guns.

222.   *The employment of horse artillery in co-operation with cavalry acting dismounted.*

1. In the dismounted attack the cavalry commander will usually take advantage of his mobility to move portions of his force round the enemy's flank or flanks, and seize successive positions from which to bring enfilade fire to bear on the enemy. To oppose such outflanking movements the enemy may attempt to change the disposition of his force, in which case the horse artillery should concentrate as heavy a fire as possible on him with a view to pinning him to his ground.

Horse artillery must be ready to assist in securing any ground gained by the cavalry, when necessary pushing forward on its own initiative.

2. When acting on the defensive, horse artillery will be able to assist the cavalry by compelling the attackers to deploy at a distance, and by supporting any counter attacks which the cavalry may make.

Arrangements may often be made with advantage to sweep the front of the line taken up by the cavalry with artillery fire.

3. In co-operating with dismounted cavalry in attack or defence it may be better to disperse the guns rather than to keep them massed. In order to obtain full advantage from the combined action of horse artillery and cavalry the commander should adopt some clearly defined plan with which the artillery commander should be kept fully acquainted. There must be a mutual understanding between the two and a good system of intercommunication.

223. *Other uses of horse artillery.*

1. In reconnaissance artillery fire may be used to assist the cavalry in making an enemy deploy and thus show his strength.

It will also be of use to assist cavalry in the rapid reduction of a hostile post blocking the line of advance.

2. In conjunction with cavalry, guns may be of great service in delaying hostile columns of all arms on the march, by compelling them to deploy or to change direction. For this reason horse artillery will at times be useful with a rear guard when it may often be divided into two or more portions which can fall back in succession, one portion covering the retirement of another.

224. *Escorts for horse artillery.*

1. When horse artillery is working in close proximity to cavalry no special escort is necessary. Should the guns, however, be exposed, or sent off to a flank, as will often be necessary in cavalry fighting, an escort will be required, and, if none is

provided and no orders to the contrary are given, it is the duty of the artillery commander to call on the nearest body of cavalry for an escort.

2. The principal duties of the escort are:—

    i. To warn the artillery commander of all attempts of the enemy to approach within effective rifle range of the guns or ammunition wagons.

    ii. To keep hostile bodies beyond effective rifle range of the guns.

All ground within rifle range which might afford concealment to an enemy should either be occupied by the escort or be under its effective fire.

3. It may occasionally be desirable to employ machine guns with an escort to horse artillery. But, as in such circumstances, it will often be impossible to direct their fire against the main body of the enemy, and as machine gun fire will seldom stop a determined mounted attack in extended order this method of employment will not be regarded as normal.

4. The escort commander should place himself where he can best superintend his command and see what is going on; in order to ensure that he has early information as to intended movements of the guns he should detail an officer or reliable non-commissioned officer to remain near the artillery commander.

5. The senior officer present will issue the necessary instructions to the escort, but the commander of the escort will be given a free hand in carrying them out.

MACHINE GUNS.

225. *Characteristics of Machine Guns.*

1. From a front of about two yards a machine gun can deliver a fire equal in volume to that of about thirty men firing rapidly, the frontage required for the latter being at least fifteen times

as great. It is, therefore, easier to find a concealed position for a machine gun than for the number of riflemen required to produce an equal volume of fire.

2. When well concealed the gun offers a difficult target and, as only two men are required for its service, it is not put out of action should these become casualties, provided the remaining men of the detachment are trained to take their places.

3. As regards fire effect :—

    i. The effective range of the machine gun may be taken as equal to that of the rifle.

    ii. It has been found by experiment that the fire of a machine gun is more than twice as concentrated as that of riflemen firing an equal number of rounds at the same target.

4. In the important matter of control of fire the machine gun has several advantages over the rifle. Once the gun is loaded and laid, fire can be turned on or off instantaneously, can be directed readily as required, and can be distributed in any direction by traversing.

5. On the other hand, the machine gun has certain disadvantages as compared with riflemen :—

    i. It is more defenceless when on the move, whether carried in the limbered wagon or on pack transport.

    ii. Owing to the concentrated nature of its fire as compared with a similar amount of rifle fire, the effect of small errors in aiming or elevation is greater. A comparatively small error at effective or long ranges will cause the whole of the fire of a machine gun to miss altogether a target which would probably be struck by several shots from riflemen making the same error in aim or elevation.

    iii. The mechanism of the gun is liable to temporary interruption.

    iv. The peculiar noise of the automatic firing attracts attention to the gun.

226. *Machine guns as cavalry weapons.*

1. The characteristics of machine guns as described in the previous section render them valuable for employment with cavalry for the following reasons :—

i. In co-operation with mounted action, the mobility of the machine gun; and the heavy volume of fire which it can bring from a small frontage render it suitable for supporting a cavalry charge on the principles laid down in Sec. **194.**

ii. In dismounted action—

(a) By its power of accompanying men on foot in any nature of country the machine gun is rendered well adapted for close co-operation with a dismounted attack.

(b) Its mobility and fire power render it suitable to meet unexpected or critical situations, hence, when cavalry are acting dismounted, machine guns may often be usefully employed as a mobile reserve of fire.

(c) The power of turning rapidly in any desired direction enables the gun to be brought to bear upon a fresh target without moving the tripod, and with the minimum of movement and exposure. This renders the machine gun specially suitable for employment on a flank of the dismounted cavalry.

(d) The mobility of the gun, the small frontage from which it acts, and the concentrated and accurate nature of its fire render the machine gun suitable for developing surprise effect.

(e) The small frontage it occupies also makes the gun valuable in cramped localities, such as small woods, villages, roads, and defiles.

(f) The power of opening fire at any time when the gun is once laid is valuable on outpost or for night firing, for the gun can command any required locality for any length of time and at the required moment produce and apply a large volume of accurate fire.

227. *The organization of machine guns.*

1. Machine guns are organized in sections, which form an integral part of the regiments to which they belong. When circumstances make it advisable to employ several sections together, a brigade commander may, if he so desires, detach two or more machine gun sections temporarily from their regiments and place them under the brigade machine gun officer for employment as a unit of the brigade.

2. When the machine guns of two or more regiments are required to support a mounted attack, it is necessary to ensure that all the machine gun sections act in close co-operation both with each other and with other portions of the fire attack, in order to ensure that the mounted attack and the fire attack do not interfere with each other. (*See* Sec. **194.**)

For this reason machine guns supporting a mounted attack should usually be brigaded.

3. The brigading of machine guns in dismounted action has the following advantages :—

> i. A commander is enabled to keep a powerful reserve of fire in hand to be used for any special purpose.
>
> ii. There is more probability of obtaining good results at ranges beyond 1,200 yards.
>
> iii. It is easy to ensure that the fire is directed on the desired objective.

On the other hand, there are the following disadvantages :—

> i. The difficulties of concealment are increased.
>
> ii. At ranges shorter than 1,000 yards the control of more than one section usually becomes difficult, more especially in attack.
>
> iii. The combined movement of a number of sections against a dismounted enemy at effective and close ranges is only possible when the ground is very favourable.

4. Generally speaking when a considerable force of cavalry is acting dismounted, it will operate on an extended front and consequently it will generally be preferable to leave the machine gun sections to co-operate with their units. It will often be advisable for a cavalry commander to adopt both methods and while leaving their machine gun sections with those units which are engaged in the first line, to brigade the sections of those units which he keeps in his own hands. This will give him a mobile and powerful reserve of fire, which can be employed to meet eventualities.

228. *The tactical handling of machine guns in a mounted action.*

1. When machine guns are employed to support a cavalry charge, the concealment of the guns in the fire position is of minor importance. The chief object to aim at is to keep the guns hidden until such moment as they can be brought into action suddenly from a position whence the fire of every gun can be concentrated on the enemy just before the moment of impact.

To effect this the machine gun commander must act with promptitude and decision and clearly understand the cavalry commander's plan of action.

2. The position of the machine guns during the approach march has been described in Sec. **197.** The senior machine gun commander should accompany the cavalry commander and hear the latter's general instructions for the attack. He must then act on his own initiative on the general principles which have been described in Secs. **220** and **221** for the employment of horse artillery. As the effective range of machine guns is less than that of horse artillery, they will normally be employed in advance, and on the outer flank, of the latter. The machine gun commander must exercise special care not to mask the fire of the horse artillery.

3. A portion of the machine guns may be employed occasionally during a mounted attack as escort to the horse artillery or to the first line transport. (*See* Secs. **200** and **224.**)

229. *The tactical handling of machine guns in a dismounted action.*

1. Machine guns will usually find opportunities for supporting dismounted cavalry in attack, iu assisting the advance by means of covering fire; in covering the flanks of the attackers, more especially if positions can be found for them, whence they can bring fire to bear on the objective of the attack and at the same time be available to safeguard the flank if required; and in assisting to secure localities seized during the advance.

2. Machine guns should rarely attempt to move forward with dismounted cavalry beyond a certain point. When they have gained a position from which they can give effective support, they should only be moved for good and sufficient reasons. The difficulties of ranging and of concealment on the move usually outweigh the advantages of decreasing the range.

3. When cavalry is acting dismounted in the defence it may be required :

    i. To deny a position to the enemy.

    ii. To delay the enemy's advance.

In the first case where the cavalry will be required to make a resolute stand the machine guns, being unsuitable for long sustained action owing to the expenditure of ammunition entailed, should often be kept in hand as a reserve of fire until a favourable target presents itself. When time admits, covered positions approached by covered communications should be arranged. Such positions should be selected with a view to bringing a fire to bear on exposed places which the enemy must cross, or on roads or defiles by which he must advance, especially when he is threatening the flank of the position. The concentrated nature of the fire produced makes accuracy of ranging on such points of great importance.

Iu order to make full use of the guns, alternative positions should be allotted to sections. These positions should be thoroughly recomroitred and all necessary arrangements should be made for rapid occupation and quick opening of fire.

These arrangements should include previous preparation of cover, information as to the shortest route to the various positions, preparation of range card, and selection of the most suitable position from which to control and observe fire.

In the case where a force of cavalry is required to delay an enemy's advance rather than to hold a position, the machine guns may be more usefully employed in close support of the firing line from the first, instead of as a mobile reserve of fire.

230. *General instructions regarding the tactical handling of machine guns.*

1. In the pursuit the utmost endeavour must be made to turn the enemy's retirement into a rout, and machine guns should be handled with the greatest vigour and boldness, endeavouring to come into action against the enemy's flanks at decisive range.

2. In retirement close engagements should, as a rule, be avoided, and machine guns should be used to delay the enemy by bringing fire to bear on roads, defiles, or open spaces, by which he must advance, and thus forcing him to deploy. They may be especially useful in delaying any effort to turn the flanks of the rear guard.

3. Owing to the liability of the mechanism to interruption, the guns of a section should rarely be employed beyond supporting distance of one another; while when sections are acting independently and are not under good cover the guns should usually be not less than twenty-five yards apart, the average width of the area of ground struck by the bullets of an effective shrapnel.

4. Machine guns will not as a rule require a special escort beyond the provision of a few scouts.

231. *Fire position of machine guns.*

1. The choice of a fire position depends upon the tactical requirements of the situation.

2. In support of cavalry engaged in mounted combat important considerations for a fire position are, that it should afford an extensive field of fire and be capable of being approached out of sight of the enemy. For this purpose a commanding position will often be the best; but time is of the first importance.

3. When co-operating with cavalry acting dismounted, a commanding position is usually favourable for the development of covering fire, but otherwise the gun should be sited as low as is compatible with obtaining the necessary field of fire.

4. A clear field of fire, facilities for observation, a covered approach, concealment and cover for the guns and their detachments, and facilities for ammunition supply are advantages to be looked for in a good fire position, but one position will rarely unite them all.

In arranging for the concealment of the guns it is important to consider the background. The neighbourhood of landmarks and the tops of prominent features should be avoided.

232. *Reconnaissance of fire position.*

1. The commander, accompanied by range takers and orderlies, should usually be well ahead of his guns so that he can keep in touch with the tactical situation and complete the reconnaissance before the guns arrive.

2. Before the commander moves forward to reconnoitre a position he should give the officer or N.C.O. next in command all the information he can as to the probable fire position, and indicate to him the pace and the initial direction to be followed. If the route to be followed is liable to be mistaken, he must leave men at doubtful points with instructions for the detachment.

3. When concealment is of importance, careful mounted reconnaissance should be made to determine the point to which horses may advance without exposure, and careful dismounted reconnaissance to ensure that each gun shall have a clear field of view and a good platform.

4. Alternative positions to which the guns may be moved to meet changes in the situation or to avoid artillery fire should be selected.

233. *Advance for action.*

1. During the advance advantage should be taken of any existing cover to conceal the approach of the guns from the enemy's view.

2. The guns should not be brought on to the actual ground where it is intended to come into action until the exact position to which the horses may be brought has been selected. There will be little delay in the occupation of the position if the commander has kept well ahead of his guns.

3. The carriage of the gun into the fire position should be carried out secretly and rapidly.

4. The commander will select a position for the wagons whence ammunition can be replenished, and where the men and horses will be under cover. This position should not be directly in rear of the guns if it can be avoided.

5. When the guns are coming into action to support a mounted attack and time is of the first importance, it will often be impossible to make preliminary reconnaissances and to take advantage of all cover when coming into action; the guns must in such circumstances be handled with the greatest boldness and every effort made to deliver an effective fire before the shock takes place.

234. *Machine gun in action.*

1. When a machine gun is in action, only those numbers required to work the gun should be with it. The remainder when not employed as rangefinders, scouts, ammunition carriers, or on similar duties, should be in covered positions in the vicinity. Groups of men close to machine guns render concealment difficult and make a vulnerable target.

2. In many cases the observation of fire will be impossible from the gun's position, and it will be necessary for observers to signal results from a flank.

3. The question of opening fire, speaking generally, depends on the tactical importance, range, and vulnerability of the target.

In supporting a mounted attack to open fire at the correct time with every available machine gun directed on the main body of the enemy about to be attacked will be the chief consideration.

Once a machine gun opens fire its presence is disclosed to the enemy, who will watch for its re-appearance. The chance of effecting surprise subsequently will therefore be diminished.

Fire should not be opened at ranges beyond about 1,200 yards unless a particularly favourable target offers or a number of guns can be employed (see Sec. **227**). Between 1,200 and 800 yards good effect may be anticipated from machine gun fire, and within 800 yards the greatest effect can be developed. If the firer can himself obtain observation, the effect of machine gun fire is appreciably increased. The more conspicuous parts of the target usually attract the attention of the layers, When the target entails much distribution of fire it will usually be advisable to allot a portion of a target to each section.

4. Except under special circumstances, machine guns should only open fire upon targets which are sufficiently large and dense to promise an adequate return for the ammunition expended. Thin lines of dismounted men in extended order are not a suitable target.

If there is no satisfactory indication of effect, and no special justification for firing at long range exists, it will usually be better to await more favourable opportunities for effective intervention.

5. When sections are brigaded and the guns are engaging a moving target of which the range is altering, it is often difficult for the commander to pass his orders. In such cases it will usually be advisable to order rapid bursts of fire followed by short pauses.

235. *Methods of fire.*

1. The following are the methods of fire:—

    i. Ranging fire.
    ii. Rapid fire.
    iii. Traversing fire.

2. In ranging fire bursts of from ten to twenty rounds are used to obtain observation. When the conditions for observation are favourable a burst of ten rounds should be sufficient. Under less favourable conditions bursts of as many as twenty rounds may be necessary, but if observation is not then obtained it is unlikely to be obtained with larger bursts. Single deliberate shots are of little value for ranging.

3. Rapid fire is used when the greatest volume of fire is required. It is produced and applied by means of a series of long groups of from thirty to fifty rounds. The firer pauses momentarily between each group to ensure that the sights are correctly aligned, and continues until ordered to cease fire or until he considers it necessary to do so.

4. Traversing fire is employed against a linear target and is applied by means of a series of small groups with the object of covering as wide a front as possible with only sufficient volume to ensure effect. In this case a group should consist of from five to ten rounds only, because against a linear target, greater volume will not produce greater effect. Traversing may either be horizontal or diagonal. (*See* also Sec. **48.**)

236. *The use of combined sights with machine guns.*

1. When two or more guns are working together, the depth of the effective zone can be increased by ordering different elevations to be used by each gun, while each uses the same aiming mark. By this means, while the effective zone is increased, the density of fire is considerably reduced.

The difference of elevation used depends chiefly on the number of guns available. For general guidance, when one section only is available, combined sights differing by 100 yards should be used from 800 to 1,200 yards inclusive; beyond 1,200 yards the difference in sighting should not exceed 50 yards between guns. With two or more sections the difference of sighting between guns should not exceed 50 yards.

When both guns of a section are sighted to the same elevation "combined sights by sections," differing by 100 yards, may be used.

With Mark VI. ammunition, the normal difference between guns will be 50 yards with a section, and 25 yards with two or more sections.

With Mark VII. and Mark VI. ammunition, these differences may be regulated according to requirements.

2. Machine gun commanders when ordering combined sights should give out the highest range and the difference in sighting to be used. The highest range in the first place will always be taken by the right-hand gun of the section or sections as the case may be. The No. 1 of that gun will pass to the No. 1 of the gun on his left the range he himself is using and difference ordered, and so on down the line.

3. When the target to be engaged is a narrow one, and all guns are using the same aiming mark, it will generally be impossible for the firers to observe their own particular cone of fire. In these circumstances no alteration in sighting is usually advisable except under the orders of the machine gun commander. In other circumstances each firer should endeavour to correct his elevation from observation of the bullet strike. If, as a result of his observations or for other reasons, the machine gun commander wishes to alter the sighting, the quickest method is to bring the elevation of the left-hand gun above that of the right-hand gun or to lower the elevation of the right-hand gun below that of the left-hand gun according as to whether he wishes to increase or decrease the elevation. If the machine gun commander is directing the fire from the opposite flank to that of the

gun or guns whose elevation he wishes to alter, it will be necessary to cease firing momentarily for his order to be received, after
which he will immediately give the signal to continue. This
will often not be necessary when he is on the same flank.

ENGINEERS.

237. *Field troops with cavalry.*

1. The field troops with the cavalry division receive their
orders through the commander of the cavalry divisional engineers
when they are concentrated, and from the brigade commanders
when they are attached to brigades.

2. The field troops of the division may be employed for :—

    i. The passage of rivers or other natural obstacles.
    ii. Assisting in the preparation for defence of a position.
    iii. Strengthening localities which it may be required to
        hold.
    iv. Assisting advanced or rear guards to remove or create
        obstacles or to improve or block river crossings or
        roads.
    v. Carrying out demolitions of a considerable nature.
    vi. Arranging the water supply.

3. The principle guiding the employment of the field troops
is that they are grouped by the commander of the cavalry
division according to the requirements of each situation. When
employed on field works the engineers direct and give technical
assistance to working parties furnished by the cavalry. The
work cannot be done by the engineers alone.

4. Field troops are trained for dismounted action and are
available for fighting purposes when required.

CHAPTER XIV.

NIGHT OPERATIONS, BILLETING, AND REQUISITIONING.

238. *Night operations.*

(*See* also " F.S. Regs., Part I., Chapter IX.)

1. Though it is unlikely that cavalry will be required to carry out assaults in strength by night they will frequently have to move secretly by night in order to operate at distant points suddenly the next morning; and in carrying out such movements it may be found necessary to overcome and capture by assault small posts of the enemy in the dark.

Opportunities for minor night operations to harass the enemy by disturbing his repose may often be found by enterprising cavalry, and when well conducted such operations may affect the enemy's moral seriously, especially when he is resting after a long march or severe fighting. On such occasions the enemy may be entirely deceived by means of rapid fire as to the strength of the force engaging them.

Reconnaissance by night, as well as movement by night in order to reach a locality whence reconnaissance can be undertaken by day, will also frequently be necessary.

2. Night marches must be designed on very simple lines, for every complication increases the risk of failure. Combined movements of two or more forces acting in co-operation are liable to miscarry.

3. When marching by night columns must move well closed up, distances between the advanced guard and other portions all being less than those necessary by day.

The head of the column should move slowly when leaving the billet or bivouac in order to allow the rear units to take their places correctly in the column. A short halt should be made as soon as the column is clear of its billet or bivouac.

With a force larger than a regiment, the rate of marching at night will seldom exceed two miles an hour.

4. Secrecy is one of the chief factors leading to success in night operations. As a rule the orders for a night march should not be issued beforehand, although it will usually be advisable to explain the leaders' general plans and intentions secretly to subordinate commanders in sufficient time to enable them to understand what will be required of them. Any necessary instructions to the remainder of the force can usually be given after the troops have been ordered to turn out.

The presence of wheeled transport and guns may endanger the success of a night march.

239. *Billeting and protection in billets.*

1. Instructions for billeting are contained in " F.S. Regs., Part I " and in " Special instructions for the utilization of the local resources of a country by an army in the field."

2. In temperate or cold climates, as many horses as possible should be brought under shelter at night, bivouacking being avoided as far as practicable.

In critical situations, however, cavalry may not only have to bivouac, but men may have to stand to their horses ready to mount at a moment's notice.

3. When in the vicinity of the enemy, cavalry may be withdrawn some distance at night in order to lessen the risk of being disturbed. The greater security and rest resulting from such movement is ample compensation for the increased distance that may have to be traversed on the following day. Commanders should remember, however, that such action in no way diminishes the necessity for maintaining touch with the enemy.

4. In billeting cavalry it may often be possible to distribute them in such a manner that the advanced line of billets serves as a line of protection for the rest of the force.

5. Except in the case of very small forces billets, if liable to attack, should not be so concentrated that all may be surprised, or brought under artillery fire at the same time; on the other hand, they should not be so scattered that part of the force can be overwhelmed before assistance can arrive from the remainder.

6. The general principles of protection are given in " F.S. Regs., Part I," Chapter V. It is impossible to lay down definite

rules as to how these principles should be put into execution in regard to the protection of cavalry during the hours of darkness, for no two situations are similar and each situation requires separate treatment. Such questions as the advisability of saddling the horses on the alarm sounding, the choice of the place of assembly, and the action to be taken in case of attack can only be decided by the commander on the spot after considering all the circumstances of the case.

It should be remembered, however, that owing to the extent of ground over which a force of cavalry must usually be dispersed if all the horses are to have shelter, it may often be advisable, instead of pushing the protective troops out well to the front, to make the perimeter of the villages occupied by the troops the line of resistance to be occupied in case of attack by night. In such circumstances each unit should usually be made responsible for the protection of the perimeter which it occupies. If this method of protection is adopted, the need for a thorough system of reconnaissance is if possible accentuated, and the commander in addition to despatching patrols or larger detachments to keep in touch with the enemy, must arrange to watch all approaches open to his opponents in such a manner that ample warning of an intended attack can be given.

7. If billeted in a town, orders should be issued as to the time at which horses may be unsaddled, an alarm post fixed on, and orders for dispositions in case of attack given out, before the men are dismissed to their billets. No officer should leave the parade until the men are told off to their billets. Squadron officers should visit the whole of the stables in which their horses are billeted.

8. In billets all arms should be removed from the stables and taken to the rooms. The bridles should also be taken from the stables and kept by the men.

240. *Requisitioning.*

1. Instructions for requisitioning are given in " F.S. Regs. Part I " and in " Special instructions for the utilization of the local resources of a country by an army in the field."

2. Whether the army is operating in a hostile or friendly country, requisitions and demands for billets will be effected whenever possible through the local civil authorities, or in their absence, through the principal inhabitants. Direct contact between the troops and the inhabitants will be avoided.

3. In carrying out requisition services it is important that economy and foresight should be exercised so that the resources of the country may be utilized to the best advantage, that strict discipline should be observed in enforcing requisitions, and that careful records should be kept so that speedy settlement of all claims can be made.

The knowledge that early payment is to be made will tend to facilitate requisitioning.

4. As a general principle only officers of the administrative service concerned and detailed for the duty are authorised to requisition, but in cases of emergency requisitions may be carried out by the commander, the circumstances being reported without delay to superior authority. Indiscriminate requisitioning and granting of receipt notes are forbidden.

Requisitions will generally be made on the prescribed form.

5. Authority to requisition will not be delegated to any but a commissioned officer, and requisitioning on the part of warrant officers, non-commissioned officers, or men will be treated as plundering under the Army Act, unless the case is one of extreme urgency, and no commissioned officer is present.

6. Surprise is an important factor in successful requisitioning, for not only does it decrease the opposition, but it also prevents the concealment or removal of supplies before the arrival of the troops. As soon as a requisitioning party reaches the town or village in which it intends to requisition, the commander of the escort should guard all the outlets, post sentries over places in which supplies are seen to exist, form a reserve of men in the town so as to be ready for any opposition from the inhabitants, and take one or two hostages if necessary. With the remainder of his force he should take up suitable positions outside the town or village and in the direction of the enemy.

APPENDIX I.

The following syllabus of recruit training is given as a guide to officers charged with the training of recruits. It is not intended that it should be followed rigidly.

1. SYLLABUS OF TRAINING.

Employment.	Hours.	Remarks.
First Fortnight.		
Physical training -	10	Arms and equipment to be issued. Course as laid down in the Manual up to and including Table IX Cavalry. Gradual according to physical condition of men under qualified instructors.
Foot drill without arms	24	Secs. 15 to 28.
Map reading	5	Explanation of map, elementary conventional signs, scales, 4", 2", 1". ("Manual of Map Reading and Field Sketching.")
Lectures	2⅔	8 lectures of 20 minutes each. For subjects of lectures *see* Appendix I, 2.
Second Fortnight.		
Physical training	10	Physical Training under qualified instructors.
Foot drill with arms -	12	Secs. 29-34 and 40-45.
Musketry instruction -	8	"Musketry Regulations, Part I," Secs. 9, 10, 37, 38, 47, 48, and 54.
Semaphore signalling -	10	"Training Manual—Signalling," Sec. 16.
Map reading	5	All conventional signs. Scales. Measurements along roads, on map, etc. Identifying objects on the map. ("Manual of Map Reading and Field Sketching.")
Lectures	2⅔	

Employment.	Hours.	Remarks.
Third Fortnight.		
Physical training -	10	Physical Training under qualified in-structors.
Foot drill - - -	9	Secs. 29–34 and 40–45.
Musketry instruction -	6	" Musketry Regulations, Part I," Secs. 2, 3. 9, 10, 11, 14, and 15, 37 to 44, 47 to 50, and 54.
Visual training and judging distance.	4	" Musketry Regulations, Part I," Secs. 65, 66, and 67.
Semaphore signalling -	6	
Map reading - -	5	Setting map with compass. Explaining difference between true and magnetic north. Setting map with sun, watch, and two points.
Wooden horse - -	8	
Fourth Fortnight.		
Physical training -	10	Physical Training under qualified in-structors.
Foot drill with arms -	9	Secs. 29–34 and 40–45. Additional in-struction in the use of the lance should be given at this period to lancers. The time will be utilized in the case of hussars and dragoons for elementary instruction in horse-mastership in stables.
Musketry instruction -	5	" Musketry Regulations, Part I," Secs. 37–55, 59, and 60.
Visual training and judging distance.	3	" Musketry Regulations, Part I," Secs. 65–68.
Semaphore signalling -	10	
Map reading - -	5	Setting map by other means day and night. Finding position on map when set. Revision.
Wooden horse - -	6	

Employment.	Hours.	Remarks.
Fifth Fortnight.		
Physical training ·	10	Physical Training under qualified instructors.
Foot drill with arms ·	9	Secs. 29 34, and 40–45. Additional instruction in the use of the lance will be given to lancers. The time in the case of hus-ars and dragoons being utilized for elementary instruction in horsemastership.
Musketry instruction ·	5	"Musketry Regulations, Part I," Secs. 51–54, 59, 60, 63 and 64.*
Visual training and judging distance.	3	"Musketry Regulations, Part I," Secs. 65–68.
Semaphore signalling ·	10	
Map reading · ·	3	Hill features and contours, with special reference to finding lowest point on map and then highest point from it. Contours more advanced.
Elementary instruction in night operations.	2	Sec. 158.
Fencing · · ·	8	
Sixth Fortnight.		
Physical training ·	10	Physical Training under qualified instructors.
Foot drill with arms ·	9	Secs. 29–34 and 40-45. Additional instruction in the use of the lance will be given to lancers. The time in the case of hussars and dragoons being utilized for elementary instruction in horsemastership.
Musketry instruction ·	7	"Musketry Regulations, Part I," Secs. 54–60, 63 and 64.*
Visual training and judging distance.	3	"Musketry Regulations, Part I," Secs. 65–68.

* If a recruit fails to qualify in any of the Tests of Elementary Training he should receive further instruction before he is further tested.

Employment.	Hours.	Remarks.
Sixth Fortnight—cont.		
Semaphore signalling -	10	Average standard attained 8 words per minute.
Map reading - -	3	Contours more advanced. General revision.
Elementary instruction in night operations.	2	Sec. 158.
Fencing - - -	8	.

2. LECTURES TO RECRUITS.

1. Lectures should frequently be delivered by officers ; with a view to retaining the attention of the recruits they should not as a rule exceed half-an-hour in length, should take place at suitable hours, and should be made as attractive as possible.

2. The lectures at the commencement of the recruit's course of training should be mainly on elementary interior economy, sanitation, discipline, regimental distinctions, the meaning and importance of a military spirit ; subsequently they may also be on the work of the period, and should then if possible be illustrated by incidents taken from actual warfare, which should emphasize the value of a military spirit in war.

Some time during the lecture hour should be devoted to catechism on previous work and lectures.

3. The following are some of the subjects suggested as suitable for lectures to cavalry recruits :—

Barrack room duties. Cleanliness and smartness expected from the soldier. Dress and clothing. Local orders. Good name of the regiment and army. Conduct when out of camp or barracks. Position of provost, and duty to obey and support him. Duty when ordered as escort. Names, rank and position of officers. Regimental colours. Saluting. Manner of making a complaint. Reporting sick and hospital rules.

General conduct while in the army. Immediate physical and material advantages of moderation and sobriety. The advantages of physical fitness. Prospects of civil employment in after life affected by conduct while in the army. Registration for employment dependent on good character on discharge, preference being given to exemplary or very good characters. For police or post office employment an additional certificate of absolute sobriety is necessary.

Fitting equipment. Laying down kits. Elementary instruction in animal management. Sanitation and hygiene.

The rifle and elementary theoretical instruction in musketry.

Duties on guard.

Co-operation, comradeship, disregard of self and their importance in war.

Observation and the use of the ears and eyes by day and night.

NOTE.—No reference to drill is made in this index. Headings of sections dealing with drill will be found in the contents.

INDEX.

A

G

I.

M

O